MISHIMA'S SWORD

Also by Christopher Ross

Tunnel Visions: Journeys of an Underground Philosopher

MISHIMA'S SWORD

Travels in Search of
a Samurai Legend

CHRISTOPHER ROSS

FOURTH ESTATE · London

望へ、愛と感謝をこめて

First published in Great Britain in 2006 by
Fourth Estate
An imprint of HarperCollins*Publishers*
77–85 Fulham Palace Road
London w6 8jb
www.4thestate.co.uk

A catalogue record for this book is
available from the British Library

isbn-13 978-0-00-713508-0
isbn-10 0-00-713508-4

TPB isbn-13 978-0-00-722811-9
TPB isbn-10 0-00-722811-2

Typeset in PostScript Linotype Janson by
Rowland Phototypesetting Ltd, Bury St Edmunds, Suffolk

Printed in Great Britain by Clays Ltd, St Ives plc

'In fact the whole of Japan is a pure invention.
There is no such country, there are no such people.'

Oscar Wilde, 'The Decay of Lying'

CONTENTS

ACKNOWLEDGEMENTS

The writing of *Mishima's Sword* took place during a time when I had no home, causing a peripatetic existence. I am deeply grateful to a number of friends who generously invited me to stay, lending me a room, an apartment or even a house, in some cases repeatedly. In London: Michael Ivey; Claire and Aidan Hartley; Celia and Lloyd Evans; Rupert Seldon, John Seldon and Leda Lignos. In Valencia: Salud Botella and Jason Webster. In Paris: John West. In Tokyo: Kenichi Hiramatsu; Tomoko and Hiroshi Takase.

A great many individuals helped me in my struggles to understand the suicide of Yukio Mishima, his writing and the history of the samurai and the swords they wielded. Some did so insisting they remain unacknowledged, but I would like to thank them here in general terms nevertheless. The help and friendship of Henry Scott Stokes was invaluable throughout this project. In Seki: Kaneko Magoroku agreed to see me when most others would have refused. Keiji Igarashi was a friendly and helpful host who opened every door in town. I would also like to thank Kiyomi Uehara. In Tokyo: Kenji Mishina patiently explained many things I did not then understand. Professor Takashi Inoue cleared up a number of points related to Mishima's work. Andrew Rankin was kind enough to discuss with me his ongoing Mishima biography. Jonathan Watts of the *Guardian* (then based in Japan, now in China) made many helpful comments and was good company over a beer. William Howell, who began aikidō with me more than ten years ago and has now far surpassed me, supported me whenever I needed cheering up. Nakayama-san and her staff at the FCCJ library were always willing to do whatever ridiculous things I asked of them to help in my search. Whatever Donald Richie says about Japan is worth paying close attention to and I am grateful he let me listen. In Nagoya: I would like to thank Fukui-san of the Atsuta Shrine for explaining about the Imperial Treasure sword (Kusanagi) and more generally helping me understand the connection between swords and Shinto rituals. For a deeply practical and truthful explanation of the limits and possibilities of Japanese swords in combat I remain indebted to Taisaburō Nakamura Sensei, founder of Nakamura-Ryū, and one of Japan's greatest masters of budō.

My parents, Marion and James Ross, provided me with ceaseless love and constant support, often rendered in practical forms. In Nicholas Pearson I found a wise and supportive editor. Steve Cox is a good man with a blue pencil. My friend Robert Twigger read the manuscript and kept me going. Georgia Garrett remains the best agent anyone might be lucky enough to have. At Fourth Estate I should also like to thank Silvia Crompton, Robin Harvie, Vera Brice, Julian Humphries, Richard Bravery and Jeff Cottenden for making this book better than it would otherwise be.

DEATH IN TOKYO

Events are the froth of things, but my real interest is the sea.
PAUL VALÉRY

A young man, just twenty-three, lies in a coma position, prone on a rocky beach. His body is broken. The stones of the seashore beneath the body trace the base of a white cliff more than one hundred feet high and extend into the endless ocean. We can hear the sounds of the sea and the calling of seabirds. The regular susurrating waves lull, like the rocking of an infant's cradle. The horizon, lit by the rising sun, seems to stretch towards infinity, punctuated only by the occasional anvil cloud. Our gaze returns – how can it not? – to the prone body, legs twisted grotesquely beneath it, like the hanged man on a tarot card.

Then, as if drawn by some magnetic force, a strange motion begins, focused on the body, which starts to move quite unnaturally. The body jerks backwards, suddenly stands, as if raised by invisible strings, like a puppet. The scene resembles a film running backwards. Yes that's it! Someone is running the movie in reverse.

A trickle of blood, which had leaked from the corner of the shattered mouth, flows back into the mouth, now unblemished, and disappears. Bruises fade and vanish. Like a rocket launched into the sky the figure leaps upwards, ascending the face of the cliff to land at the top, one hundred feet above, a vantage point overlooking the stone-strewn beach and out towards the restless sea. The young man stands on the edge of the precipice, once again living. Suicide has occurred, but in reverse.

London – 1990s

It takes about ten minutes to walk from the Tube to The Studio, a modern building that combines social and sports clubs and has added grooming facilities: there is a sauna, a solarium and odd rooms for hire. I was carrying a small brown valise and a vinyl bag whose shape suggested that I played billiards, or perhaps belonged to a gun club. No one had ever guessed its contents.

Inside the customised bag was a katana, a samurai sword. I was on my way to a class in Eishin-Ryū *iaidō*,[1] a four-hundred-year-old school of Japanese fencing that focuses specifically on what to do if you are surprised with your sword still sheathed – how to draw, cut, kill and resheathe, all the while supremely indifferent, the fastest sword in the East.

But the sword in the bag was not a real one. The blade was made of a softish zinc alloy and had no edge; it would not cut tofu. Following the American occupation of Japan after the Second World War, when all martial arts were banned and swords confiscated, a kind of practice sword began to be made, shaped and weighted closely to resemble a real blade, but incapable of being sharpened. This was the *iaitō*. It looked real, and if need be I suppose you could poke someone in the eye with the *kissaki*, the sharpish tip.

Once you entered The Studio the quiet autumn evening street sounds gave way to an enclosed world with its own atmosphere and noises. The building throbbed to dance music of a kind you only ever encounter in exercise classes. Aerobic disco. I struggled to adjust to the din. When I first visited The Studio I was shocked, finding it hard to believe that in such an environment I could find calm enough to concentrate on practice. I was used to Japan, where even when dōjō were badly situated – say in a building next to a construction site – the sounds were only natural big-city noises. The problem with music, even music you like, is that it usually makes you want to dance – and fencing has rhythms of its own.

I went to change and soon emerged with my street clothes repacked in the small case – there were no lockers – and carrying my sword. I was wearing an *uwagi* and *hakama*, a cotton top, like the top half of a karate suit, but dyed black and tucked into a pleated black cotton skirt that is really a huge specially folded pair of trousers, formerly worn by samurai to protect their clothes from dust while on horseback.

Standing there, a few minutes early, waiting for the others to arrive, I gazed round the room. A step-aerobics class was about to begin. About twenty fluorescently clad young women and a solitary, rather tubby man in soccer shorts and a singlet were milling around and positioning small wooden platforms. One woman, who might be new as I had never seen her before, dressed entirely in dayglo pink, was listening to a Walkman and sported a set of pink-framed wrap-around sunglasses, like skiers' goggles. She stared at me, with eyes that seemed indignant, behind the pink-tinted lenses. I stared back, standing squarely and leaning on the handle of my sword, my face a blank. The gulf between us was immense – hundreds of years, thousands of miles, a shift of cultures. She had come here to dance, to have fun, to exhibit her fondness for pink and to keep 'in shape'. I had come to study how to kill with a single spectacular slice, dressed in the clothes of a Japanese feudal warrior, a caste long since extinct.

In the small second-storey room, we knelt to prepare our swords. An oil[2] scented with cloves, *chōji* – a spice I now associate with the dōjō, *kiai* shouts and fencing – is applied to the blade to lubricate the draw and, with a real sword, protect against rust. Any surplus is wiped off with specially hand-made paper, *nuguikami*.

A rule of practice is that even edgeless weapons, even *iaitō* or wooden swords, are to be handled with cautious respect and treated as if razor-sharp. It is a good rule, designed to deter bad habits that might at some later time cost a finger or worse in a lapse of concentration.

After bowing to the enshrined gods, to the teacher, and lastly

– responding to the order *tōrei* – to the sword itself, we warmed up with a variety of practice cuts, *suburi*, and then knelt down to absorb today's lesson. The hard wooden floor caused me a kind of pain that I secretly welcomed: it cleared my head and helped me to concentrate. Today we were to practise *kaishaku* or *juntō*,[3] the correct form for assisting at a suicide, where the second must lop off the *seito*, or principal's, head after he himself has cut open his stomach in the notorious act of ritualised suicide, hara-kiri.

Hara-kiri is more correctly written – and reversing the order of the Japanese characters – 切腹 – *seppuku*. As with all traditional activities in Japan there is a definitive form to follow when doing this – a *kata*. The purpose of the second is to avoid propelling the head across the room like a dropped melon, which is considered vulgar. A tricky task, requiring considerable skill and nerve, as you must cut the neck but stop the blade just short of completely severing it, so that the flap of skin at the throat remains intact, allowing the head to flop neatly onto the suicide's chest.

Kaishaku is the seventh of a series of seated sword draws taught in the Eishin Ryū. Each of these begins from the formal kneeling position *seiza*.[4] The sheathed sword is worn edge-up, pushed through your belt at the left side. As you rise onto your toes the blade is drawn out about two-thirds of its length. Standing up smoothly you complete the draw, stepping back with your right leg; next you raise the sword so that it is held behind the head and angled down, gripped only with the right hand. Stepping forward you cut at an angle of about 40 degrees to the neck. You stop the blade by bringing the left hand to the sword handle to meet the movement. Now you have severed the head. It only remains to shake the blood from the blade[5] and resheathe slowly in a stylised set of motions called *nōtō*, breathing quite calmly and naturally, and projecting the stable, imperturbable spirit known as *zanshin* – 'lingering mind'.

Tokyo – Ichigaya Hill,
Ground Self Defence Force,
Eastern Army Group Headquarters,
25 November 1970[6]

Yukio Mishima steps back into Room 201, where General Mashita sits tied to a chair. He is followed by his Shield Society cadet student captain Masakatsu Morita. Mishima's face is a grim mask. He looks at the floor, shaking his head, saying: 'I don't think they heard me well.' Outside the noise continues, soldiers shouting – *Konoyaro!* (You bastard!), *Chinpira!* (Gangster!), and perhaps most woundingly, *Eiyuu kidori shiyagatte!* (You're just a phoney hero!). Outside there are police sirens and the din of hovering helicopters. Within Room 201 it seems, by contrast, almost silent.

Stooping, Mishima begins to unlace his boots. He had already begun to unbutton his uniform jacket as he re-entered the room. 'What are you doing?' asks General Mashita, realising exactly what Mishima is about to do. A veteran of the Second World War, Kanetoshi Mashita had already witnessed two acts of formal suicide by disembowelment. 'You must stop! This is madness.' Tiny Koga looks towards his commander to see if he should replace the General's gag. A small, nearly imperceptible, nod indicates it is unnecessary.

Mishima removes his uniform jacket, folds it neatly, pulls down his trousers and quickly kneels in *seiza* facing the direction of the Imperial Palace. Beneath his uniform he is wearing only a *fundoshi* loincloth which he also eases down at the front, feeling with the tips of the fingers of his right hand, like a doctor performing a critical examination, searching for the place on his tightly muscled belly. A cadet tries to hand him a writing brush and a stiff square card, *shikishi*, on which he had planned to brush the character 武, *bu*, martial, in his own blood, but he waves it away. The thing is to die, and quickly, before something else goes wrong, before someone tries to stop him. Details of form seem unimportant now.

He removes his watch, as if to stop time, and passes it to Old Koga – not an old man but a youth nicknamed for the way he writes his family name. Morita has taken the long sword and is beginning to hyperventilate. His hands are sweating and he wipes each in turn again and again on the sides of his uniform trousers, moving the sword from hand to hand as he shuffles on the spot, waiting for the signal, positioned to Mishima's left and slightly behind him.

Mishima half turns to look at Morita for one last time. *Kimi wa yamero* – 'Don't do it,' he tells him, imploring Morita to let him die alone. Then, picking up the *yoroidōshi*, an armour-piercing knife, he places its point against his left side, breathes sharply three times in quick succession – advice from the *Haga-kure*[7] when facing 'difficulty' – then exhales fully before pulling back on the handle, a sudden jerk, and sliding the blade through the wall of flesh and muscle into his body. Four inches of metal enter his belly and he slowly forces the edge from left to right and then up at the end, to open a flap of skin. Blood floods the floor. A coil of greyish-pink protrudes from the wound. A lavatory stink pervades the room.

Mishima nods. Morita cuts with the sword, pulling it down as hard as he can. His posture, coupled with his urgent need to vomit, causes the blade to miss its target; it glances off Mishima's shoulders and bites into his back instead of his neck. Mishima slumps forward as Morita slices again, this time a harmless cut into the blood-soaked carpet. Morita raises the sword a third time as his horrified comrades yell: '*Mō Ikkai*' – 'Again!' He swings again, a silver ellipse in a flash of sunlight, this time entering Mishima's neck, but not at the proper angle. The edge stops cutting as it collides with Mishima's jawbone, one of the hardest bones in the human body. The blade edge chips and Morita struggles to wrench it free. He turns to Old Koga, who immediately takes the sword from him, raises it briefly to take aim, and in one motion cuts off Mishima's head. It comes to rest, more than a yard away. The writer's blood pulses from the neck arteries, arches like the jets of a fountain, spraying across the wall-mounted air conditioner.

Now Morita kneels, like Mishima naked but for a loincloth, his uniform trousers pulled down below his thighs. He has retrieved the knife, and slides the blade across his stomach. A shallow cut exudes a line of blood. Old Koga, answering his friend's signal, slices off his young head and ends another life with one clean cut of Mishima's sword.

At the time of his spectacular death in 1970, Yukio Mishima was Japan's most famous man of letters, three times nominated for the Nobel Prize. His literary output had been immense, and from the date he started work as a full-time writer – 25 November 1948 – covered a span of twenty-two years to the day. In this time he wrote forty novels, hundreds of essays and twenty volumes of short stories. He also penned eighteen major and many minor plays and saw them all staged and performed.

Mishima had reached outside his study to engage in other activities. He had conducted a symphony orchestra and acted in movies – both those based on his works and others. He appeared on stage, performed songs he had written. He posed for countless photographs, sometimes nude and always calculated to shock the staid literary establishment and play to his public, almost all of them themed around the erotics of death and pain and suffering. He became a body-builder and an exhibitionist, transforming his appearance through force of will and ceaseless work, and took up Japanese traditional martial arts in his early thirties, studying first kendō, then *iaidō* and finally karate. He conducted a failed experiment with boxing. He danced, badly.

Mishima had a genius for publicity and was seldom out of the news. In 1966 he formed a private militia, one hundred strong, the Tate no kai, Shield Society, comprised of students with right-wing views and a taste for military training. He used his celebrity and political contacts to gain permission to train with Japan's de facto army, the Jieitai or Self Defence Forces. He completed courses with special forces ranger units and was instructed on intelligence procedures, learning how to shake off a tail in the busy streets of Shinjuku. He was taught how to use a crossbow for silent killing, and was the only Japanese civilian ever to be taken up in an air force jet.

Anyone who met him could not fail to be impressed by Mishima's energy and vigour, his zest for life. And yet from an early age death obsessed him. The phrase he used to describe his preoccupations in *Confessions of a Mask*, his breakthrough book published in 1949 when he was twenty-four, a time when he was contemplating suicide, is 'Death and Night and Blood'. It is possible to view his work as having occurred during a gap in his resolve to die.

I wondered if this strange man, his life and literature, and his even stranger death, had anything to teach me thirty years on. There were links with my own life. I was now a writer – albeit of another sort. I too practised the martial arts and was deeply affected by ideas of the body and its correct relationship to the mind. My mental landscape, while not Gothic or especially morbid, was also far from conventional. The place to ponder this question must be Japan, a country I had lived in for nearly five years. I would have to go back.

PRIMARY

Word(s)

But words are things, and a small drop of ink,
Falling like dew, upon a thought, produces
That which makes thousands, perhaps millions, think . . .

LORD BYRON, *Don Juan*

... selbst dann bin ich die Welt.[8]

WAGNER, *Tristan und Isolde*

One morning in August 1966, Hiroshi Funasaka, owner of Tai-seidō Bookshop in Tokyo's Shibuya and Mishima's senior at the kendō dōjō they both attend, asks Mishima if he might have time to look at a memoir he has written of his wartime experiences. It is the first time he has acknowledged Mishima's status as a writer. Funasaka's book is called *Cries of the Heroic Dead* (*Eirei no Zekkyō*, 1966), a title that coincidentally echoes that of a work Mishima has just completed but not yet published – *Voices of the Heroic Dead* (*Eirei no Koe*, 1966). Mishima agrees to read it, admires the book and writes a laudatory preface.

On the strength of Mishima's involvement Funasaka's work is accepted for publication. It is impossible for him not to thank Mishima. Japan has a gift-giving culture. A few days later, after another kendō session, Funasaka asks Mishima a question. 'Do you perhaps have a good sword?'

'No, I have nothing special,' Mishima replies.

Not long afterwards, one day in September, Mishima arrives at Funasaka's house and rings the doorbell. Funasaka answers the door himself: he has been waiting, knowing that Mishima is always prompt and will arrive exactly at the time agreed.

'Please come in, Mishima-san,' he says, gesturing to a plain pair of slippers, the right size for Mishima's tiny feet, laid out just beyond the *genkan*, the raised entrance to the house.

After a cup of green tea Funasaka leads Mishima down a corridor into a small tatami room, empty except for a number of wooden stands and racks. Displayed around the room are twenty-five swords. Some are in *shirasaya*, plain unvarnished wooden storage mountings, the scabbards removed a few minutes earlier so that the blades will be visible. Other swords are mounted in various styles of *koshirae* – sword furniture, including the handle, scabbard and fittings. One or two are naked blades, displayed on stands draped in white silk, with the tang – the *nakago* – exposed to reveal the smith's signature and file marks.

Mishima gazes round the room, begins to examine the swords one by one. After a moment or two Funasaka comes to stand next to him, starts to describe each sword in his collection. He hands Mishima a soft clean cloth with which to wipe the surface of the blades should he need to, and a small silk square for holding the tang of any sword where the handle has been removed.

'This blade here has a small chip, no look, there are two,' says Mishima, pointing. 'How did that happen?' He indicates a shortish, thin-bladed sword with a pronounced *sori* – curve. Now he picks up the sword by the handle, weighing it in his hand, locating its balance point and then turning the blade into the light.

'In battle. It is a Mino-den *kotō* by Seki no Magoroku.⁹ Sixteenth-century. It was used in battle.'

'Ah,' says Mishima pausing. 'Then this, I think, is the one for me.'

Later, in the early hours of the next morning, Mishima is alone in his study. He sits at his metal desk, a Peace cigarette burning in the ashtray in front of him, the one source of light a small desk lamp. On the desktop lies the sword. The Seki no Magoroku. He releases the *habaki* from the mouth of the *saya*¹⁰ with an upward push of his thumb against the sword guard, draws the blade out from the scabbard, angles it to catch the light, the *hamon*, the temper line, flashing – the forging marks playing along the curve of the polished metal. Mishima imagines blood running down the blade towards the sharp tip, wonders if anyone really has died under its edge. He shudders just a little as he resheathes the sword, as if something invisible has passed between metal and man.

Satsujin no ken, a murderous sword, is a sword misused in committing acts of wilful evil. It is usually contrasted with *katsujin no ken*, literally a lively, reviving or life-promoting sword. *Katsujin no ken* represents the concept of employing a weapon solely for the defence of the weak. It presumes a state of mind the opposite of arrogant, since there must always be arrogance in choosing to kill or injure when there is no need.

Japanese sword techniques evolved on the battlefield and focused on efficiently dispatching an enemy. During the Pax Tokugawa, an enforced peace of nearly three hundred years spanning the seventeenth, eighteenth and two-thirds of the nineteenth century, fencing fell under the influence of Zen thinking. The swordmasters Miyamoto Musashi and Yagyū Munenori[11] were famously influenced by the Zen monk Takuan Sōhō, and their exchanges on the higher concerns of fencing explore the idea of the morally correct employment of armed strength.

Most arts and crafts of that time were co-opted as means for self-improvement, or Ways – *dō* or *michi* in Japanese. So there is a way of serving tea, *sadō*, a way of writing, *shodō*, even a way of loving boys, *shudō*, and there is, of course, a way of the sword, *kendō*. Modern forms of *budō* and the surviving ancient forms of martial arts – *koryū* – all represent themselves as means to polish man's spirit and produce a more evolved human being.

At the end of his life Takuan wrote down the Chinese character 'dream', dropped the writing brush and died. He taught that anxieties and lusts, fear and greed, which litter the mind, act to distract us in life, and in combat may cause a fatal mistake. Takuan's response was a state of mind known as *mushin* – literally no-mind,[12] a generalised awareness that resisted fixing onto any particular object and promoted a natural and non-reactive mastery in martial disciplines. Takuan, in addition to leaving sixty volumes of his writings and many works of calligraphy and other craft arts, such as the famous tea scoop called *Buji*, invented the pickled daikon radish, which is eaten to this day all over Japan.

Oddly, Mishima was quite dismissive of the mystique surrounding the Japanese sword. I doubt that he paid much heed to the idea that a sword possesses a spirit, or even several spirits – that of the smith who made it, its owners, anyone who died under its edge. He once described a sword as nothing more than a 'man-killing kitchen knife', a specialised tool with only one purpose, unlike, say, a weapon such as a bow and arrow, with which you might also hunt for food. For Mishima then, a Japanese sword was meant for just one thing – to kill another man.

Mishima was no expert on Japanese swords. There is no evidence of connoisseurship and he may not have been aware that his term *hōchō tetsu*, kitchen steel, is a term of abuse for a type of Japanese sword manufactured between 1870 and 1930 using soft untempered steel.[13] These were tourist swords, flashy; they looked impressive but lacked the qualities of a true weapon. Typically they were mounted with an intricately carved handle made of ivory or bone and with a matching carved *saya* in the same material. Just such a silly sword illustrates the UK paperback edition of an historical potboiler set in Japan – *Sensei*, by David Charney – which is like illustrating a war novel with a child's toy pistol.

But the view that a Japanese sword is concerned solely with killing is a cynical one and ignores the development of *budō* as a system of spiritual self-discipline.

The *Nihon Sansaku* or *Tenka Sansaku* (Three Greatest Sword-smiths of the Land) were so designated by the eighth Tokugawa Shogun[14] Yoshimune, who commissioned the Hon'ami, the leading sword-polishing and sword-appraising family, to compile a work of the best Japanese swords of all time. Their three-volume 1719 work *Kyōhō Meibutsu Chō* (Catalogue of Famous Things) adjudged three smiths as peerless: Etchū Matsukura Gō Umanosuke Yoshihiro, usually called Gō Yoshihiro; Awataguchi Toshiro Yoshimitsu; and Gorō Nyudō Masamune. Gō Yoshihiro and Toshiro Yoshimitsu each had sixteen blades listed. Masamune had sixty-one. The ruling Tokugawa family grew so obsessed with collecting the swords and knives of Masamune that it would often block the fortunes of anyone possessing one, so as to encourage them to sell.

In his story 'The Estate of Maximilian Tod', Bruce Chatwin refers to a sword dated 1279 and made by another of the Three Greatest Smiths, Toshiro Yoshimitsu, whom he misnames Toshiru. Chatwin tells us that the sword had been tested on the dead body of a criminal: a practice known as *tameshigiri* had been used to cut him from left hip to right shoulder in a move Chatwin calls *iai*. Sword blades of much later periods sometimes contain details of *tameshigiri* inscribed on the tang, but there is no cut called *iai*.

A number of myths and stories has built up around named swords, *meitō*,[15] or swords made by famous smiths. The idea that a Japanese blade might be dipped into a stream to see if leaves floating down on the current will be cleaved seems to derive from a story about Damascus scimitars. In its Japanese version there is an elaboration contrasting the good and evil reputations of the swords of two smiths, Masamune and Muramasa.[16] The Muramasa blade easily cuts leaves using only the force of the current. The Masamune blade, however, fails to cut the leaves: as each leaf nears its razor-sharp edge, something causes each one to detour intact past the blade. The suggestion here is that the Masamune blade is charged with a righteous spirit: it will not cut unless it has to.

The reputation of Muramasa swords as evil-omened derives from their use in killing and injuring several members of the Tokugawa Shōgun's family.[17] To counter the supernatural threat of Muramasa swords a Masamune *tantō* dagger would be worn as a protective talisman. Yoshimitsu *tantō* also had talismanic properties.

Apart from the work of expert sword-appraisers another more practical method evolved for evaluating the qualities of a sword. *Tameshigiri*, test cutting, has already been referred to in one of its forms, cutting the dead bodies of executed criminals. There were, however, several versions of the practice: *iki-dameshi*, cutting a living man; *shini-dameshi*, cutting a dead body; and *katamono-dameshi*, cutting a hard object such as an iron *tsuba* sword-guard or a helmet. None was a test of swordsmanship, although the skill required of the tester was assumed to be of an advanced order. *Tameshigiri* was considered to be a test of the cutting qualities of a blade – how far it could cut, its technical limits, without chipping, bending or breaking.

The hereditary sword-testers and executioners for the Tokugawa shōguns were the Yamada. Yamada Asaemon, known as Yamada Kubikiri, or Yamada the Beheader, together with two others in the later eighteenth century tested over two hundred blades. The results were published in 1797 in a work called the *Kaihō Kenjaku*. In this text four classifications of sharpness were defined:

> *saijyō ōwazamono* – superlative sharpness
> *ōwazamono* – superb sharpness
> *ryō-wazamono* or *yoki-wazamono* – excellent sharpness
> *wazamono* – good sharpness

Ranking the sharpness of a sword involved cutting more than one body tied down on a special mount on a sand pile, called a *dodan*. Particular points on the body were cut, each deemed to have varying degrees of resistance. The greatest number of bodies entirely severed in a single cut is said to be five or possibly six piled on top of each other, cleaved at a point around the navel. A cut through three stacked bodies was sufficient for a sword to be declared *saijyō ōwazamono*. Another testing system was based on the extent of a cut at a particularly hard point on a single body, a complete cut being required for *saijyō ōwazamono*.

Among the swords designated *saijyō ōwazamono* by Yamada Asaemon were those made by the two Seki no Magoroku smiths, Kanemoto I and Kanemoto II.

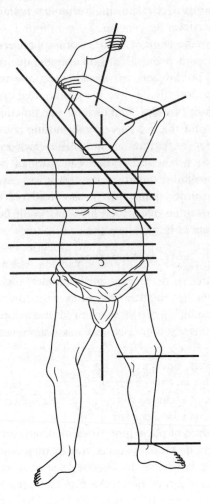

Lines of cutting on a tied-down human body in *tameshigiri*

The keys came in a small padded envelope festooned with too many stamps, as if they had been used not just to pay for transit but to repair the package, to hold it together. I counted seventeen stamps, eleven 80-yen, one 90-yen, four 110-yen and one 130-yen. The illustrations on the stamps were all different – a Red Fuji ukiyo-e print, a cartoon elementary schoolboy in a blue uniform holding an outsized yellow nib pen with a fat white olive-bearing dove flying over his head, a festival dancer from the far north of Honshu, Akita Prefecture, in an elaborate costume dancing for the rice harvest and another boy, naked except for a *fundoshi* and swimming mask and clutching a string of freshly caught fish, standing between wooden boats with the kind of oars you only see in the Ryūkyū Islands of the far south. Inside the envelope, along with the keys, was a coloured postcard with a picture of an ANA jumbo jet taking off from Tokyo. A single sentence in English explained:

'Need to move, take my place. Ken.'

The keys, three of them in a bunch, all big brass security-type keys, were attached to a key fob I had seen before. It was silvery, metal and moulded into the shape of a *kanji*, a Japanese character, *makoto*. Ken used to joke this was because *makoto* was the 'key to the Japanese character', punning in his heavily accented English. *Makoto*, sincerity.

Kenichi Hiramatsu – everyone abbreviates his name to Ken – Ken-san, Ken-chan, Ken-kun or just plain Ken – is the chef/owner of a small *sunakku* bar in Shibuya, the kind that serves coffee and a bite of something to eat during the day, switching to booze at night, and is perhaps two or three years older than me. We have known each other for seven years. He used to cook at a grand Tokyo hotel, the Imperial I think, saved some money and, as he put it, 'Got his life back.' We became friends during the time I spent in Tokyo in the mid-Nineties. I managed the impossible, infiltrating the closed world of a small Tokyo drinking den, had made Ken laugh enough to become a regular, a small group of faces whose food and drinks were subsidised by overcharging anyone else who ventured inside.

Once Ken had needed some help and I pitched in. It seemed the only thing to do at the time, but as it involved danger to myself and some cash, Ken and I were now, in the Japanese way, bound together in an unexpressed and unbreakable bond of mutual obligations and rights. He liked to shut his bar suddenly and go walkabout without notice, just a line or two on a scrap of card pinned to the locked door. Sometimes there'd be a date when he'd be back, sometimes not even that. Ken didn't say much generally, but he cooked instinctively, smiled a lot and was easy to like. The way he hummed helped me relax after the madness of a Tokyo day. Only a few minutes at Ken's were needed to feel the tension slough off like a discarded skin. Some-one must have told him I was looking to come back to Tokyo and needed somewhere to stay. I wondered if he had really gone anywhere or just cleared out to stay with a friend to help me out. Any answer to that would have to wait.

I am on a plane now, a Virgin plane, cattle class as usual, seated in the small space the cheapness of the ticket buys me. Having browsed the in-flight magazine for a few minutes I am reduced to staring at a tiny monitor built into the back of the seat in front of mine. I am not alone in doing this, for there is little else to do in a steel tube about to be shot across the planet. A small control console is inset into the right armrest of my seat. With this device you can look at an electronic map of the journey or choose from a selection of music or movies or even play video games.

For eleven hours non-stop, as we steadily cross Europe, Asia

and the oceans blue, the Japanese man in his early twenties
sitting next to me plays a golf game. I can hear the muffled
bleeps as he strikes the virtual balls. I doze, he plays. I drink, he
plays. I read, he plays. I eat, he plays, eating. I plan his imminent
death, he plays on, oblivious to danger. I leave my seat to use
the lavatory as he begins a new game and find him still playing
it on my return. He remains in his seat, doesn't need to pee,
only to play. *Otaku*, I mutter under my breath – nerd, with an
extra Japanese twist. *Otaku* simply have no off switch.

The lack of an off switch is a key metaphor in trying to understand the various excesses of recent and less recent Japanese
history. Even today the political machine, the bureaucracy and
government, resembles a plane set in motion after the war by
the SCAP[18] occupation authorities and whose cockpit has since
remained empty. The plane is on autopilot. To alter course – in
this case to deviate from an all-out pursuit of economic growth –
is next to impossible.

So here I am once again on my way to Japan; and this time in
search of the sword used to cut off the head of Japan's greatest
modern novelist in his suicide thirty years before. I was ten
at the time and my priorities were children's television – *Blue
Peter*, *Noggin the Nog*, *The Magic Roundabout* – and looking after
a red-haired pet guinea pig named Rusty.

Mishima's life was unusual, and in setting out to examine it I wondered whether Ian Buruma[19] might be right in declaring that its oddity robs it of broad significance, that it stands for nothing at all, or at any rate only for Mishima himself and his own (and possibly pathological) personal obsessions with Death, Blood and the Night, the product of a Gothic imagination incubated during over a decade spent in his grandmother's sickroom.

One of Mishima's English-language biographers, John Nathan,[20] in the preface to a new edition of his 1974 work, disagrees with Buruma. He argues that 'Mishima's life might properly be seen as a paradigm of the cultural ambivalence which has plagued Japan since the country was pried open 140 years ago,' and adds: 'I refer to the national struggle to find an authentic *self* by reconciling two disparate and often irreconcilable cultures – one native, inherent and grounded in tradition, the other foreign and intractable.' Here is a Mishima seen as a paradigm of his nation, his life spent struggling and searching for a comfortable self, one that sits easily.

Yukio Mishima was born Kimitake Hiraoka on 14 January 1925 and died on 25 November 1970. He lived for just forty-five years, a life that straddled the Second World War, the American occupation of Japan and the student riots of the 1960s. He took the pen-name Yukio Mishima at the age of sixteen with the publication in *Bungei Bunka* (Art and Culture) of his short story *Hanazakari no mori* (A Forest in Full Bloom). In his writing career he became Japan's most successful novelist and playwright, and then its most widely translated author. In 1970 *Esquire* magazine cited Mishima as one of the hundred most influential writers in the world, without saying who he was influencing. He was three times shortlisted for the Nobel Prize for Literature,[21] and might well have won but for his unpalatable and possibly misunderstood politics and his relative youth. His friend and mentor the novelist Yasunari Kawabata, himself awarded the Nobel Prize in 1968, described Mishima as a talent that comes along only once every three hundred years. And yet foreign writers and critics have consistently sought to downgrade his stature, Gore Vidal labelling him a B-list author with only one topic, himself.

Mishima was not, however, content simply to write while remaining largely out of the public eye, like Kawabata, who lived in self-imposed exile in Kamakura. He was, as I have suggested, like twentieth-century Japan, searching for an authentic *self*. And, like Japan, he chose to conduct much of this search in the gaze of a mystified public.

Another way to put this is to say that Mishima was profoundly troubled by the question: How can I feel that the life I am leading is real? If I experience my life as a fading reality, a process whereby things change their coloration, fading, reducing in savour, can I reverse this process? If so, how? If life is a process where we begin as a *tabula rasa* and take in a torrent of sensory experience, then arguably early life and young adulthood are bound to feel more real than what comes later, a time when you have tried most things, usually a process of narrowing down to what you like or at least to those things that attract you. Is this then one way to gauge the tragic nature of human life? Life as a performance that starts off in full sound and vision, in technicolor glory, then gradually fades, as the sensory organs grow slowly less able to do what they once did intensely well – a slow process of preparing to be unable to hear properly, see well and feel fully and with passion: a drift towards death?

How can I feel more alive? was Mishima's question, and it is also my own. The answer was not some programme of continent restraint – eat healthily, ride a bicycle, have modest, mild and regular habits, hope for a long life. For Mishima drama, offering to pay with his life for something more worth while than mere survival, being involved in something larger than himself, seemed a better way to make an exit. A good death might be viewed as the goal of a disciplined and productive life. What could be more magnificent?

Thinking about all this in the dimmed light of the aircraft, in the state between waking and sleeping that descends on me on long-haul flights, I realised that there were certainly overlaps with my own life. And the more I mused the more I wanted to discover, to really try to know, why on earth Mishima killed himself. So I would look for the sword, but more than that, I would search for answers to a large and multiplying number of questions posed by this man's anachronistic death.

. . . there are two kinds of human beings: those who keep death out of their thoughts to live better and more freely, and those who, on the contrary, feel their existence more wisely and more

strongly when they watch for the signals death gives . . . These
two kinds of spirits do not mingle. What one calls a morbid
mania is for the other a heroic discipline.

MARGUERITE YOURCENAR

Death, for many cultures and societies, is a taboo. Enquire of a
new acquaintance met at a party how he would like to die, and
the conversation might stop right there, never to be continued.
Yet it is a reasonable question, and as the moment of your death
frames your life it ought to matter a great deal.

The circumstances of one's own death are, suicide excepted,
unknowable, although we can look at statistics and express odds
for various sectors of society. There are books cataloguing
bizarre deaths: a woman in Spain quietly knitting in her front
room when a three-ton bull crashes through a window and gores
her still seated in her armchair; a retired actress smothered by
a file of her notices kept as a memento in a box on a shelf above
her bed. Most deaths are not so dramatic. Most of us will die in
bed at home or in hospital, from cancer, or heart failure or
stroke, the so-called diseases of civilisation.

I also wanted to examine Mishima's life afresh, to dig into his
obsessions. Some of his aims and activities overlap with my own,
and through looking at him I hoped better to understand why I
am drawn to such anachronisms as learning how to fight with a
sword in an age of guns and bombs and hi-tech death-at-a-
distance warfare. I also wanted to think about Japanese craft
skills and the way they are transmitted, how they are taught and
learned. One way to do this was by considering a single object:
Mishima's sword, the Seki no Magoroku sword used to cut off
his head, its history and manufacture, its role as a symbol of the
culture and warrior heritage of Japan. In considering all this, I
also hoped to learn about myself.

Mishima's life was characterised by a series of unlikely transformations. He was always on the way to becoming something
else, a chameleon character, taking on his hue from the territory
he chose to inhabit. He more or less started life as a girl, and
had to struggle to learn how to be a boy. Having looked fated
to die young from ill health, he had to find a way to live when
he did not die. At school his awkward gait and feminised language and mannerisms separated him from the brute boys he
found sexually alluring and forced him back into his own imagination and the creative zone of making things up. His natural
intelligence was responsible for legends, such as that while still
a schoolboy he memorised an enormous dictionary of *kanji*
characters. Perhaps he did – more likely he did not – but his
vocabulary was extraordinarily wide, and throughout his writing
career Mishima seemed to delight in the use and employment
of archaisms.

In early adulthood, like most males of his generation, Mishima
had once again expected to die – this time in battle in the service
of the Emperor – but he presented himself as someone unfit
even as cannon fodder, and mistakenly diagnosed as tubercular
was rejected. After a brief career as a bureaucrat in the Ministry
of Finance, he acknowledged his latent desire, the only thing he
had ever wanted to do since the age of fourteen and set out to
transform himself into a writer. Soon further transformations
were required. He would discipline himself physically and command his sexuality so that he could make love to a woman and
marry and father children. He would further punish himself,
and set about the largest transformation in his life, by making
himself a new body to occupy, through bodybuilding and later
through the demands of *budō*.

I arrived back in Tokyo in the month without gods. They, like my friend Ken, had gone on vacation, but unlike Ken they did so every year at this time, 11 October. *Kan na zuki*, the godless month, when all the gods – except Ebisu, who is deaf – obey the heavenly summons to Izumo Taisha – Shinto's oldest shrine – as part of a shrine tour.

Narita, Tokyo's international airport, is a godless place all year round, a ghastly concrete shed more than 60 kilometres from the city. This trip I had plenty of money, a brand-new visa-stamp-free passport and a return ticket, so there was absolutely no reason for the unsmiling immigration functionaries to give me a hard time and deny me entrance. This was a new feeling. Up to now I had always felt vaguely guilty in this situation, a hustler about to be unmasked, paranoia convincing me that I would be kept out, that I was smuggling myself in, as I stood behind the white line – 'Stop!' it screamed in silent Roman lettering – waiting my turn to be scrutinised and approved. My passport is riffled with a practised thumb and then stamped, the normal good for 90 days visitor's visa, and passed back across with only the faintest nod. *Nihon ni yōkoso* says a sign on the wall – Welcome to Japan.

I picked up my bag and had a brief exchange with the Customs man, he in his faltering English. Where had I come from and where was I bound? If he only knew what he was asking. I replied in English, never speaking Japanese to officials. Why give them an edge?

I took the Keisei Line into town, the cheapest option and I wasn't in a rush. Tokyo has a way of accelerating you, like hyper-peristalsis in an upset stomach, and I wanted to start slow. Drugged-looking, but just tired, schoolkids in Prussian uniforms boarded the train and collapsed on the benches, instantly slumping into sleep in the overheated carriage as we slid through the Chiba countryside, swathes of brilliant green exploding above the horizon, dotted with isolated blue tile-roofed buildings, the tree line the last natural thing before the concrete and neon of Tokyo. At Nippori Station I changed over to the Yamanote Line and arriving in Shibuya took the Hatchiko exit.

Ken's place was in a side street not far from Senta-Gai. I found the keys in my bag and let myself in to a darkened room that hadn't changed at all in the three years since I was last here. I flipped a light switch. Everything looked neat and ready for another day's business. Glasses and plates washed and precisely stacked. Ashtrays and rows of CDs placed to hand, ready for use. Ken liked classical music and organised his collection, which was huge, by the chronology of the compositions. You had to know just when Mozart composed his 23rd piano concerto to find it at once. I had answered this one before, like a question remembered from a game of Trivial Pursuit, and I reached down Mitsuko Uchida's 1986 version and slid it into the player.

There were two six-mat rooms and a small cubicle-style bath-room unit on a second storey above the bar. The lavatory was in a small annex accessed through the bar. The kitchen, really just bottle gas burners and a couple of electrical toaster ovens, was behind the bar. Everything was carefully stowed, shiny cop-pery pans hanging on hooks, cleverly fixed and angled shelves, piles and stacks. It was the best use of a small space I had ever seen and had the feel of a custom-built cabin on board a yacht.

The efficient use of nooks and crannies had to ignore the very real danger of an earthquake. Unless your customers didn't mind drinking out of plastic mugs and eating off paper plates, you stood a fair chance of being decapitated by sharp shards of falling glass and china. I paused and held my breath for my ritualised silent request to the seven good-luck gods[22] to preserve me from the next big one.

Upstairs I opened a built-in wardrobe. There were rows and rows of black clothes hanging on parallel rails extending deep into the space. Ken only wore black, like someone perpetually prepared for a funeral, claiming it saved time by removing both choice and complex laundry questions. In recessed drawers there were dozens of pairs of black socks, black underwear, and more oddly, black handkerchiefs, the ubiquitous *tenugui* every Japanese carries as a makeshift towel and never to blow their noses on. I couldn't resist examining the labels – almost everything was Yohji Yamamoto, Comme des Garçons, the odd item by Helmut Lang or Prada. Ken was better dressed than I had ever realised.

I slid my bag into the cupboard and closed it, thinking I'd unpack later. Feeling hungry, I decided to go round the corner in search of a Mos Burger.

I don't eat fast food, at least not American fast food, but Mos Burger is different. Mos – short for Mountain Ocean Sun – has taken the basic burger concept and subjected it to the Japanese genius for *kaizen*, continuous refinement, producing the best burger sold anywhere in the world. This branch was just around the corner. Signs on the counter and tables announced that it was the thirtieth anniversary of the founding of the company. And thirty years, nearly thirty-one, had passed since Mishima died. I had already found something out. Mishima killed himself before he had the chance to try a Spicy Mos with Cheese, so I ordered two, one for me and one by proxy for my quarry.

Nihilism was, for Mishima, both a personal issue, an insight or even simply a nagging doubt that his life had meaning, and a more general concern, a manifestation of *yūkoku*, a state of regret about the decline of the spirituality of Japan. In Mishima's view nihilism was the inevitable result of abandoning the Emperor as a divinity, and hence as a centre of ultimate value, a source of immutable otherness: a focus of meaning in an otherwise meaningless world of transitory things.

I began to wonder whether by his death Mishima hoped to stimulate a return to the values of a Cultural Emperor, a concept very different from his country's fascistic worship in the Thirties of the flesh-and-blood man who occupied the Chrysanthemum Throne. I doubted whether he had any clear idea of how this might actually be achieved, but perhaps the details did not matter. Mishima could confidently rely on a truly Japanese tradition of disregarding pragmatic concerns where an idealistic goal is being pursued. In addition there was *yōmeigaku*[23] and its central notion – that a sincere heart will yield *ryōchi*, infallible direct insight into the worth of any action contemplated. It is worth while to point out that this capacity was theoretically limited to the mind or heart of a Confucian sage. For anyone short of sagehood, self-deception seemed much more likely, especially when you were planning a coup d'état.

Sonnō jōi, Revere the Heavenly Sovereign, Expel the Barbarian, is a nineteenth-century slogan coined to summarise the twin objectives of a radical political movement inspired by Yoshida Shoin, a student of Yōmeigaku Confucianism. *Sonnō* invoked a desire to unite anti-Shogunal factions so as to restore the Emperor to direct rule; and *Jōi* expressed a reaction to foreign encroachment on Japanese domestic politics.

The invitation he carried, inscribed on a stiff card headed by a raised gilded Imperial Chrysanthemum *mon*, was tucked inside the pocket of his tailcoat, though he did not expect to have to show it. There would be lists of those invited and his face was a familiar one. Fame had few advantages, he thought, but not needing to remember invitations might count as one. Yōko had taken care in the selection of a formal kimono; she had sought advice from the Prime Minister's wife, an arbiter of style and thoroughly grounded in matters of protocol. The car would deposit them at the designated entrance to the Akasaka Imperial Palace. Despite the early onset of autumn it was a bright warm day, and it would be pleasant to walk in the serene precincts of the Imperial Gardens, albeit in the company of 2,000 other guests.

Mishima had discreetly enquired about the security arrangements, so it did not surprise him that after they had been ticked off on a list held by an Imperial Household functionary they were bowed to by the gate policemen rather than searched.

Imperial Garden parties are held twice a year, in the spring and autumn. At these events the Emperor and Empress accom-

panied by the Crown Prince and Crown Princess and other
members of the imperial family mingle and conduct 'warm and
friendly conversation' with selected members of the 2,000-
strong crowd. Those invited comprise the great and the good:
politicians, including the Prime Minister and other ministers,
senior judges, captains of industry, heads of diplomatic missions,
and individuals identified as making significant contributions in
the fields of the arts, sciences and community works. This year,
1966, Mishima was among those honoured.

Mishima was talking to his friend Yasunari Kawabata, who
unlike most of the male guests was wearing a kimono and *haori*
jacket. He never wore Western clothes and had received specific
permission from the Imperial Household Agency to ignore the
strict instructions as to clothing that accompanied the formal
invitations. Kawabata was, after all, like Mishima himself, said
to be in the running for the Nobel Prize. He was a man to be
indulged.

The group led by the Emperor, flanked by the Grand Chamberlain, approached the section of manicured lawn where
Mishima was waiting. Everyone was bowing in succession, like
the rising arms of a Mexican wave. Mishima bowed, remem-
bering having practised various angles before the war while bowing to photographs of this same man, and recalling that a ninety-
degree bow was a mandatory minimum to demonstrate respect
to His Imperial Majesty.

The Grand Chamberlain moved to introduce Mishima.

'We have met before, Mr Mishima,' said the Emperor. 'Both
of us were much younger I recall, and I was then able to hand
you a silver watch to reward your scholarship. Since that time
you have achieved so much for the nation, for which we can
only thank you.'

Mishima bowed. The party started to move on towards Kawabata, the next stop on a carefully choreographed drift through
the thronging crowd, other parts of which were being worked
by other members of the imperial family with their pre-scripted
'warm and friendly conversation'.

Mishima reaches within his tailcoat, round to the small of his back where the knife is hidden, and uses his thumb to release the scabbard. Simultaneously he breaks into a run. A few bounds are all that he needs to catch up with the thin grey old man in unbecoming Western formal dress. Gasps go up from the dozens who see the knife, the Emperor half turning as Mishima reaches him. 'Heaven's Punishment!' screams Mishima as he thrusts the knife into the Emperor's chest with an upward twist to sever an artery close to the heart, a means of ensuring an instant kill.

Withdrawing the knife from the collapsing Emperor, Mishima slashes his carotid artery and sinks into a kneeling position as the blood jets from his neck. For a moment a small amount of imperial blood and Mishima's own blood commingle on the blade. Within minutes, just as policemen arrive at a run, their pistols drawn, two men lie dead on the grass. An author and a former God. The sky remains bright and the sun shines on as if nothing untoward has occurred.

Mishima bowed. The imperial party moved off towards Kawabata. Mishima shook himself, ceased fantasising about assassination and accepted a glass of champagne from a passing servant.

In the morning, waking after a sound and dreamless sleep, I had forgotten about earthquakes and the prospects for sudden death. I had to decide what to do next and sat musing over a cup of coffee, doodling possibilities on a pad of paper, whilst munching my way through a plate of spongy super-thick toast, a kind found only in Japan. My decision to come back here, back to Tokyo, was straightforward enough: the clues to the Mishima puzzle I had set myself were here, if they were anywhere.

But I didn't have a fixed plan of action. Instead I hoped to make contacts and be passed along the links in a human chain of connections in the usual manner of such things in Asia. Previous experience had taught me that a rigorous and logical attack on problem-solving – lists and prospectuses, letters and petitions – just doesn't work very well in this part of the world. A better approach is to put the word out person to person that you want to talk about something, to see anyone who will consent to meet you and to try to make the best possible impression on everyone encountered. You need time and patience to do this. How much time did I have?

Patience was just as related to the idea of time running out as to any inner sense of urgency. I glanced down at the pad. I had unconsciously sketched the kanji *dai* 大 – large, which is written in the shape of a stick man, arms outstretched, headless.

By the time I found I could drink no more coffee and stepped out into the street there were tens of thousands of people shuffling up and down the hills of Shibuya in the brilliant autumn sunshine. I merged with the flood.

The first adjustment anyone must make on arriving in Japan is to the sheer volume of human traffic in cities. Too many people in too small a space. Yet pavement discipline is good. Not many collisions. Not even spaced-out teens, viewing video downloads on mobile phones as they clunk along on six-inch heels, convincingly dressed as Little Bo Peep in head-to-toe Vivienne Westwood, bump into anyone.

My first port of call was the FCCJ, Foreign Correspondents Club of Japan, a place I had heard about but had never visited. I had a letter of accreditation from the *Observer* appointing me as a special correspondent for Japan and hoped to use the club as an office, to delve into its press clippings and archives and ask around. I knew that Mishima had visited the club and spoken there in the late 1960s. It seemed a good place to start.

I walked down towards the station and the entrance to the subway in no particular hurry, telling myself to relax. If you don't do this, just being in Tokyo provokes a major stress reaction – a rash, a compulsion to drink too much, lethargy, far too much time spent asleep, or all of these symptoms combining. I doubted if I had enough time to adjust to this naturally, as the process takes roughly six months in the ordinary way, and I had to be back in England in four or five months' time.

In the subway I bought a transfer ticket to Yūrakuchō, hitting the right sequence of keys on the Japanese screen quite automatically, reading the alien text on the display without thinking, as if it was the easiest thing in the world.

When I first came to Japan it was as if words had been mysteriously eliminated, had vanished from my life. I couldn't understand what anyone was saying, but there was nothing especially new in that, it was an experience I had had many times before in the countries I had visited or lived in. What was unique for me was that I couldn't read anything written. Not one word could I make sense of, or even hazard how to say it.

For a literary person this is a disturbing feeling, a traumatic realisation. It is like being rendered illiterate or blind – as by the wave of a magic wand. You feel helpless, thrown back onto the dependencies of childhood. There is nothing for it but to work out methods for answering the questions usually resolved by language without recourse to language at all: by heightened observation, and by careful preparation and planning before leaving home, relying on others more than you otherwise would wish to.

In those days there were far fewer, if any, bilingual machines in stations, banks and ticket restaurants – ubiquitous cheap eating houses where you buy your meal ticket before sitting down to eat. Romanisation of Japanese was not common either. And so I struggled with the 'Devil's language' as the Jesuits dubbed it – claiming a Satanic conspiracy to keep out Christianity – and quickly resolved to learn the two Japanese syllabaries at once.

Japanese employs three writing systems in combination. *Hiragana* and *katakana* are syllabaries whose purpose is to supplement the Chinese character-based bedrock (*kanji*) used to convey essential meanings. I would learn the *kanji* too, but all in good time. I wrapped a metaphorical wet towel around my head, and after a five-hour struggle had vanquished the hundred or so squiggles.

Unlike alphabet-based languages, where letters combine to create sounds which, once rules of pronunciation are understood, can on the whole be read aloud even by someone who does not understand what they are reading, Japanese requires understanding just to vocalise it correctly. Written Japanese uses *kanji* or ideograms, characters imported at various times from China, and which have a range of possible pronunciations –

sometimes as many as thirty. Further, the very basis of an ideo-
gram is a visual one, not simply that you can see it – a character-
istic of all writing systems – but in Japanese a text can be read
and understood without the reader knowing how to pronounce
it aloud at all, or at least with any confidence. So a preliminary
understanding can be gleaned almost at once simply by scanning
the *kanji* in a text.

Many *kanji*, originally, were simple pictures of whatever they
represented. As the hieroglyphic possibilities are somewhat
limited, more complex shapes were adopted, adapted and combined to yield thousands of symbols that could either stand alone
or be used in combination to form compound words and ideas.
The character for a jewel, say, combined with the character for
a seat, yielded the compound character for throne.

In Japanese the beauty of a sentence does not come simply
from how it sounds and the ideas it contains. It also derives from
the look of the characters on the page, the subtle effects that
occur when particular characters are read. A fascination with
the correct order of writing the strokes that make up a character
is a part of being literate in Japanese and is often discussed when
an unfamiliar *kanji* is encountered. Despite the use of computers
and printed texts, calligraphy, one of the core skills of an educated person according to Confucian thinking, remains univer-
sally admired.

Interviewed by Robert Trumbull of the *New York Times* about
the difficulties of translating from Japanese into English and the
differences dictated by the nature of the Japanese language itself
for a writer who works in that language, Mishima explained that
sometimes the chiché about poetry being that which is lost in
translation is quite true. In a sense it is not possible to translate
from one language to another. For example, as there is only a

small number of sounds in Japanese – just over one hundred syllables (English has over four hundred) – there are many homonyms, words pronounced exactly the same, and because of this Japanese literature abounds not only in poetic effects but also in word play and puns. The title of one of Mishima's most widely read novels, *Gogo no Eikō*, literally means 'Afternoon's Tow' – referring to a tugboat pulling ships into harbour in the late afternoon, a common sight in the port of Yokohama where the action is located, but the sounds can also mean 'Faded Glory'. In English this allusion could not be maintained, and an entirely different title, *The Sailor Who Fell from Grace with the Sea*, was adopted.

Mishima condemned the use of rōmaji – the use of romanisation (as in this book) – as simply awful. The word *bara*, which means rose, is written with a rounded multi-stemmed character – 薔薇 – that seems to contain the essence of the rose itself, as Mishima saw it. 'A writer loves to give such effects to his readers,' he said.

I suppose the first character does rather resemble an inverted rose and its trailing thorny stem, like the flower clamped between Mishima's teeth in Eikō Hosoe's remarkable portrait in his 1963 nude photo-essay *Barakei* (Ordeal by Roses).

In modern times Japanese has twice been overhauled. In 1868 during the establishment of the Meiji state, when everything was being reformed and updated, a member of the oligarchy, whilst Minister for Education, seriously suggested that Japanese be abandoned in favour of English. Another equally august person counter-proposed German as the key to a successful transformation from a feudal to an industrial society. A further reform took place in 1945 under the American occupation, when many *kanji* were simplified and older forms abandoned. Mishima enjoyed using pre-1945 words, and when his manuscripts were typeset it was usual for the printer to return the galley proofs with *geta* marks – two lines like the imprint of wooden clogs in mud, signalling where a character not in stock will appear. The archaic *kanji* metal type had to be specially manufactured in order to print the book.

Among the most interesting aspects of ancient vocabulary is the so-called hapax legomenon, a word, or in the case of ancient Chinese/Japanese a character, which is found only once and whose meaning and pronunciation can only be guessed at, as the missing context is truly decisive. In such a case, where no comparison exists, and there is no precedent to base anything on, we are forced to improvise.

In Yūrakuchō I found the building in which the FCCJ occupied two floors and took a lift to the reception area. When I explained that I was a journalist seeking temporary membership, the bearded Westerner behind the front office counter told me in Canadian-accented Japanese that I needed a sponsor, someone who was already a member. He would see if he could find a member who might be prepared to sponsor me, and would I mind waiting for a moment or two?

    After a few minutes the Canadian returned and said that a member would be happy to help. Would I mind having a quick word with him now? I followed him into the dining room and café area and was directed towards a man just finishing his lunch, a cup of tea to hand, with several others at the table drinking bottles of beer, one smoking a large cigar. Together they looked like classic foreign correspondents.

When I walked over and introduced myself, the gentleman who had apparently been selected at random to endorse my membership turned out to be Henry Scott Stokes, an English journalist who had written an excellent biography of Mishima[24] and had been close to him in the last years of his life. Serendipity? I was delighted, and mumbled a phrase or two of thanks for the kindness he was extending to a stranger.

Henry seemed to wince as he sipped his tea, and I asked him if he was all right. He told me that he was recovering from a hernia operation. 'I should never have had it,' he said, without explaining why. I was conversing with a man who had allowed others to cut open his stomach, on the subject of another man who had done it for himself, and without anaesthetic, one seeking healing, the other destruction.

The library was on the floor below the FCCJ reception. The entrance, accessed down a nondescript corridor, passed a door leading into a small private cinema which showed Western movies to enhance the social life of the members' families. Inside the library itself, to the left, there was a further room equipped with small booths where journalists could work undisturbed, as well as a soundproofed box for filing stories by phone. I walked up and down the narrow space glancing down at the abandoned laptops and piles of papers – it was lunchtime – and then returned to the main room and introduced myself to the librarian, Mrs Nakayama.

The library proper had two or three computers connected to the internet and rows of metal and wooden filing cabinets indexing the library's collections. There were stacks of shelved books, of course, and in an area arranged in a square there were several centrally placed low tables strewn with magazines taken from nearby racks and surrounded by armchairs. In three of the chairs, middle-aged Japanese men in suits sprawled fast asleep. One man was snoring. I glanced around the stacks and then enquired about clippings, which were kept in the librarian's office.

My request for the Mishima file brought me three large bundles. The papers were date-stamped, and some – both photocopies and original cuttings from newspapers and journals – were yellowed with age. I settled into an armchair opposite the snoring man, and began to sort through the files. What was I looking for? Any mention of the sword, I supposed, anything strange, names, faces, maybe places. Something to follow up.

There were hundreds of pages. After only a few minutes I realised that this would take hours of concentrated effort and decided just to skim the files for now and to come back another day for a detailed review.

A quick scan yielded:

> A blurry photocopy taken from the *Asahi*, a left-leaning paper, with a photograph of Mishima's and Morita's heads, carefully positioned on the floor of General Mashita's somewhat Spartan office.
>
> An account dated a year after Mishima's death reporting that someone had stolen his ashes from his grave. After an extensive search had failed to find it, the missing urn was accidentally discovered buried in a shallow hole a few hundred metres away and still within the cemetery. The hole was next to a public lavatory.

The sword was also mentioned. Hiroshi Funasaka, the owner of Taiseidō Bookshop, had given the sword to Mishima in September 1966. Funasaka let Mishima have the pick of his collection, a sixteenth-century sword by the famous smith Seki no Magoroku.

Later that afternoon at Ken's, feeling jittery and unsettled, I decided I needed some exercise. What could be more appropriate than sword cutting? But I couldn't afford a sword, even a cheap one, and anyway owning a *shinken*[25] in Japan meant registering it with the police to comply with the Sword and Gun Control laws. I wasn't even sure if someone on a visitor's visa could do this. It made more sense to buy a *bokken*, a wooden sword, and try to find somewhere to swing it, preferably early in the morning before anyone came to wonder at the foreigner. I remembered there used to be a kendō shop visible from the edge of Yoyogi Park, only a ten-minute stroll away, and decided to walk across to check.

I found the shop without any trouble. Crossing the park I was surprised at how many encampments of homeless people there were, most of them gathered under improvised tents, blue plastic sheeting tied to trees and fencing to form a shelter from the wind and the rain. Inside the shop were a great many wooden swords, most of them cheap red and white oak imports from China. I asked if there were any superior *bokken*, and eventually selected a white oak fairly heavy Japanese-made sword. It was straightish, like the swords used in some kenjutsu styles such as *Kashima Shin Ryū*,[26] and as I bought it I was given a cloth sword bag and a kendō headcloth on which the word *heijōshin* was written in bold calligraphy. *Heijōshin* – a man with a stable heart, a fixed character, morally steadfast. The goal of *budō* training.

It is nearly 6 a.m. I have found a small Buddhist temple with a courtyard and graveyard about five minutes from Ken's. The gate is always open. It is always deserted, at least I have yet to see anyone there the three or four times I have popped inside to eat a sandwich or just sit away from the clamour of the streets. I take out my sword, remove my jacket. I have decided that a thousand cuts, *kiri otoshi*, straight cuts down the centre line of the body, will do as my morning exercise. The aim is to make each cut exactly the same as the last. No variation. It is very hard to do this. After I finish I notice that I am being watched. In a line are three black figures staring at me. The crows are perched on three grave markers, nodding like tiny mourners. As I return their gaze they fly off cawing.

I place the box on the counter in the main room at Ken's. I have just bought a mobile phone, or to be precise, have just been given one, having signed up for a connection service and voice-mail account. Unlike in the UK it is possible to terminate a phone rental agreement within a month. No twelve-month minimum contract. Over a cup of coffee I browse the instruction booklet. 'Do not get dew on phone,' it says in nicely poetic *Japlish*, Japanese English. I scroll through the ring tone options, with all the usual bleeps and whistles and snatches of music, but finally go for the oddest choice on offer, something I have never seen elsewhere. I set the phone to alert me to incoming calls by cawing like a crow.

Shishi, Men of High Purpose, were a mid-nineteenth-century terrorist movement committed to direct action as the means to achieving their political goals – largely the *Sonnō jōi* agenda. Their methods included attacks against government property, the assassination of state officials and foreigners and the destruction of foreign property. Even statuary was beheaded to make powerful symbolic points, as in a famous incident where the heads of three wooden statues of the Ashikaga shōguns kept inside the Tōji-in, a Kyoto temple, were cut off and displayed on Sanjō Bridge, like executed criminals, alongside messages citing treason against imperial rule more than five hundred years earlier. They operated throughout the 1850s and 1860s and were responsible for dozens of killings – between the years 1862 and 1864 there were more than seventy murders attributed to *shishi*.

The League of the Divine Wind rebellion occurred in Kumamoto in Kyūshū in 1876. A group of fewer than 200 samurai opposed to Meiji government reforms decided to attack Kumamoto Castle, the major army garrison in Kyūshū. They killed the garrison commander, Major General Masāki Taneda, and severely wounded the prefectural governor.

At first imperial troops were taken by surprise, but because the rebels refused to use firearms and were few in number, the defenders were able to regroup, and within three hours repelled the attackers. By the end of the following day the rebellion was crushed, and nearly all the rebels had been killed or had committed seppuku.

The anti-Western ideology of the rebels meant that the timing of their attack was determined by consulting a Shinto oracle – a ceremony called *Ukei* – as a means both to demonstrate the sincerity of their intention and to ask for divine sanction.

The two chief events that spurred such ultra-traditionalists into open rebellion were the Hito-rei Edict of 28 March 1876, a government decree which ordered that only members of the army and the police forces might henceforth carry swords – everyone else was banned from wearing a sword in public; and the compulsory conversion of samurai stipends into low-yield government bonds which reduced the income of samurai, in many cases already impoverished, by as much as 30 per cent.

In *Honba – Runaway Horses –* the second volume of his *Sea of Fertility* tetralogy,[27] Mishima uses an account of the Divine Wind rebellion as the ideological inspiration for his protagonist Isao's group of 1930s terrorists. Isao names his group the Showa League of the Divine Wind. (Showa was the reign name of Emperor Hirohito.) He sees the issues for which they will fight and die as a clear war of values: Japan's traditional culture versus Westernisation. He and his small band of boys are angry at the lack of justice in the modern industrialised world, a world where rich industrialists work hand in glove with corrupt politicians. The concepts they adopt suggest that assassination as a means of purging the national body of an imported poison is both urgently necessary and fully justified – one or two deaths to save the nation. They acknowledge that their purity of intent requires that they too must die. Even to be captured and imprisoned would provide a personal advantage – staying alive – and corrupt the purity of their efforts. They must gain nothing, lose everything, to benefit Japan.

Although the events of the Divine Wind rebellion are historical, the descriptions in *Honba* are fictionalised by Mishima. His language mimics that of the nineteenth century.

The Rite of Ukei

The story begins in 1873 at Shingai village, five miles south of Kumamoto in Kyūshū. Four men are gathered at the Shingai Imperial Shrine, a branch of the Grand Shrine at Ise, and the most sacred place in the prefecture. After their devotions the men retire to the priest's dwelling to await the results of his performance of the rite of *Ukei*. Harukata Kaya, Kengo Ueno, Kyusaburo Saitō and Masamoto Aikyo – all of them samurai.

The priest of the shrine, Tomo Otaguro, is a student of the former priest Oen Hayashi, now dead, who writing about the *Ukei* claimed:

Of all the rites of Shinto, the Ukei is the most wondrous. As to its origin, the ineffably awesome goddess *Amaterasu*, together with Lord *Susano-o*, conducted the first *Ukei* in High Heaven, when it was transmitted to our land of Yamato.

The practice of the *Ukei* had by this time been forgotten, having lapsed into abeyance, and Oen struggled to reintroduce it as the means for men to govern their affairs in accordance with divine will. Special chanting invoked the gods. The *Ukei* was 'worship by words fraught with sacred power'.

Oen's teachings can be summed up by stating that worship of the gods and government are the same. To serve the Emperor is to serve the gods, 'the distant gods of the world hidden to men'.

In the early years of the Meiji restoration we see the rising tide of foreign learning and technology: an imperial prince studying in Germany; the prohibition of the wearing of swords and the decree that samurai should cut their distinctive hairstyles; treaties with foreign powers; the adoption of the Western calendar. These trends were not progress but a rush towards destruction.

A League is formed and named the League of the Divine Wind, a reference to the idea that sincere living and purifying your heart will cause the gods to send a divine wind (*kamikaze*) as they did in the past to sink the invading Mongolian fleets, in this way purging toxic foreign influences. Members of the League refuse to walk beneath telegraph cables, as they are foreign innovations. They carry salt to self-purify in the event of encountering someone dressed in Western clothing – or a Buddhist or a funeral procession – and only with chopsticks will they pick up money which has a foreign design.

This Shinto fundamentalism is transcendental, promising a direct ascent into heaven, free from the corruption of death, as a reward for anyone living a pure life, avoiding defilement and worshipping according to the ancient ways.

The edict against the wearing of swords in the eighth year of the reign of the Meiji Emperor – Meiji 8 (1876) – triggers a crisis. The young men of the League wish to fight. 'If their swords are snatched from them what means will remain to guard the honour of the gods they revered?' In a key passage Mishima highlights the significance of the dissolution of the samurai feudal class, to be replaced by a conscript army:

> The defence of the land would no longer be entrusted to the manly warrior bearing at his side the swift thunderbolt of the immortal gods. The national army created by Aritomo Yamagata gave no preference to the samurai class, nor did it honour the ideal of the Japanese as individuals rallying spontaneously to the defence of their native land. Rather, it was a Western-style professional army which, in ruthless disregard of all tradition, ignored class distinctions and depended upon a draft system to support its manpower. The Japanese

sword, giving way to the sabre, had lost its soul. Now
it was fated to become a mere decoration, an ornament.

Harukata Kaya presents a petition to the authorities, protest-
ing against the Prohibition of Swords Edict. His petition is
ignored, and separately the League leaders gather to consider if
it is permissible to rise up, to try to kill the military and civilian
officials of the prefecture and to capture Kumamoto Castle. A
further *Ukei* is arranged. This time the gods sanction the proposed uprising, transforming the League into 'an army of the
gods'.

That the enterprise is doomed is displayed by the numbers –
fewer than 200 men of the League facing ten times that many
government troops. They choose to arm themselves solely with
traditional weapons, whereas the garrison is armed with modern
firearms. The sole non-bladed weapon adopted by the League
is a traditional kind of grenade needed to blow up the arsenal.

Into battle they will bear a simulacrum of the God of War,
Hachiman of Fujisaki Shrine, who will act as their unseen commander.

The Combat of the Ukei

The League gathers at Fujisaki Hachiman Shrine overlooking
Kumamoto Castle. There is no moon. At 11 p.m. they set off.
They attack the castle, killing Lieutenant Sakaya and suffering
their first fatality, a youth of seventeen, Motoyoshi Aikyō. The
artillery barracks is captured, its garrison utterly routed in a
single hour of combat. Many of the surrounding buildings, and
buildings in other parts of the city, are burning – the bulk of
the castle looms dark against a crimson sky.

The infantry barracks is attacked and also the main garrison
force, an infantry regimental base. The government soldiers,
though vastly superior in numbers, have no ammunition – none
is issued in peacetime – and can only respond with sabres and
bayonets. The fighting is a bloody business – there is a limit to
how many men can be felled with blades. Soon it grows clear to

some of the defending officers how few are their opponents, and they start to regroup and to offer effective resistance.

The regimental commander escapes an assault on his residence and flees disguised as a groom, eventually to make his way to the barracks, where he resumes command of his troops. The main magazine is raided and the defenders obtain ammunition for their rifles. Reinforcements arrive and a murderous crossfire pins down the men of the League. A series of heroic charges attempt to close the distance and engage the defending troops, but each time the men of the League are shot down. Eighteen men are killed in this way, twenty others wounded. The leader of the League, Tomo Otaguro, is mortally wounded. He asks his brother-in-law to behead him and bear his head along with the simulacrum of the God of War, Hachiman, to the Shingai Shrine.

One with the Gods

The League has been defeated in a battle that lasted only three hours. The fleeing survivors attempt to escape by boat but cannot launch the vessels, which are stuck fast in the mudflats. Instead they retreat to the top of Mount Kimpo. It is early morning and the vistas afforded from such a vantage point are spectacularly beautiful. 'All was clear and fresh and tranquil.' They are being pursued in earnest and must quickly decide what to do.

Some of the men reflect on the teachings of their deceased Shinto master, Oen, who wrote that there are only two routes into heaven. You must either make use of the Pillars of Heaven or the Floating Bridge of Heaven. Both of these, through lack of purity, have become invisible to mankind. The gathered men consider their choices – to fight again or to commit seppuku. Escape seems both impossible and undesirable.

Seven of the company are boys of sixteen or seventeen. It is decided that they should withdraw, but of course they are the most fervent and protest, only reluctantly agreeing to leave after they have been ordered by their elders to do as they are told.

After sending out scouts the remaining band of around thirty men try to cross the bay in a fisherman's vessel, but it is too small to take them all, and so they decide to split up. Each is to make his way as best he can. The rebellion is over.

The men on Mount Kimpo are less than a third of the original number of rebels. All the others have died in battle or committed seppuku when seriously wounded or about to be captured by government forces. The survivors, one by one, cut open their stomachs, choosing death and ascent into heaven, perhaps by way of the Floating Bridge, as a fitting conclusion to their struggles as the defeated army of the gods.

Only one member of the League survived. He was Kotaro Ogata, who consulted the gods and was told that he ought to surrender. Ogata allowed himself to be captured and was imprisoned for life. He wrote a book about the uprising, *The Romance of the Divine Fire*, which considered the question of why the *kamikaze*, the Divine Wind, had not blown to aid the rebels, why the *Ukei* had seemingly proved fallible. In lamenting their efforts he wrote:

> How wretched and pitiable that men so splendidly faith-ful should, counter to all expectation, perish in a single night, like blossoms scattered by a storm, like the fleet-ing frost and dew, and in an enterprise conceived and executed under the guidance of the divine will!

The samurai spirit is defined in the last line of Ogata's book: 'Were we to have acted like frail women?'

It was Mishima's belief that most Japanese literature, including the works of Kawabata, came from the 'tender-soul or feminine tradition,'[28] represented by peace, the beauty of elegance and refinement'.

But I am trying to get back to the rough-soul tradition
of the samurai – warrior stories from the medieval age,
samurai poetry since the 15th century, and even some
kabuki and noh plays . . . Since World War II, the feminine tradition has been emphasized to the exclusion of
the masculine. We wanted to cover our consciences.
So we gave great publicity to the fact that we are a
peace-loving people who love flower arranging and
gardens and that sort of thing. It was purposely done.
The government wanted to cover our masculine tradition from the eyes of foreigners as a kind of protection. It worked. The wives of American occupation
officers became enchanted with the flower arranging
and the rest of *Japanese culture*. But we have also hidden
this rough-soul tradition from ourselves.

It's odd how a culture passes through phases in the way it is
regarded and characterised by outsiders or non-native observers.
In the period after the fall of the Tokugawa Shōgunate and the
restoration of the Meiji Emperor – the last three decades of the
nineteenth century – the newly arrived merchants and news-
papermen and adventurers in Tokyo, Yokohama and Nagasaki
were at pains to stress their fascination with the vestiges of the
samurai class. Japan's was a martial culture in the same way that
Prussia's was a martial culture – and at the same time. This
viewpoint persisted until the Second World War, when Western
attitudes towards Japan were coloured by the battlefield experiences of members of the Allied Forces captured and imprisoned
in POW camps. Admiration was now supplanted by utter loath-
ing at the brutality and perceived cruelty inflicted on these
prisoners in captivity. What was little understood at the time is
that a cultural assumption was operating. From the viewpoint

of Japanese martial culture, to have submitted to capture demonstrated low self-worth and a lack of honour worthy of abject contempt. The duty of a soldier facing capture was clear – to die, taking with him as many enemy soldiers as he could.

Can you pick and choose and say that you want some but not other aspects of a culture to survive, and so to provide the necessary continuity to constitute a national identity? Why not? Who would argue for, say, female infanticide, however traditional, simply for the sake of historical continuity and preserving a consistent way of life? The martial culture of Japan that Mishima mentions developed over centuries of perpetual warfare – mostly during the *Sengoku Jidai*, the period of the Waring States during the fifteenth and sixteenth centuries, when all the regional states were at war. After the establishment of the Tokugawa hegemony in 1603, when Japan was finally united, a condition of enforced peace lasted for 264 years. During this time the military arts began to stagnate. Pragmatism was displaced by display, substance by form. A conversion from battlefield warriors to feudal administrators was the fate that befell the samurai. The pen became mightier than the sword.

Mishima worked at his desk from 11 or so at night until the early dawn every day from the age of sixteen until he died at forty-five. He divided his time to give part of each night to writing commercial works to pay the bills, and part to real literature. He said of himself that he was upside down in relation to reality, working during the dark hours of night and sleeping during the day, hidden away from the life-giving light of the sun.

Societies, like individuals, need to be in balance. There can be predominantly male or predominantly female societies, but every society has to balance a 'male' and a 'female' ethos to be stable. Mishima claimed that the feminine side of Japan, displayed in the arts of ikebana and the tea ceremony, in kimono design and the institution of geisha, in haiku and ceramics, had been deliberately stressed since the American occupation. But this side was not the whole of Japanese culture. There was also an immense historical and cultural investment in the arts and attitudes of the warrior: the sword was needed to balance the chrysanthemum. To ignore this was to be cut off from both a genuine and a romanticised past and to be cast adrift into an unknown identity as a nation, to dissolve historical connections. Yet historical features that might evoke an era inevitably fade and disappear when the conditions to sustain them have vanished.

One way to think about this is that Mishima was simply projecting his own problems and concerns on to the nation. He was obliged to struggle to become a man, having been brought up as a sensitive feminised girl-boy, a mother's boy, soft and intelligent but as unphysical as one can imagine. So instead of being satisfied with developing his own muscles and martial skills he felt himself compelled to insist on the same preoccupations for Japan as a whole. How else might a homosexual narcissist love his country, other than as an image of a muscle-man, a reflection of himself?

The last thing Yukio Mishima wrote, after a lifetime of prolific writing, was a short note, a single sentence, left on his study desk at home before leaving en route to his long-anticipated encounter with a spectacular act of suicide:

Human life is limited, but I want to live for ever.

With these words, Mishima states the first concern of a mortal artist, of anyone, sums up the tragedy of mankind, of all individually held values, of any kind of love: that each of us must one day die.

Mishima wrote an odd essay titled 'How to Live For Ever' in October 1968 – a time when he had certainly decided to engineer his own death – and I opened it eagerly, hoping to discover his views on the familiar notion that an artist creates partly to achieve fame and adulation that will outlive him. A writer writes 'to live for ever', in the words of Mishima's last note. Yet this is not at all what the essay reveals. It meanders in a stylistically Japanese manner, with no systematic analysis, no logical development. Instead Mishima launches into a critical attack on any writer who works with half an eye on posterity. If I have understood his point, it is that this causes a falsity, a self-consciousness that will falsify what is being written, and this will come between the writer and life itself.

Mishima claims he has never done this himself, that he is unconcerned with posterity. He considers whether a work lives on in the hearts of readers but realises that they too die. Books live on as objects; for a time they continue to exist. But can an object, a book, be said to be a form of life, especially if no one reads it? He does not elaborate this point, but compares this situation to the accumulation of objects by the doomed Flying Dutchman who gathers for the last judgement.

Having been passed a number of ideas to hold on to, we see each of them taken away, so that by the end of the essay we are left holding nothing at all. Which I am sure is Mishima's point. Live for ever? There is no way to do so.

Death poems are mere delusion – death is death.
TOKŌ KANZAWA, eighteenth-century poet

A blazing August sun reflects off the white concrete of the Tower Building of the Hotel New Otani in Tokyo. Mishima, wearing sunglasses, is lying back on a lounger, having completed his swim. The outdoor pool is magnificently sited in a Japanese garden 400 years old and expensively maintained. A cold glass of *mugi-cha*, barley tea, beaded with condensation, stands on a table beside him as he scribbles intently on a pad of paper. His skin is bronzed from his stay at the Tokyu Hotel in Shimoda on the Izu peninsula, where he always spends around a month with his family in the summer. He returned to Tokyo a few days ago. There are many things to manage in the few months that remain to him. Although he has finished the final part of the fourth and final book in the *Sea of Fertility* tetralogy, *The Decay of the Angel*,[29] in Shimoda, he intends to hold on to the manuscript until the last day.

Only the sounds of children laughing and splashing in the pool lap at the edge of his concentration. Even those who may have recognised the famous writer will not have guessed what he is working on.

Mishima was writing a death poem; the first of two he would

carefully inscribe and leave to be found after his suicide. The form he used, dictated by tradition, was *waka*, a 31-syllable poem in five lines of 5, 7, 5, 7, 7 syllables. The poetic conventions of a *waka* death poem stipulate that it should be graceful, use natural imagery and express transient emotions. There should be no hint of the fact that its author is about to die.

After several lines had been written and scratched out, Mishima finally settled on a poem turning on his acquisition of the Seki no Magoroku sword.

> *Masurao ga*
> *Tabasamu tachi no*
> *sayanari ni*
> *Ikutose taete*
> *Kyō no hatsushimo*

> A strong man
> gave me a sword which didn't fit in its scabbard
> provoking an urge to complete a task
> I have endured several years of this feeling
> Today's first frost

Is this a good death poem? Following its publication after the incident various critics said that it was not – it hinted at the suicide. Perhaps even Mishima realised this, as he composed a second death poem, though not this time while sunbathing by the outdoor pool of a luxury hotel. The second poem was more naturalistic, contained more feelings of *mono no aware*, the pathos of the transience of things.[30]

> *Chiru o itou*
> *Yo ni mo hito ni mo*
> *Sakigakete*
> *Chiru koso hana to*
> *Fuku sayoarashi*

> A small night storm blows
> Saying 'falling is the essence of a flower'
> Preceding those who hesitate

Here Mishima restates his romantic credo, that only by an early death may you enhance life itself.

In *Forbidden Colours*[31] Mishima writes:

> The process in which a writer is compelled to counterfeit his true feelings is exactly the opposite of that in which the man of society is compelled to counterfeit his. The artist disguises in order to reveal; the man of society disguises in order to conceal.

My first job on my original visit to Japan in the early Nineties as for most native English-speakers, was teaching English at a small language institute in Shibuya called the Rose of York School of English. During gaps between lessons and on any meal break when there was enough time I would book-browse in *Taiseidō*, spending hour after hour there *tachiyomi*[32] and fighting an ever-present urge to go home instead of returning to work.

The Rose of York had two 'campuses' – one in Tokyo and the other in London. The London school, in Baker Street, was a thriving enterprise, and the entrepreneur who owned it had sought to expand by opening a second school in Tokyo. She placed her brother in charge of the Tokyo venture, a decision that turned out to be disastrous.

Ura-san was small, thick-set, and wore his hair in a punch-perm, the preferred hairstyle of more old-fashioned yakuza mid-rankers. I never saw a tattoo, but would not be surprised if he had one. I knew he was a gambler, but doubted he was a gangster, despite his affected appearance. Later, and much to my surprise, I found out that his true passion was for ikebana, Japanese flower arranging, in which he held an advanced qualification. There were always enigmatically beautiful flower displays in the school.

Ura spoke poor English, was good with the students, and permanently suspicious of the gaijin – non-Japanese – teachers whom he only grudgingly admitted into his world, forced to concede that to teach English, English-speakers were unavoidable.

During the six months I spent working for Ura I met Ken and would bitch to him in the evenings at his bar about my boss and the indignities of teaching English to schoolgirls who would rather do just about anything else, but had no choice. Two of my students were at Gakushūin, the exclusive school Mishima had attended. One girl had delusions of grandeur, claiming descent from an imperial princess, and I delighted in setting her embarrassing language exercises to try to put a dent in her haughty demeanour. You are a pig, I would tell her, and to her nicer friend: You are a sheep. What would you say to each other in the farmyard? Eventually she realised what I was doing and complained to Ura. I was told off and my lessons restricted to the amazingly dull exercises printed in a range of boring textbooks.

Shibuya had been my stamping ground. I knew my way around this fashionable neighbourhood, and any visit to the multi-storey Taiseidō always had to include a brief diversion into the basement. This was not part of the bookshop but was leased to a number of strange businesses. One specialised in Nazi memorabilia – SS ID cards, Iron Cross medals, helmets, swastika armbands, videos and books about the Nazi war machine, along with small models of soldiers and their weapons, vehicles and equipment. I had never seen so much stuff of this kind gathered together in one place before.

There used to be two other kinds of material in the basement: martial arts and military books and videos, including large selection of Paladin Press militaria; and kinky sex stuff – female mudwrestling videos, sado-masochistic magazines featuring a bewildering array of restraint and knotting techniques, naturist videos and magazines with a stress on naked children.

I had dedicated hours to browsing the Paladin Press military titles. I recall *How to Kill* in about six volumes, segueing into *Do It Yourself Undertaking*, which explained how to get rid of a body after you *have* killed someone. One of my favourites was *Breath of Death*, not about the dangers of halitosis, but a treatise on building your own blowguns. The manuals, many of which explained how to perform illegal crafts – such as how to make plastic explosives or modify a rifle into a machine gun – always carried the statement 'For Academic research purposes only'. I liked that. 'Knowledge is power, and power leads to freedom' was the corporate motto of this subversive publisher, presumably paraphrasing Bacon.

The basement had hardly changed. The kinky section had contracted – no obvious child porn any longer – but the Nazi stuff was still going strong. A new range of foreign-language videos and music CDs – in Farsi and Urdu – had materialised. The Paladin titles were also depleted. Was this an indication of a shift in society from subversion to shopping, or had there been a police crackdown? After a nostalgic few minutes I walked back to Ken's, resolving to drop Funasaka a line to ask him if he would meet me.

Last Day   6.30 a.m.

Mishima rises early on Wednesday morning. His usual habit is to work through the night, waking around noon after five or six hours' sleep. But last night he went to bed earlier. Yōko has already left the house to take the children to school. Mishima empties his bowels, bathes, applies some clear lipstick and light rouge to his cheeks.[33] He lays out his Tate no Kai winter uniform, which has been cleaned and pressed. Dressing he steps into the trousers right leg first, following the tradition of reversing the usual order for putting on a *hakama*, which is left leg first. The exception to this traditional order is limited to dressing on the day of committing seppuku, stepping into the death *hakama* or *shibakama*, where it is right foot first, a symbolic acknowledgement that you are already dead, since the left over right, or left before right, order is only reversed when dressing a corpse before cremation.

The sky beyond Mishima's study window is bright and clear and cloudless – a good day to die, he thinks. But whatever the weather his resolve won't weaken now and he gathers up the letters he has written – to friends and family, his editors, publishers – and places them where they will be found later in the day. He also writes a short note and props it on his desk. He makes two phone calls, both to journalists he knows and likes. Munekatsu Date is a TV journalist with NHK, whom Mishima has dined with a few months before when he asked him if he would film and transmit him committing seppuku. At the time, seeing Date's shocked reaction, he turned the remark aside, passing it off as a joke. The other man, Takao Tokuoka, is a reporter for the *Mainichi* newspaper who took Mishima to a brothel in Bangkok after Yōko had returned home to Japan. He urges both of them to come to the Ichigaya Kaikan, a building adjacent to the SDF base and where the Tate no Kai hold meetings, saying only that 'something is going to happen'.

Just before 10 a.m. a white Toyota Corona pulls up outside the front gate to Mishima's house. Tiny Koga gets out of the driver's door, enters the courtyard and approaches the house as Mishima opens the door. Mishima passes Koga his briefcase and several envelopes. There is one for each of the Tate no Kai cadets waiting in the car and another for Koga. Mishima picks up his uniform cap and gloves and with his left hand holds his sword in place. It hangs from his uniform belt in a leather *guntō* military mount. The previous night, after Yōko had gone to bed, Mishima had carefully hammered flat the *mekugi* pins in the sword handle, a precaution to prevent the blade and the handle separating under the impact of a blow.

Mishima gets into the car and waits while his followers read their letters. They have all prepared themselves to die on this day and three of them, the two Kogas and Ogawa, are now ordered to survive, to ensure that Mishima's final message is not covered up or distorted in the subsequent trial. Mishima passes across an envelope containing money to pay the initial costs of a defence lawyer. The money, like a cash donation made at a funeral, is nine perfect unused 10,000-yen notes.

Albert Camus famously declared in his 1942 philosophical essay *Le Mythe de Sisyphe*:

> There is only one really serious philosophical question, and that is suicide. Deciding whether or not life is worth living is to answer the fundamental question in philosophy. All other questions follow from that.

Henry stirs his tea and meditates. I watch the spoon go round and round. I have just asked him if he considers Mishima a violent man.

'Whilst researching *The Sailor Who Fell from Grace with the Sea*, Mishima wanted to know what it was like to kill. Of course, he couldn't just kill someone, so he decided to kill a cat. He enlisted the help of his friend, the novelist Kobō Abe, who had trained as a doctor, and together they caught, killed, skinned and dissected a cat. Mishima claimed he found it hard to write about anything he had not experienced or at least witnessed. He also said that if he had not become a writer he would certainly have murdered someone.'

'I suppose these feelings were overwhelming,' I reply. 'That he needed a release for violent and sadistic urges, so he wrote them down.'

Henry sips from the steaming teacup. Some journalists on the other side of the room are loudly disputing over a couple of beers. We are enjoying a quiet pot of English tea in the FCCJ dining room. Henry had sent the pot back once when it was not prepared to his specifications. I don't remind him that killing animals, particularly pets, is a well recognised form of behaviour for nascent sociopaths. The practitioner often goes on to prey on human victims.

I like to walk while reflecting, and so decided to spend the afternoon looking at statues. It was a bright day, and the open air would freshen my sagging spirits. There were two particular statues I wanted to see, two more short journeys to make.

I rode the Yamanote line round to Ueno. In the carriage sitting opposite me was a teenage girl outlandishly dressed. Outlandishly dressed teenage girls are a common sight in Tokyo, but I couldn't stop staring at her hands. It was her nails that were especially odd – long and obviously artificial, they were covered in black fur. A friend I asked about this told me they were called Yeti nails, came from France, and had just caught on.

After the girl got off, her place was taken by a student, this time a boy. He wore a Reebok windcheater and jeans and carried a sports bag. He was tall and stocky, so physically different from his grandfather's generation since the arrival of high-protein diets in the 1970s. His left ear was, I noticed, cauliflowered and I realised that he was a serious practitioner of judo, the damage to his ear resulting from hours of ground fighting, *ne waza*. Beneath the logo of his jacket it said 'Life is not a spectator sport.'

It was no great distance from the station to the park. As in most of Tokyo's parks, a significant number of homeless people had set up camp here and were sheltering under improvised blue tarpaulins. Like everyone else in the park I ignored them and walked on towards Saigō's statue, not unconscious of the idea that Saigō would not have passed them by.

The statue, a famous gathering point, stands on a stone plinth and shows Saigō Takamori in a light summer kimono striding forward with a favourite hunting dog, a short sword in his belt. He was incredibly broad, bull-necked, with sturdy legs. His other famously distinguishing feature, his enormous testicles, are not visible. Saigō was a hero who had preoccupied Mishima. Sometimes called the last samurai, he died a hero's death in his fifties, and this convinced Mishima that it was not too late for him too to die a hero.

The second statue I wanted to see was in the Outer Gardens of the Imperial Palace. It was a large figure of the imperial loyalist samurai hero Kusunoki Masashige, clad in full armour and mounted on horseback. The statue had been paid for by the Sumitomo family to celebrate the bicentennial of the firm and used copper from their mines in Ehime. It was installed in 1900. As I stared up at the fierce fourteenth-century warrior, memorialised in European military equestrian style, I wondered if Mishima had a single trait in common with him. I doubted it. This was a man of another age. We could only guess at his beliefs. Who could unearth an authentic account of his life from under the thick blanket of hagiography and legend? Kusunoki was simply an abstract idea now – and in that sense ideally suited to co-option by Mishima as something to emulate.

Understand Saigō and you will understand Japan is nearly a proverbial expression, but Saigō is not easy to understand. Much of what is known of him has been revised and trimmed to fit the model of *Dai Saigō*, Saigō the Great, a national hero, and a good deal of what ordinary Japanese imagine as Saigō's story derives not from history but from hagiography, from popular novels of his life and a television mini series first screened in the 1990s. This is like trying to grasp the details of the Israeli/Palestine conflict on the strength of the movie *Exodus*. Was Saigō the last samurai, the last in the heroic tradition that Ivan Morris describes as embodying the idea of the nobility of failure when coupled to other virtues, such as a sincere effort purely motivated?

That Saigō Takamori is a national hero is certain. In a poll conducted shortly after the end of the Second World War, while Japan was still under US occupation, Saigō was chosen as one of the ten most respected figures in Japanese history. Twelve years later he was still popular, counted among the eighteen most splendid personalities who had ever lived. His appeal is strangely flexible. He has been adopted as a model on both the far right and the far left, and by everyone in between, and has even been put forward as a kind of unconscious Christian.

Saigō Takamori was born in 1827 in the southern island of Kyūshū, in the southernmost *han* of Satsuma. Ever since fighting off a Mongol invasion in the fourteenth century, with the assistance of a 'Divine Wind', or *kamikaze*, the Satsuma samurai were famously militant, a significant power in the land. It was also the domain with the longest uninterrupted rule by successive generations of the same – Shimazu – family. Geographically isolated, by distance and mountains, it was a deeply conservative environment and excessively proud of its traditions and heritage. It was also in a financial crisis, having the highest ratio of 'unproductive' samurai to peasants of any *han*. The national average was 6 per cent; in Satsuma it was 40 per cent, and 70 per cent in the castle town of Kagoshima. The need for reform had become irresistible by the time Saigō was born.

Saigō rose from modest circumstances as a poor lower-ranking samurai in Satsuma to Commander of the Imperial Guard, a Field Marshal and Counsellor of State in the Meiji government, having played a pivotal role in the overthrow of the Tokugawa shogunate and the imperial renewal which paved the way to Japan's transformation from a feudal society into a modern industrialised state. Having risen so far, in order to fulfil his role as a Japanese tragic hero he now had to fall. And so the alienated hero of the Meiji nation became a rebel and led the last great armed uprising against central government until the attempted coup by the Young Officers in 1936, for whom Saigō was a model. Naturally, if it is to be a Japanese tragic event, the hero must die – and so he did, on the battlefield, according to legend by seppuku, though this distorts the truth.

Charles Yates, one of Saigō's English-language biographers, sums up contemporary opinion:

> all Japanese who value the image of the Great Saigō share the belief that he was the perfect embodiment of the ideal samurai. He was stoic, gentle, and fearless, a master of the martial arts and a brilliant military leader. His intellectual powers, and the scholarly originality he achieved through them, were second only to his military abilities, and he was a master of all the important intellectual currents of his time, including Zen Buddhism and both of the dominant traditions of Neo-Confucian thought. He was physically imposing: larger than life, exceptionally strong, and in complete control of his body. His character was likewise flawless: he was scrupulously faithful to his ethical code, obedient to those above him in status and benevolent to those below, and he always placed his duty to others above his own needs. And in the best hagiographical tradition, he came by all these qualities early in his childhood, and exhibited them consistently throughout his life . . .[34]

Saigō was tall: nearly 6 feet in height at a time when most Japanese men were closer to 5 feet or even shorter. He was bulky from his boyhood, weighed 240 pounds as an adult and had a 19½-inch neck. One biographer coyly mentions that he also had testicles of truly heroic dimensions, but this feature is most likely the result of elephantiasis, possibly contracted from filarial worms transmitted through insects when in exile on the Amman Islands rather than an emblem of superhuman potency.

Saigō became an intimate retainer of the son of the daimyō, feudal lord, of Satsuma, Lord Nariakira, and as a mark of having been noticed was appointed chief gardener to the Shimazu mansion in Kagoshima, a post that drew no suspicion from other close retainers and those of opposing factions but permitted Nariakira to talk to and get to know Saigō whilst at leisure in his gardens. Saigō was later appointed Keeper of Birds at the Satsuma mansion in Edo (Tokyo) more or less as a cover to enable him to undertake confidential missions on behalf of his master. Whilst out on one such mission in Kyoto, canvassing for support to overthrow the Tokugawa shogun, Saigō received the news that Lord Nariakira had died. He was devastated and resolved to commit *junshi* – seppuku to join one's lord in death, and long since outlawed. He was dissuaded from this course of action, which would have rebounded badly on his family, by an influential monk called Gesshō, who told him that he must survive because he was the only one who understood his lord's policies and must work to implement them.

Shortly after, Saigō was to meet Gesshō again, when the monk became implicated in a plot against the government and was on the run. Saigō promised to protect him and Gesshō travelled to Kagoshima hoping to be sheltered by the Shimazu. Instead of sanctuary he was told he must cross the border into a neighbouring domain under escort. This was usually a euphemism for being deported and then murdered, so Saigō took Gesshō on a boat with a few friends, having resolved to die with him in an act of joint suicide. Such a suicide was probably motivated by several things – his failure to keep his promise to protect the monk, his desire to protest against the decision of his lord, his unhappiness since the death of Lord Nariakira. After writing death poems Saigō and Gesshō jumped into the sea, but were rescued and taken ashore for first aid, whereupon Gesshō was found to have drowned and Saigō to have survived. There is little doubt that Saigō felt guilt, even shame, at having failed in his resolve to die. He developed a death wish, and from that time focused only on the idea of a fitting death.

Saigō had deeply imbibed the action philosophy of *yōmeigaku*, the neo-Confucian system of thought developed by the Chinese general Wang Yang-ming. The most famous idea – possibly all that is extant today – of this system is summarised in the tag, 'To know and not to act, is not to know.' There must be a harmony between knowledge and conduct. True knowledge frees you from the difficulties of choice: there is no choice, only a correct way, one way to act and to behave. Saigo understood the Confucian perspective which is primarily concerned with groups, societies, nations, rather than with individuals. Even today Eastern cultures are more sympathetic than Western cultures to the idea of group conformity: the source of this is not rice-harvesting, but Confucian thinking. Saigō was big on two essential notions: the need to be sincere, and the idea of purity. On sincerity, *makoto* or *shisei*, a concept somehow reaching deeper than that word does in English, he commented:

> A man of true sincerity will be an example to the world even after his death . . . when an insincere man is spoken well of, he has, so to speak, got a windfall; but a man of deep sincerity will, even if he is unknown in his lifetime, have a lasting reward: the esteem of posterity.

There is no doubt that samurai culture valued renown, heroic deeds and qualities that would inspire songs and poems and artists in later generations. Like the Vikings, samurai saw this as a form of immortality. The idea of a good death was central to their self-image. To die fighting bravely in battle, or where you sacrifice your life for honour, as in the famous story of the Forty-Seven Rōnin, was considered the ultimate good.

Saigō's most famous slogan is *keiten, aijin* – Revere Heaven, Love Mankind. This is not quasi-Christianity, but again a Confucian concept based on the twin notions of justice (desired by

Heaven) and benevolence to the childlike masses over whose welfare the superior man, the samurai, watched and administered as a task for which he alone was fit. Despotism failed in both cases, offending the notion of justice and betraying a lack of honour towards one's duty to practise virtues such as *nasake*, a compassion felt for the helpless and weak, the unarmed, swordless peasant whose work fed the mouths of everyone.

Saigō's last stand, during the Satsuma uprising, resulted in the deaths of 30,000 men over a period of seven months. Legend has it that at the end, cornered on Shiroyama, a hill overlooking Kagoshima, his home town, Saigō chose to commit seppuku facing the direction of the imperial palace and was beheaded by Beppu Shinsuke as his *kaishaku*. In fact from the official autopsy report it is clear that: Saigō was beheaded; did not cut his own stomach; had sustained a fatal wound – he had been shot in the thigh and the bullet had passed through his pelvis. The beheading was more than likely either a coup de grâce or an attempt by Beppu to prevent his master's head from falling to the enemy – bodies of enemies were often treated with extreme disrespect, often displayed in public. The head was buried, but was later found by the imperial forces, ordered to be treated with the utmost respect, washed and carefully delivered to the commanders of the imperial troops.

Saigō was dead, but his reputation had only started to grow. In the years immediately following his death he was apotheosised as the planet Mars, which was renamed *Saigōboshi*, Saigō's star. Newspapers carried polls asking the public if they believed Saigō was actually dead, or had escaped into exile. He appeared in a painting, *Saigō Nehan Zu*, as a Buddha. Like so many mythic heroes, Saigō would, it was said, return to deliver the nation from evil in the event of great danger. He had become immortal and had been right about sincerity . . . it does have staying power after all.

*The goal of my life was to acquire all the various attributes of
the warrior.*

YUKIO MISHIMA, *Sun and Steel*

When I was eleven, or perhaps twelve, I formed the firm conviction that I should become a kung fu master. I had not thought very hard about what this meant in practical terms, but was certain that in this commitment I had solved a number of pressing problems, in particular the urgent need to acquire magical powers, mystical skills, with which to hold off the unwelcome and always malign attentions of bigger boys. In the jargon of the times, these boys were 'hard' and I was surely not.

Apart from being small in stature – I am still small, but have grown a lot wider – I was also fairly obviously brainy, a swot in the making, and this served to mark me for bullying. Crucially, I also lacked the will to inflict pain on enemies. I lacked a killer instinct, which in later life I identified as underlying my indifference to worldly ambition. The bullying, it seems to me now, at a distance of thirty years, was not so bad; but to a small boy used to a loving home and mild friendliness all round, it took on an extra significance, looming large in a young life. So, a kung fu master I would have to be.

Thinking about this unlikely ambition I am forced to wonder at my sources of information. I can recall that I formed an obsessive interest in Bruce Lee – even now I can, if pressed, recollect the Little Dragon's shoe size. Yet I am quite sure I had not then seen a single Bruce Lee movie, or even a trailer.

The television series *Kung Fu*, starring David Carradine, was, however, staple viewing, and I had no way of knowing that I was watching a very badly acted and poorly choreographed pastiche of genuine martial arts. For me the romance of the Shaolin Temple, repeated each week in the title sequences while a bamboo flute played a stirring and vaguely oriental theme tune, was deeply seductive. Did I ever fantasise about running away to such a place? I cannot recollect, but I can remember desiring for myself the distinctive badge of a Shaolin priest – indelible scars inflicted by lifting a red-hot brazier that barred the narrow exit from the temple, a process which branded you with impressions of a dragon and a tiger, forever burned into your forearms and, for those who knew, whenever glimpsed, a flag of deadly omen.

A magazine was published to feed on the frenzy of interest in kung fu, and I eagerly bought the first issue. On the cover was a free gift, a coppery metal pendant shaped like a crude oriental dragon. It became an item of treasure, and I stored it in a shoebox under my bed, the hiding place for my coins and shells and the other significant rubbish of an ordinary boyhood.

I began to pester my parents to allow me to join a kung fu school, having picked out a few institutions by thumbing through the Yellow Pages. Naturally, I was most attracted to a school called 'The Bruce Lee School of Kung Fu'. Was Bruce alive or dead at the time? I have no idea. Did I expect him to be teaching? I don't remember. But it seemed obvious to me then that there must be some connection. This implication also seemed obvious to Linda Lee, Bruce's widow, when she sued the school a few years later for passing off – for there was no connection at all to the King of Kung Fu.

I was thrilled to learn that in return for my joining fee I would receive a pair of black cotton drawstring trousers and a white T-shirt. Once I had donned this uniform, plus a pair of white socks and black cotton 'kung fu shoes' which were amazingly comfortable and came in a variety of types – either with plastic soles (slippery) or with rubber soles (the best) or with white coiled rope soles (the best-looking and worn by the senior Chinese teacher) – I felt that very little distance remained on my journey to mastery. Surely I would be shown the secrets, would memorise how and where to strike my enemies, and that would be that. It was just a knowledge thing, a transaction. The idea of painful training to acquire slowly won skills did not occur to my magically inclined mind.

Our first instructor was not Chinese but Jamaican. He was a large muscular man and counted in Chinese with a West Indian

accent, something I did not realise at the time. We were made
to exercise: push-ups, sit-ups, running circuits of the small room
that smelled powerfully of male aromas, an admixture of feet,
stale sweat and adrenalin. Then push-ups again, this time on
clenched fists, then on fingers, then on two fingers and thumbs
– was this the secret of the deadly *Eagle Claw*, I wondered on
the bus home afterwards. After the exercises we were shown
four techniques and paired off to practise, while the teacher
walked slowly around to correct us. I had begun a journey which
has yet to end.

The Bruce Lee School was formed by a number of Chinese
friends who had pitched up in England to work and send money
back home – either to Hong Kong or to the mainland People's
Republic. Most of them were waiters in the city's restaurants.
They had studied some kung fu and thought to combine their
expertise and open a school. Although I was not to stay long at
the Bruce Lee School I learned later that the syllabus was more
or less bogus, a patchwork of real kung fu styles grafted onto a
fake history of a system which had become extinct in China in
the early nineteenth century. This mattered not at all in the
heyday of Bruce Lee mania, a time when hardly any reliable
information existed in English and the real experts, traditionally
minded to a man, had no intention of teaching *gwei lo* – round
eyes – their secret fighting arts.

After I settled in to the Bruce Lee Kung Fu School in the city
centre I noticed an advertisement in a local newspaper for a
kung fu course which was to be held in a local church hall much
closer to my home. It mentioned that the system to be taught
was *Bak Hok Pai*, the White Crane style – a northern Chinese
art, formerly reserved for the Imperial Guard of the Ching
Dynasty and with a mythic origin in Tibet. Tibet! The Imperial
Guards! Tibet! How could I resist?

The advert announced a formal demonstration the following
weekend in a park not far from my home. I murdered the time
in between, willing it to pass at an implausibly accelerated pace,
daydreaming scenarios where I pecked my enemies to death in
a deadly Crane boxing manoeuvre.

On the day of the demonstration the sun was shining, promising perfect conditions. The newspaper advert identified the school as the Chinese Martial Arts Centre and the teacher I had come to watch was called Christopher Lung. I expected from his name that he would be Chinese, or possibly Chinese-American, but when I saw him, despite his swarthy looks, I realised that he was Caucasian, and perhaps in his late twenties or early thirties. He was small and wiry and appeared with his younger brother Michael, who was closer to my own age, in his mid- to late teens, also short but noticeably muscular.

The demonstration included boxing forms performed alone and in pairs, weapons forms with a variety of interesting equipment I had never before set eyes on – the *sam jeet kwun*, or three-sectional staff, used by Michael Lung in an amazing display of skill and speed, a feat unmatched until I saw the Chinese national Wu Shu team some years later and the early Hong Kong action movies of Jet Li. There were multi-edged steel whips, swords and daggers, broadswords, double-edged swords and swords with cruel hooks at the end and blades extending out of the handles wielded in pairs.

Christopher Lung performed a monkey boxing staff pattern – The Iron Staff of Heaven – seemingly transformed into a monkey, rolling and flipping and screeching, while spinning the staff around his body so fast it was a blur. Huge metal shields with wicked points were hefted effortlessly in a Hung Gar pattern and a White Crane form was demonstrated by a tall young student with an innocent ruddy-cheeked face and corn-blond hair, dressed in a black mandarin cotton jacket buttoned to his throat and matching cotton trousers. I noticed that Christopher Lung had tied a red sash around his waist, which I learned is worn by kung fu teachers for good luck rather than as a badge of rank. Most kung fu styles have no ranking system – at least no rank indicated by belts or other visible symbols.

I was amazed at the skills displayed. What I had seen at the Bruce Lee School had resembled the slow and ugly kick and punch routines of the *Kung Fu* television series. Nothing had prepared me for the elegance, speed and power of the Lung brothers. And then, to cap it all, Christopher Lung demonstrated *chi gung*, internal power. He announced he would bend a sword on his throat. At first I thought I had misheard – bending a metal sword with soft flesh just seemed impossible. The sword – a Thai blade with an ornate carved wooden handle – was passed around the crowd for examination. The point was extremely sharp and a man cut his palm before handing it back convinced that it was real. Michael Lung held the blade carefully against his brother's Adam's apple and then began to push. I could hardly bear to look, certain it must end in death. But the blade refused to enter Christopher's throat and miraculously began, slowly at first, to bend. A grunt, a final thrust and the blade was bent into a dog-leg shape. He held it high for everyone to see. There was a red mark on Christopher's throat, just above his windpipe, but no other sign of injury. I was hooked, reeled in and in the basket.

My involvement with the Lung brothers lasted a decade. To say that it was an odd association barely comes close to the truth. As I got to know them I was able to piece together an official and a likely more truthful version of their history. I began to suspect that Christopher Lung's kung fu was improvised. Whilst embodying a high level of skills – extreme flexibility, *chi gung* power, and a very severe fighting technique – it did not seem to resemble anything which I could verify from external sources – videos and magazines for example. Michael Lung was quite different. His forms were all precise and authentic. He seemed to be his brother's student, but I began to suspect it might be the other way round. Or had Christopher progressed to a level where patterns and forms were not necessary and he just made it up on the run?

I began to train every day. At first I studied White Crane. Then I asked to study Northern Dragon Boxing. Then Pa Kua. Then Wing Chun. Next Tai Chi Chuan. And finally, Hung Gar boxing. I was indulged. The Lung brothers seemed to have an encyclopedic knowledge of dozens of distinct Chinese boxing styles. It was the only school I know of – except for the Ching Woo Association in Hong Kong and Shanghai – which taught so many varieties of kung fu.

Towards the end of my time with the Lung brothers a lot of my social life was spent in their company. The business fortunes of their kung fu schools varied, sometimes doing well but mostly badly, as students left after finding the classes too demanding. Christopher was getting steadily odder. He expressed a keen interest in Satanism after we had all attended a late-night preview of the movie *Damien, Omen I*, and began to dress in black and sport an inverted crucifix around his neck. Although this seemed peculiar it did not matter that much to me if I studied martial arts from a worshipper of the Devil as long as he had real skills and was willing to pass them on. I was mostly being taught by Michael, who was more mainstream in his tastes, using his physical genius to attend discos and nightclubs and effortlessly outdance anyone on the floor, having observed their moves and learned them at a glance. It was a sure-fire way to impress girls, and Michael was soon a young father, with children by more than one mother.

Christopher had married a large lady to whom he taught Wing Chun kung fu. She was thick-set and wore her hair in a short cropped style. Within a year of their wedding a baby girl was born, and I spent less and less time with the Lungs as the domestic routines absorbed their life and my academic studies mine.

What came next was a major shock. My kung fu teacher, Christopher Lung, a man who had torn off the ear of a fourth-degree black belt tae kwon do fighter in a full-contact tournament in Florida and could bend swords on his throat, decided that he was not a man at all, but a woman trapped in a man's body. To liberate his or her real self he or she decided to become just she. At the same time his wife Anne had come to a similar conclusion. Her bulky body, so much larger than the slender form of her husband, although nominally female was, she was sure, a mistake. She was a man. In time both would seek gender reassignment through hormone therapy, counselling, and finally surgical intervention.

It was not long before the *News of the World* got wind of the first married couple in the UK – they said the world in their World Exclusive front-page headlines – to exchange gender roles as parents. He became their daughter's mum and she her dad, perfect tabloid material.

Although I believed in liberal values and still do, and was certainly not hostile to transsexuals, I felt that a double sex change linked to the practice of satanism was a heavy hint that I should direct my energies elsewhere. Soon afterwards I moved away from home and my kung fu days were over.

. . . today bushidō is passé.
Yukio Mishima, *Seventeen Years of Warlessness*

Shidō, the way of the military or knightly class, describes a code of values or behaviour that in some way defines the standards by which samurai lived and died. It is neither a religious system nor strictly a philosophy, but a number of its ideas and practices derived from Buddhism and Shinto, which are religions, and from Confucianism, which is a philosophy of conduct.

The domination of warriors in the life and government of Japan dates from the end of the twelfth century, when Minamoto no Yoritomo established his 'military camp government' – *Bakufu* or Shogunate – in Kamakura. In the subsequent Period of the Warring States, no codification of the behaviour of samurai was developed, beyond manuals of military tactics and weapons strategy. It was not until the re-establishment of peace, the unification of Japan and the eventual domination of the Tokugawa clan in the seventeenth century – a time when warriors were faced with the fundamental problem of justifying their role as warriors in an age without warfare – that samurai began to be seen as moral exemplars and the values that set them above and apart from the rest of society were first described. If samurai were to have an elite status at the top of a rigidly hierarchical feudal society without risking their lives, or doing any work, they would have to earn it by their disciplines and moral rectitude. Samurai were declared an object lesson in how a man might best behave.

In the Tokugawa or Edo period (1603–1867) the word *shidō* was used interchangeably with a number of other expressions: *mononofu no michi, masurao no michi, tsuwamono no michi, yumiya no michi, musha no michi, yumiya toru mi no narai, bushi no michi, samuraidō* and *bushidō*. There are several written accounts that provide insights into the thinking of the time.

Kakun, house codes, were detailed rules of the individual regional domains ruled by feudal lords, or daimyō. These included rules about hygiene, security of domain secrets, and idiosyncrasies of the individual daimyō – such as the blunt prohibition 'A samurai who is caught dancing shall be killed,' which was a house code of Kumamoto Castle, decreed by Kato Kiyomasu.

Yet individual daimyō had more philosophical preoccupations also revealed in their *kun*. Takeda Shingen expressed his regard for Zen:

> Pay proper reverence to the gods and the Buddha. When your thoughts are in accord with the Buddha's, you will gain more power. If your domination over others issues from your evil thoughts, you will be exposed, you are doomed. Next, devote yourselves to the study of Zen. Zen has no secrets other than seriously thinking about birth-and-death.

Hōjō Sōun esteemed literacy at a time when it was the exception, not the rule, for samurai:

> Whenever you have a little bit of time for yourself, read a book. Always carry something with characters written on it with you and look at it when no one's looking. Unless you accustom yourself to them, asleep or awake, you'll forget them. The same is true of writing.

In addition to the house codes there are four main written sources of *shidō* and a number of minor ones that date from the Tokugawa period.[35] The four main ones have been translated into English, in some cases more than once. They are: *Gorin no sho*

(*The Book of Five Rings*) by Miyamoto Musashi; *Shidō* and *Bukyo yōroku* by Yamaga Sokō; *Hagakure* by Yamamoto Tsunetomo; *Budōshoshin shu* by Daidoji Yūzan.

Shidō, literally 'the Way of the Warrior' (synonymous with *bushidō*), was not the only behavioural code, but had counterparts in feudal Japanese society for each level of the social hierarchy – there was a Way of the Merchant, an Artisan's Way, and rules for the role expected of farmers and workers on the land. However, only the role of the warrior had been radically altered by the Pax Tokugawa. Warriors were now required *not* to fight. Their primary role had, in a sense, been abolished – or more accurately was in abeyance, pending any armed uprising or other form of conflict, such as a foreign invasion. Like a professional standing army in peacetime, it was not unusual for those dedicated to war and killing never to see any action at all. This inevitably led to enormous introspection and a self-referential crisis – what we would call today an identity crisis. Just what am I, what am I for? asked the samurai of the seventeenth and eighteenth centuries.

The term *bushidō* has been thought by some Western scholars not to have been in use before the early twentieth century, following the publication of Nitobe Inazō's book *Bushidō: the Soul of Japan*, which was written in English and first published in Philadelphia in 1899, targeting a Western readership. But this is a fallacy, and the word can be found, along with many other words for the same thing, as early as the sixteenth century. The concepts of *bushidō*, as we now understand them, were not universal. It is more accurate to speak of competing ideas of how a samurai should behave to deserve his rank in society.

The written sources of *bushidō* were not distributed throughout Japan – apart from Shōgunal Edicts – and often had the status of secrets restricted to members of a particular *han*, or domain. The *Hagakure* was not known outside the Nabeshima domain of Saga in Hizen province, Kyūshū. Not one universal *bushidō* then, but several, distinct, approaches to the challenges for the samurai class in general.

The central government had its own concern – how to neutralise a large armed class from which all previous rebellions had arisen. How, in effect, to disarm the samurai. An edict issued in 1615, Regulations Concerning Warrior Households, assigned a duty for samurai to study and master the literary arts with the same vigour as they devoted to the martial arts. The authority for such a reorientation was the Chinese classics, and in particular a statist orthodox Confucianism.[36] This is the origin of such tags as *bunbu ryōdō*, the twin paths of the pen and the sword, which was promoted to counter the belief that military specialisation was all a samurai should concern himself with.

It is worth while to summarise the three major competing versions of *bushidō*, together with the works that evoke them:

(1) The Pragmatic School – Miyamoto Musashi, *Gorin no sho* (The Book of Five Rings)
(2) The Statist School – Yamaga Sokō, *Bukyo yōroku* (Essentials of the Warrior Creed)
(3) The Idealist/Romantic School – Yamamoto Tsunetomo, *Hagakure kikigaki* (What was heard in the shadow of leaves)

Pragmatic Bushidō

Miyamoto Musashi is often called Japan's greatest ever *kensei*, or sword-saint. That he is well known in both Japan and the West is due to two factors – in Japan the publication of the world's best-selling novel, *Musashi*, by Eiji Yoshikawa, sometimes said to have sold 120 million copies in all editions, and in the West the modern interest in Musashi's most famous work, *The Book of Five Rings*, a technical text on fencing skills and their wider application. Yoshikawa is responsible for many of the myths which have grown up around Musashi, and there have been a number of films and television series which have built on his fictionalised personality.

Musashi first killed, by his own account, at the age of thirteen. He fought on the losing side at Sekigahara[37] and was obliged to become a rōnin and to engage in *musha shugyō*, a wandering pilgrimage to improve fencing skills by challenging any worthwhile opponents encountered. By the age of twenty-nine he had won sixty death matches. There is only one account of him having been beaten, in a rematch with the founder of Shindō Musō Ryū *jōdō*, Musō Gonnosuke Katsukichi, but no one is certain that this fight actually took place.

Musashi had developed the capacity to hold and wield a katana in his right hand only – usually both hands are employed in a strong two-handed grip – while using his left to wield the *wakizashi*, or short sword. This technique, which became a secret method in the Niten Ichi Ryū, employed a number of unique skills that no one unfamiliar with Musashi had ever encountered before, especially a kind of 'x' block that could be used to trap and control the opponent's sword before administering a coup de grâce. Musashi is sometimes called the Leonardo of Japan. This refers to his desire to be fully rounded and his extraordinary skills in anything he decided to take up – calligraphy, painting, metal-working, poetry. He claimed quite simply that what he had learned about fencing could be applied to absolutely anything. In the end, having retired to a cave and given up fencing to concentrate on his Zen studies, it is believed that he was poisoned by one of his many enemies.

Musashi was a pragmatist. He declared that the principal goal of a samurai was to succeed in the interests of his lord: not to die and certainly not to die needlessly in a selfish act to garner a hero's reputation for himself and material advantages for his descendants. The means used to achieve your aims were irrelevant – as long as you did, in fact, succeed. There is something almost American – with its emphasis on winners and losers – in such an ethos, and it is not hard to understand the re-emergence of the *Book of Five Rings* as an American bestseller. His tactics on fighting duels might be summed up as: know your opponent and fight only on your own terms, having calculated how to exploit a weakness.

Musashi always adopted psychological tactics, which even today some Japanese regard as underhand, such as arriving to fight late or early, in order to disrupt the concentration of his opponent.

Statist Bushidō

Yamaga Sokō was born in 1622 and died in 1685. He was a rōnin, a masterless samurai, and a teacher of military science and Confucian studies. His students included the long-lived Daidoji Yūzan, whose *Budōshoshinshu* is perhaps the best translated account in English of the values and concerns of the samurai class.

Yamaga is an example of statist bushidō not because he was a member of the ruling authority – he was not and was for a time in exile because he opposed the neo-Confucian Shu-shi Gaku school sponsored by the Tokugawa government. He was statist because he saw the need to transform the unoccupied samurai class in peacetime and would have agreed with the second Tokugawa Shōgun in his *Buke Shohatto*, Edict to Ruling Daimyō and their Samurai Retainers, where the first article declares:

> 1. Literature, arms, archery and horsemanship are, systematically, to be the favourite pursuits.
> Literature first, and arms next to it, was the rule of the ancients. They must both be cultivated concurrently. Archery and horsemanship are the more essential for the Military Houses. Weapons of warfare are ill-omened words to utter; the use of them, however, is an unavoidable necessity. In times of peace and good order we must not forget that disturbances may arise. Dare we omit to practise our warlike exercises and drill?

In his work *Shidō*, written in 1665, Yamaga summed up the new peacetime role of a samurai:

> The business of the samurai consists in reflecting on his own station in life ... It would not do for the samurai to know the martial [*bu*] and civil [*bun*] without manifesting them. Since this is the case, outwardly he stands in physical readiness for any call to service and inwardly he strives to fulfil the Way of the lord and subject, friend and friend, father and son, older and younger

brother, and husband and wife. Within his heart he
keeps to the ways of peace, but without he keeps his
weapons ready for use . . .

It was Yamaga who provided a convincing case for samurai to
render service through administration work. He believed that
they should aim to become sages and be fully rounded. He
stressed loyalty to the state and opposed individualism. Here is
Yamaga on the characteristics of a sage:

> In order to know what the real master of the Way is
> like, you should first have a very clear understanding of
> what the sage is like. The sage, according to the prevail-
> ing notion among conventional scholars, is one who has
> a mien of moral superiority – a distinctive personality,
> remarkably conspicuous in a crowd of men. His inner
> excellence being so eloquent of itself, the fact that he is
> no ordinary man is sensed immediately. Endowed as he
> is with supernatural and superhuman qualities, his
> speech and conduct are anything but human. Amidst
> whatever sensations of sound or sight, his emotions
> remain unmoved just as if he were a dead tree or burnt
> ashes. To him personal gain and a fat salary are more
> fleeting attractions than a snowflake on a red-hot stove.
> And in scholarship, he is versed in almost everything.
> Therefore, when entrusted with the government of the
> land, he will sweep away in an instant evils that have
> festered and bred for years; sweet dewdrops will gather
> on earth, while [such lucky omens as] giraffes and
> phoenixes will be constant visitors; all the people will
> follow the Way, practising humanity and righteousness.
> Just one interview with the sage, and a man of plain
> mediocrity will shine with intelligence; overnight he
> will become unselfish and pure in body and mind – or
> so it is thought.
>   Now this indicates a lack of real knowledge concern-
> ing the sages. Upon studying the utterances, the actions,
> and the political ordinances of the Duke of Chou and
> Confucius, we find that they were not at all like this.

The sage represents only the best of humankind and is not a bit different from other men. He is fully accomplished in those things which make a man a man, is well informed of things and affairs and not perplexed by them at all. As to his personality and character, he is amicable, humble, frugal, and self-sacrificing. A model of decorum, to parents he is filially pious in wholesome measure. In liberal arts he can express himself well when writing; in military affairs he is preparedness itself, being warm-hearted but not hot-headed, commanding respect without being violent, working hard when at work but relaxing fully when at rest. He takes what is due to him, gives to others what is due to them, is generous when liberality is called for and sparing when to be sparing is in order. His sayings and actions are hard to characterise in simple terms. Those who do not know him well call him unselfish at the sight of his charity; but take him for a miser when he is sparing. They think him flattering when he is merely truthful and consider him arrogant when he is not flattering. They fail because they are ignorant of what the sage is really like.

Idealist/Romantic Bushidō

Mishima said that Yamamoto's *Hagakure* was his favourite book and one he had consulted all his life. In 1967 he published a commentary on it, *Hagakure Nyūmon* (Introduction to the *Hagakure*), whose most famous line is 'The way of the Samurai is to be found in death.' This sentiment appealed to Mishima enormously, but what did Yamamoto actually mean by it?

Yamamoto Tsunetomo was a lower-ranking samurai prevented from committing *junshi* – seppuku on the death of your lord – at the beginning of the eighteenth century. Instead he retired and became a monk living in isolation. Peace was a century old at this time, and it was a common belief that samurai were weakening and becoming decadent. The main difference between Yamamoto's idea of bushidō and that of Yamaga and Musashi is that he was less interested in the effects of a samurai's actions and much more concerned with the purity of his motives, advocating utter disregard for oneself in advancing the interests of one's lord. The best way to remain pure and to disregard your own selfish inclinations, such as the desire to survive in a dangerous situation, was to embrace death.

At school Mishima hated the hearty boys of the Kendō club. He was aesthetically inclined and thin, weedy and a swot. His nickname was 'asparagus' for his floppy way of standing and sitting. His skin was so pale that the veins of his arms were conspicuous purple lines. His vocal mannerisms were those of his grandmother: feminised speech, excessively polite and elliptical, nothing like the banter of boys of his age, always engaged on an adolescent quest to be taken seriously. Even the way he walked was mocked. His PE teacher at the Peers School called him *bā-san ahiru*, a grandmother duck. He laughed self-consciously in a high-pitched whinny.

In his early adult years Mishima systematically remodelled himself, piece by piece, struggling to transform the girlie-boy into a macho man. He acquired a masculine, mocking laugh, fully refined by the age of twenty-five – a mannerism that many remarked on for its mirthless frigidity. He corrected his walk. He began to exercise, attracted to the methods of Hitoshi Tamari, a physical training instructor at Waseda University, who could move the muscles of his chest in time to music. In time he became an obsessive body-builder. He sunbathed to change his pallid complexion into a healthy year-round tan, like a movie star. After exercising for a number of years he was able to stop using the injections of pain-killing drugs he needed to control severe stomach cramps. He began to get well, to turn himself into a hypertrophy of maleness. This preoccupation with the meaning of his male body and the proper role of a Japanese man, a would-be warrior confined within an era of peace, would obsess him for the rest of his life – and eventually lead to his decision to commit suicide.

For many years Mishima's grandmother, Natsuko, had brought her grandson souvenirs of her frequent visits to watch Kabuki and Noh performances. She would tell him the plots of the plays, comment on the splendour of a particular actor's gestures or vocal range, pass on rumours and gossip about theatrical circles. There can be little doubt that by the time of his first outing to the Kabuki-za, the main Kabuki theatre in Tokyo, Mishima would have been suffering from a frenzy of excitement and anticipation. The first play he saw, aged twelve, in 1937, was the *Chūshingura*, the Kabuki retelling of the Akō Incident, usually called the *Tale of the 47 Rōnin*. It had everything Mishima could have hoped for – most particularly blood and gore, bravery and sacrifice, death and a sense of justice – and a large number of heroic men who cut open their own stomachs quite willingly.

Mishima became an aficionado of Kabuki from an early age. He understood its archaic language and poetic conventions and was perhaps the only playwright of his generation who could produce new repertoire written in the style of Grand Kabuki. He wrote eight Kabuki plays and directed the last of them, *Chinsetsu Yumiharizuki* (The Moon Like a Drawn Bow), at the National Theatre in Tokyo in November 1969. In the seppuku scene Mishima insisted that the pools of shed blood should glisten.

Act: (1) to do something; (2) to pretend to do something, as on a stage.

Oxford English Dictionary

One of the five styles of Noh drama is known as *Shura-mono*. The narrative always depicts the pleading of the ghost of a warrior tormented in hell and seeking to be released, his pleas often addressed to a priest encountered in the world of the living. Warriors, having based their conduct in life on notions of worldly honour, ignoring a higher honour, reap the karmic effects of their battlefield cruelty. The hell to which they are confined is sometimes described as raining fire.

One of the things that most interested me about Mishima was that he was said never to revise. He simply wrote down in longhand – on Japanese squared paper, rather like graph paper – what he intended to say, neither changing much as he went along nor separately producing a clean finished copy. This is similar to the way Mozart wrote music, sometimes described as taking dictation from God – but is possibly unique for a writer.[38]

In wondering about this I remembered accounts of Mishima's childhood, and his lack of reaction when his father held him in the path of an oncoming train to test his physical courage. There was no reaction from the boy at all, when most children would have cried in fear. No screams. No struggling. This incident suggests mild autism or a related condition such as somewhere on the Asperger's Syndrome spectrum – where there is often obsessive interest in a very limited range of themes accompanied by major literary talent – he swallowed a dictionary – coupled with poor social skills and few, if any, friends. All of these conditions are noted in certain types of genius, and Mishima may well have fallen into this category.

Mishima's early life involved an enforced retreat from the exterior or real world. For the first twelve years of his childhood he was more or less a prisoner of his grandmother. Obliged to sleep in her bedroom and to keep her company, forbidden boys' games, male companions and any type of dangerous play, he was judged to be a delicate child who might easily succumb to illness and premature death. To be so marked for death so young by those around him – is this the cause, or just an early symptom, of what happened three decades later?

Unsurprisingly, he retreated into an imaginary world of fantasy and fiction. Forced to stay in his small darkened sick room, he peopled it with characters of his own invention. The sources of subject matter for Mishima's fantasy world were books, stories told to him by his grandmother taken from Kabuki and Noh, the various collections of Japanese myths and legends in the *Kojiki* and the *Nihonshoki*, and the earliest anthology of Japanese poetry, the *Manyōshū*. (The last three all date from the eighth century.) He mixed in Western fairy stories, Hans Christian Andersen, figures seen in picture books – Joan of Arc, a knight in shining armour, her sex ambiguous but assumed male by Mishima. An abnormally intelligent child with a high need for stimulation, yet in a dull situation, he did the only thing possible: he made things up, created worlds and entered into them. He escaped into himself.

Once we have got used to familiar stories it is normal to want to tweak them here and there, to improve on their reality, perhaps by introducing ourselves into the action, usually in a central role. I have yet to meet a child playing with, say, an action man who declares: 'I'm a clerk in the Area Commander's office responsible for keeping field kitchens resupplied' or 'I am an infantryman in a sector of the war where nothing is happening, trying to interest my exhausted comrades in a game of cards.' Reality is not much good when it is too real and lacks a heroic potential. The main point of the imagination is that it can focus on the good bits.

I have lived in a number of odd places in my life – once in a brothel, once as the house guest of a prince in a palace – but perhaps one of the oddest periods took place in Japan in the 1990s. It was my first house move following the bankruptcy of the Rose of York School of English which had employed me and one of the friends I then lived with, Robert. We had tried to fend off the imminent decline in the school's financial fortunes by dreaming up new and attractive English conversation formats – a last-gasp effort was the '*Twin Peaks* English Course' based entirely on the David Lynch hit television series and using the scripts of episodes for vocabulary and activity exercises. We touted for business with a poster and from somewhere obtained a cardboard cutout of Kyle MacLachlan which was put on display in the street-level window of our school building in Shibuya. It attracted no students whatsoever, snaring only an unemployed Australian seeking a teaching job, and a week later someone who wondered if they could buy the cardboard Kyle. Obviously the school quickly went bust.

We had been owed our last salary, and as a precaution in the final few days had started physically removing practically anything that could be carried off and sold, even a largish stock of photocopying paper, while Ura the owner was busy at creditors' meetings or seeking funds from gambling cronies. Robert was particularly pleased at having 'distrained' our now ex-boss's collection of replica guns – his favourite was a realistic SIG-Sauer P226 – and we had even gone so far as to remove the brass name plate from the wall, which I gave to Ken to display in his snack bar as a trophy of our small act of rebellion.

Even though we were cross with Ura for not paying our final salaries, neither Robert nor I felt especially hostile to him now that the business had folded. For about a week before the last day of work we speculated that on arriving at the school one morning we would find Ura swinging from a door lintel, perhaps having arranged one last poignant display of flowers using blossoms commenting on the ephemeral nature of life itself – a sprig of cherry flowers, or a delicate mountain orchid that began to die the moment it was severed from its parent plant. Alternatively if Ura *was* a gangster and possessed a real gun he might blow his brains out – or even commit seppuku using the razor-sharp Ikebana pruning shears he kept in the office.

But Ura did not kill himself. Instead he begged his former boss to give him his old job back selling central-heating radiators, and our paths never crossed again.

We would lose the tiny flat that was tied to the job. Forced to find somewhere else to live, we moved from Yokohama-shi in the south to Tokorozawa in Saitama-ken in the northwest, having found a contact through the other friend I lived with, Frank. He introduced us to an eccentric Japanese antiques dealer who was letting rooms in a storage house he owned, a place which had once been a small factory manufacturing kimonos.

The Old Kimono Factory was about fifteen minutes' brisk walk from Tokorozawa railway station, a stop on the Seibu–Ikebukuro line. The area had the most radioactive soil in the Tokyo region – a fact I discovered only after living there – and was home to the Seibu Lions baseball team. It was a house, unremarkable, with two storeys and a garden comprising three fields of unplanted dirt. All the rooms for hire were on the second floor. The first (or ground) floor was used to store the owner's antiques prior to their transfer to his shop in central Tokyo as space became available for their display. After we had hired a room at the end of the second floor, six mats in size, with a couple of sliding futon cupboards and a small veranda where washing could be dried and which overlooked some cultivated fields, we explored the ground-floor rooms.

We didn't know then that the contents were the stock of the owner's business, but thought that it was mostly junk and decided on the spur of the moment to decorate our small new home with a few pieces that took our fancy. Robert selected a 6-foot stuffed Japanese bear, which had been fixed on a wooden base, posed rearing up on two paws with its forepaws reaching out, claws exposed; even though this would reduce our living space, we agreed it was a cool object to move in with us. I chose a small porcelain vase in the form of an erect penis, lifelike in all its details, foreskin retracted, glans bulging. I was unsure if it was made for an oddly sexy school of ikebana or designed as a small lewd sake flask, but decided it would do to introduce an aesthetic note to balance the violent maleness of the bear (although a penis was an odd choice as a feminine touch). I would use it to display small wild flowers gathered on my walk home from the station in the fading light of dusk each evening. Frank chose a scroll of *senryū* poems written in a curved hard-to-read script called grass hand which he said he wanted to use as a reading exercise – one a day. We manhandled the bear up the narrow stairs and positioned it in the corner. Before long it would become an unofficial clothes horse co-opted to dry wet towels, carefully draped over its forepaws.

In the room next to ours, a smaller room of four mats, lived a hairy Canadian called Rick Paradis. Rick was bearded, mild and friendly, a good source of jokes and happy to share our booze or ply us with his own stock in the quiet of a Tokorozawa evening. After he got to know us he started to confess. Frank was told the unusual circumstances of Rick's romantic history, that he was travelling away from his girlfriend, a German porn actress who as a keepsake had given him a copy of her most successful and acclaimed short film, *Anal-ist on the Couch*. Rick said he would show Frank the video sometime.

Rick had a small cabin on the Newfoundland mainland, not far from the sea. He told us tales of snow and freezing winds and invited us all to stay with him as an imaginary antidote to the heat of the Japanese summer.

The other rooms in the Old Kimono Factory were occupied by two other ethnic groups: one room by three Pakistanis, two others by an unknown number of seemingly nocturnal Nigerians. In the kitchen the Nigerians had a bank of rice cookers cooking rice round the clock using a plug adaptor to provide enough electrical capacity without blowing a fuse. We preferred to eat out in the cheap noodle shops of Tokorozawa and only reluctantly ventured into the kitchen for some hot water for tea or in search of a corkscrew or bottle opener, and so were no threat to the assembly-line food arrangements already in place. The Nigerians were unfailingly polite and shy and would smile as if their lives depended on it whenever met with in the corridor on the way to or from the shower or lavatory.

About a week after moving in I got into a conversation with Archimedes from Lagos, who explained that he had a Ph.D. in theoretical physics and had come to Japan to work. He was not employed, however, in the nuclear power industry or in any other scientific capacity, but as a shift worker in a small factory that manufactured plastic lavatory seats. He never said and I never asked but it was clear that the secretive nature of the Nigerians was for two reasons. Being black in Japan made you stand out and be even more noticeable (due to rarity) than being white. And none of them had valid visas to work, or had overstayed a tourist visa and were now on the run. Officially there were said to be eight Nigerians in two rooms. I abandoned my list after compiling thirty-two names.

The Pakistanis were less easy to like. They seemed in conflict with each other, usually over small sums of money, nearly all the time, and we chose to ignore them on Frank's advice. He was Iranian and had found the house through his network of rug-dealing contacts, including a Pakistani carpet-seller who acted as the Japanese landlord's rent-collector. We suspected the Pakistanis to be his spies. They also seemed to resent being ignored, and one day one of them shouted at me as I wordlessly boiled a kettle:

'I too am schooled! I have degree! Math-chem-physic.'
'Well done,' I replied, not wanting to argue. 'I am an idiot.'
To this he could think of no reply and left me in peace.

Robert, Frank and I had agreed that our indolent lifestyles needed shaking up. We were growing fat and lazy and spent far too much time sitting around smoking and drinking coffee and booze, conducting our endless conversations. The answer was some form of vigorous exercise routine, but joining a gym and running on treadmills or riding stationary bikes held no appeal for any of us. One evening I said: 'This is Japan, let's take up a Japanese martial art,' and the others agreed and asked me to make some inquiries. I did so by the same method I had used so many years before when searching for a kung fu school – I looked in the Yellow Pages.

In the section that listed martial arts schools there was a boxed advertisement for the Yōshinkan Honbu Dōjō. It included a picture of an elderly man throwing a thick-set younger man in a spectacular somersault. The Yōshinkan was an aikidō school headed by a famous master, Gōzō Shioda Sensei – he was the elderly man in the picture, although I didn't know it then. But his name seemed familiar, and before long I realised that I had read a book of his, *Dynamic Aikido*, published in 1968 and discovered by me in my local library in 1972 when I was twelve. Twenty years later I was ready to begin my studies. It was a long hesitation, but I would try to make up for having taken so long to start by enthusiastically throwing myself into learning how to throw others.

We all joined the Yōshinkan the very next day. Soon we were in the grip of an obsession, training every day, and with friends made at the dōjō spending most of our leisure time discussing techniques and dōjō gossip. I lost a quarter of my body weight in the first year and had muscles again and practically no body fat. Robert eventually went on to join the Senshusei – literally 'specialists' – course, perhaps the most intensive martial arts training programme in the world, and taught to non-Japanese and Japanese students alongside a group of Tokyo Riot Police trainee instructors. Robert wrote it all up in his book *Angry White Pyjamas*,[39] a work that deservedly went on to scoop prizes.

Since that time I have continued to study aikidō and regard it as an important aspect of my life, now that ten years have passed since I obtained a black belt. In Japan a black belt is simply a mark of seriousness, indicating that you are a serious student, and conveys nothing like the Western notion of expert status. I feel I will remain a beginner all my life.

Left/Right

I have a new pair of socks, called *tabi* socks in Japan. They are unusual in that they are shaped so as to separate the big toe from the other toes, and derive from traditional Japanese foot-wear, such as *zōri* sandals and *geta* wooden clogs, which both require that you slot a thong in between your big toe and the other toes to keep them in place. I have noticed that *tabi* socks are shaped so as to have a distinct heel too. This means that something I have done all my life, something as simple as putting on socks, now requires a higher degree of attention. Like shoes, *tabi* socks are foot-specific and must first be identified as left or right to be put on correctly.

This happened to an unsuspecting novice – a girl, but it could have been anyone – while training at the Yōshinkan dōjō in a class given by the founder, Kanchō Gōzō Shioda. Kanchō notices she has put her *dōgi* jacket on 'back to front' with the right front flap wrapped across her body on top of the left front flap. He nods to two hovering *deshi* and wordlessly they lift her by the elbows and carry her out of the dōjō at the double like removing an unwanted piece of furniture. Afterwards it is explained that a *dōgi* top, kimono or *uwagi* is worn in this way only when the wearer is dead, and it is considered very bad luck.

Mishima said to the extreme left-wing students he lectured at Tokyo University that if only they would acknowledge the Emperor he would join them. The extremes of any political pole have a tendency to meet.

Martial arts have formed part of my life since the age of eleven. If I sit down and ponder about the reasons for this continued fascination I find it easy to list a series of negative conclusions, – to say what martial arts are *not* – but immensely difficult to make a more positive statement. The negative manifesto includes:

> I am not a timid person fearful for my own protection and through martial arts seeking a means to defend myself.
>
> I have never desired to be a soldier or to fight in a war. Have never imagined myself as some sort of hero.
>
> I do not suffer unduly from aggressive urges that need to be channelled into some harmless or controlled avenue or as a catharsis.
>
> I am not especially interested in the culture or history of the Far Eastern nations that devised and developed the most advanced unarmed and pre-modern weapons combat systems the world has ever known. I find I am equally drawn to many other places, many other cul-

tures, in the quest to understand the strange and the
different.

I am not a natural masochist. In general pain is not an
attractive experience for me.

I have no desire to kill.

I do not want to be involved in any competitive or quasi-
sport forms of the martial arts and so am not seeking a
competitive outlet.

Perhaps a good explanation for my ongoing interest is simply
the continuity of self. I began my studies as a child, and as an
adult can see no reason to stop. There is so much more to learn.

When I first began to practise as a child I am not so certain
that any of these negative propositions could be asserted with
any confidence. Aged eleven I certainly imagined myself as an
heroic and powerful figure – a kung fu master. I certainly wanted
to be able to defend myself from the bullies who were taunting
me, and occasionally physically attacking me. Perhaps, once or
twice, prior to the socialising effects of my adolescence and early
adulthood, I fantasised the odd revenge killing, but if so I cannot
recall any details. I do remember how when walking down a
staircase at school, and finding my feet at the level of an
unknown boy's face as he ascended from below, I would have to
resist a powerful urge to kick him in the face. This is something I
never gave in to. Is it, I wonder, like the unbidden urge to push
someone off a train platform or a tall building which sometimes
swims into even the most pacific mind?

But as soon as I began to acquire some strength from regular
training and some ability to apply techniques that might give
me an edge in a fight, I found that I no longer wanted to fight.
The fantasies of revenge had faded. I had become tougher, even
'hard', but had at the same time lost the initial point, the theme
of nearly all Chinese kung fu movies: the transformation of the
weak into the strong in order to reverse the prevailing and unjust
order – to deal out retribution. Instead I had become absorbed
in the routines and details of a complex physical culture, struggling to acquire skills not easily won. I practised in order to

practise, trained because training was what I did. There was no goal, only effort, endless and unfathomable – like the process of life itself.

Between my twentieth and thirty-first birthdays I attended no martial arts school. I trained occasionally, revising what I had been taught, but not really keeping up the effort necessary to maintain what I had learned. I stopped training, gained weight and began to lose whatever skills I had once possessed. I shifted from concentrating on my body to working with my mind as a principal focus. Words replaced physical learning. In a sense I began to revert to my own culture.

So what did I have to show from most of a decade of obsessive study? A developed chest – with my left pectoral muscle visibly larger than the right, from the asymmetry of Hung Gar boxing patterns. The capacity to knock a man down with a very short punch – Bruce Lee's one-inch punch – known more formally as long bridge force. A nostalgia to swing a spear or handle a Chinese *dao*, or broadsword, whenever I chanced to watch demonstrations in Chinatown for the Chinese New Year. It all seemed so slight.

Ever since I had bought a black belt – without being eligible to wear one; the thrill of putting it on aged twelve was not equalled until I had earned it two decades later – from a sports shop in my home town I had harboured a desire to learn Japanese martial arts. There was something about the formal, regimented structure of a Japanese dōjō that answered to something in me. Was this a latent militarism? And if so, where did it come from? Both of my parents had served in the RAF, but it was wartime service and a normal thing to do in such emergency circumstances and represented in no sense a family military tradition. There was something calming about the silent sitting before and after practice which I had observed the few times I had seen inside a dōjō – *mokusō*, eyes closed in silent meditation. It was, I thought, without knowing why or how, somehow more Zen.

Last Day 10.10 *a.m.*

Mishima is carrying an attaché case. Inside are four books – two bound volumes of the *Sea of Fertility* cycle, *Spring Snow* and *Runaway Horses*, Mishima's difficult essay 'In Defence of Culture', and an anthology of rightist essays by a number of different authors titled *A Philosophy of Modern Revolution*. In addition to these books are copies of his written demands, a length of thin rope, some wire, a pair of pliers, a small bottle of brandy and some cigarettes, two knives – one a *tantō*, the other a *yoroidōshi* – and a quantity of cotton wool. The last item, Mishima had explained to Morita at a planning meeting earlier in the week, was necessary for them to plug their anuses to avoid fouling themselves as they cut open their stomachs.

I was intrigued by the cotton wool, never discovering precisely when, if at all, Mishima and Morita were free to introduce this precautionary plug. In the car on the way to the Ichigaya barracks whilst singing patriotic songs? In the General's office after lowering their trousers and just before kneeling to kill themselves?

I am forcing myself to live with an image of Yukio Mishima. As I am using his picture as a screen-saver I stare into his eyes every day for hours on end. The photograph I have selected for this is one of him aged forty-five, close to the moment of his chosen death, posing next to a rococo mirror in his anti-Zen house in

Magome. The mirror is wooden, carved into the form of a sunburst – more Louis Quatorze than Amaterasu Ō-Mikami.

Sometimes I can't help wondering whether or not I like this man, looking still deeper into his eyes for an answer that is not there, before dismissing it as a waste of time. Something unknowable. I am too late, I shall never meet the real Mishima. Did anyone?

Last Day 🕐 *10.10 a.m.*

Just before he and the others get into the car Mishima hands an envelope to Tiny Koga, telling him to read it and then pass it around so that the others can read it too. All the cadets had prepared themselves to die on this day – had written death poems, and as far as possible ensured they had left their loved ones on good terms. The envelope contained money and a letter ordering all the cadets except Morita to remain alive, urging them to faithfully represent the events of the day at their trial. The money was to pay for the hire of a lawyer. Despite what must have been disappointment – although perhaps admixed with a sense of relief – all three agreed to obey their leader's commands. In the letter Mishima also claimed sole responsibility for the planning of the incident, in the hope that it might lighten the charges against the Tate no Kai survivors.

The white Toyota containing the five men pulls away from Mishima's house at around 10.15 a.m. Unless there is heavy traffic they will be early.

The steam rising off the surface of the bowl of boiling soup misted my glasses as I began to slurp down the noodles with the customary loud sucking noises it had taken some time to learn to make. Everyone in Japan, from infant to grandma, slurps noodles. It is a practical skill that allows you to eat the noodles while they remain scalding hot, and I had forced myself to discard my misplaced Western table manners. The stall selling *rāmen*, Chinese-style noodles served in hot soup, was a Shibuya fixture, pitched just outside the JR station. The noodles were good and the old man who ran the stall a great source of news and gossip from the neighbourhood.

As I ate I was puzzling about my evening stroll. I had wandered over to visit the shrine to the Young Officers uprising, a monument commemorating the Ni Ni Roku Jiken, or 26 February Incident – an army mutiny that occurred in 1936.[40] The shrine itself was a kind of stepped pyramid in slabs of stone, with hedges and bushes and a tree planted around a funeral tablet or gravestone arranged with a shelf for burning incense and leaving offerings. There were fresh flowers in a pot, indicating that someone was tending the shrine. A shrine to a mutiny seemed so strange.

'Just been to see the Ni Ni Roku Jiken monument over there,' I said waving in the direction I had come.

'That so?' said the noodle man, ladling more *rāmen* into a line of waiting bowls. Others crowding into the small space under the canvas awning seemed uninterested, or listened secretly, still slurping their soup.

'Why would anyone build a monument to a mutiny?'

'It's because of the ghost.'

'What ghost?'

'They put the thing up in Showa 35 [1960]. I was there and remember the speeches. On and on they went. They were all there. Araki, Mikami too – he'd just got out [of prison], Sagoya and Konuma.[41] It was a good chance to see such a line-up of assassins, haha!'

'They were all Kōdō-ha people, weren't they? And General Araki was the leader. When did he die?'

'Showa 42 [1967].'

'So you were saying, the ghost?'

'I don't know who it's supposed to be. They say it's one of the officers. The one who shot himself after Prince Chichibu wouldn't support them.'

'A troubled spirit eh?'

'Mmm. Everyone's superstitious about such things. And of course there's a political angle. There always is haha. Excuse me.'

The noodle man turned to deal with a large group of salary-men who had just arrived, and that was that.

At the weekend I decided to do some further research. I had heard of the 26 February Incident and knew a little of the history of the times, but was curious about the details. The Incident, I discovered, was the last significant act of insubordination in contemporary Japanese history. The Imperial Army had at this time divided into two broad factions – the Kōdō-ha, or Imperial Way, and the Tōsei-ha, or Control Faction. Both factions supported Japan's military expansionist ambitions, but they differed over the direction and methods needed. The Imperial Way believed strongly that former military successes, as in the Russo-Japanese war, could be attributed mainly to Japanese combative spirit and therefore emphasised the development of physical and mental disciplines. The much more diverse Control Faction were modernists, many of whom had studied in the West, committed to assessing war potential in terms of manufacturing capacities, manpower and munitions.

The Imperial Way also argued that expansion should be directed against the Soviet Union in a strike north. The Control Faction counter-proposed a Japanese displacement of Western colonial powers in Asia, striking south to 'liberate' British, Dutch and American colonies. By 1936 the Imperial Way was losing ground in terms of key appointments to positions of power in government and the military high command and a rumour spread that army units loyal to this ideology were about to be transferred out of Tokyo to Manchuria in what would amount to a purge.

Early on the morning of 26 February 1936 twenty-one officers and roughly 1,400 men and NCOs of the First Division together with a single unit of the Imperial Guard conducted a series of politically motivated assassinations hoping to provoke a military coup leading to a Showa Restoration, their term for the Emperor assuming direct control of government, backed by his most loyal subjects, the army.[42]

The rebels seized the Army Ministry and the Metropolitan Police HQ and killed Viscount Makoto Saitō, the Lord Privy Seal, Korekiyo Takahashi, the Finance Minister, General Jōtaro Watanabe, Inspector General of Military Education, the secretary to Prime Minister Okada and five police officers. Others were wounded. Grand Chamberlain Kantarō Suzuki was shot in the testicles by Captain Teruzō Andō, who subsequently further demonstrated his ineptitude by failing in an attempt at suicide. The offices of the *Asahi Shinbun* and *Tokyo Nichinichi Shinbun* newspapers were shot up.

After the initial frenzy of murder the troops surrounded but did not enter the Imperial Palace and a temporary headquarters was established in the nearby Sannō Hotel (the guests were politely found rooms elsewhere). Following three days of negotiations with senior officers, many of whom sympathised with the Showa Restoration ideology of the rebels, the Emperor flatly refused to receive a petition from those whom he regarded as mutineers and insisted they be denied supplies and forced to surrender. The leader of the uprising, Captain Shirō Nonaka, a personal friend of the Emperor's younger brother Prince Chichibu, failing to receive the support he had anticipated, shot himself, and his force surrendered on 28 February. In the subsequent military trials seventeen were condemned to death and executed by firing squad in July 1936.

I had read Mishima's novella about the uprising, *Yūkoku*, or *Patriotism*. He called it his favourite story and wrote two further pieces themed on the events of the uprising: 'The Voices of the Heroic Dead', and the play *Tōka no Kiku* (The Tenth-Day Chrysanthemum). Why, I wondered, did this mutiny, which occurred in the tumultuous 1930s when Mishima was only eleven and still under his grandmother's close control, have such resonance for him? I bought a new copy of *Yūkoku* and settled down in a Dotour coffee shop with a large and steaming mug of *burendo kohii*, filter coffee, to read it again, scouring the text for clues.

'*Patriotism is the conviction that this country is superior to all others because you were born in it.*'

G. B. SHAW

In fewer than sixty printed pages, *Patriotism*[43] describes the circumstances of the suicide of a young army officer and his wife following the emergency of the 26 February Incident. The novella is divided into five chapters. The first, very short one serves as a kind of overture, stating quite simply that a suicide occurs, recording the ages of the couple – he is thirty-one, she is twenty-three – and commenting that they have been married for just six months. It is a tragic situation, yet Mishima insists that the story is a description of happiness, a happy tale.

We are told that anyone gazing on the bridal photograph might catch a presentiment of fate. The perfect beauty of the match is such as to evoke a sense of hubris: it is easy to believe there 'was a curse on these flawless unions'. The couple live simply in a small house with no maid. There are three rooms. The larger room upstairs is the only room that catches the sun, and is therefore used as a combined bedroom and reception room. The woman is called Reiko, the man Shinji. They did not have a honeymoon due to the circumstances of national emergency – Japan at war in China.

On their wedding night Shinji, a lieutenant in the army, lectures his wife on the nature of marriage to a soldier. He could die at any time. Is she prepared to accept this? In silent answer

Reiko fetches a dagger that formed part of her trousseau, confirming her resolve to kill herself should her husband die. It is a wordless death pact.

For the first month of their married life they are passionately physical towards each other, yet even in their passion they are sober and serious. Nothing frivolous enters into their relations. Reiko conducts herself in accordance with the Imperial Rescript on Education, which enjoined the value of harmony between a married couple. Each morning before Shinji leaves to attend to his military duties the couple formally bow before photographs of the Emperor and Empress kept on a shrine shelf. Theirs is a religious and moral life of intense happiness.

The scene is set. We have decided that the young officer and his wife are beautiful, passionate and aware of their duties both to each other and to certain ideals. They are a standard of formal perfection, a perfect Confucian couple.

The world is about to intervene. Shinji wakes on the morning of 26 February to the call of a bugle, the city carpeted in newly fallen snow. He leaves to discover what is taking place and does not return until the evening of the 28th. We are aware, of course, that a rebellion is occurring and that it will all be over by the day after Shinji's return home. Reiko finds out what is going on by listening to news bulletins on the radio. She remains at home, the door locked. Recognising that her husband may be involved, that he may die, she resolves to die too should he not return. Shinji has admonished his wife to think only of the present, to disregard the morrow. Her passionate devotion is contrasted with her childish sentimental attachment to some china ornamental animals. Yet she is not in the least afraid of death and almost welcomes it. This is bizarre given her age and situation, but it is not a matter for regret, as she is so much her husband's wife, a soldier's wife, ready to die.

The radio reports make it clear that colleagues of Shinji are involved in the rebellion. What began as a movement dedicated to restoring the nation's honour is quickly branded an act of mutiny. Will fighting break out in the snowy streets?

On the evening of the 28th the lieutenant returns home. His face betrays trauma, his sense of dejection. The denouement is clear – tomorrow his friends, the rebels, will be denounced and he will be ordered to attack them. It is a conflict of personal sentiment and unavoidable duty, following a model that crops up again and again in traditional Japanese drama. 'I can't do it,' the lieutenant tells his wife. But the situation is not a dilemma. There is no room for vacillation. Although not mentioned in the story, it is one of those situations described in the *Hagakure*: when facing a fifty-fifty choice between life and death, simply choose death.

The lieutenant experiences true peace of mind for the first time. He announces to his wife his decision to cut open his stomach, to commit seppuku, and she responds by asking permission to kill herself. The freedom he feels is a sense of having set aside the tensions that always attend making choices. When you have decided to die there are no more choices to make. Nothing concerns you. There can be no fear about the future when there is no future.

At this point in what is so far a straightforward account of a tragic situation an odd Mishima-esque twist is given to the story. Shinji tells his wife: 'We'll go together. But I want you to be a witness, first, for my own suicide. Agreed?' This is highly abnormal. In situations like this the man would kill his wife then commit seppuku, in case she may lack the strength to see it through alone. This new departure is justified as exemplifying the lieutenant's trust in his wife – in her role as a witness and in having the courage to manage her own end. He has no thought of saving her the horror of watching the person she loves die a most painful death; and the idea of her serving as a witness to endorse the propriety of his suicide is absurd. She will be dead, unable to tell anyone how he died.

There is a transcendentalism in having made a resolution to die. From Reiko's point of view 'She seemed to see only a free and limitless expanse opening into the vast distances.' Ordinary experiences take on new and enhanced significance. The caresses of her husband, his kisses, so soon to be lost to her, seem renewed and intensified.

Yet what remains of their lives is the opposite of dramatic. It is banal. Things proceed as on a normal evening. She prepares some side dishes and warms sake for them to drink as the lieutenant takes a bath.

Purity is mentioned. We are to believe that there is nothing impure about the couple pleasurably anticipating their own deaths. In a key passage, the act of patriotism – suicide in such circumstances serving loyally to remonstrate with the Emperor – is equated with physical love-making. Sex somehow merges with death.

The overlap of love-making and suicide suggests that the lieutenant desires death as he desires sex – as a kind of inborn instinct or inherent passion, Eros and Thanatos locked together in a fond farewell embrace. Such an idea also confirms the feeling of freedom. *Seppuku* as *kanshi* – a protest against the direction of government in his beloved country – which does not have to be effective provided that the motivation is pure. It is an act in the front line of the spirit, a place where there can never be any witnesses.

Shinji and Reiko make love in the upstairs room before a glowing gas heater. The act is rendered utterly poignant as both realise that they are making love for the last time. The imminence of their deaths elevates their senses, massively magnifying their pleasures.

Reiko's body is described in erotic and poetic detail as Shinji kisses it and gazes on it for the final time, etching it into his mind. Reiko, overcoming her customary modesty, reciprocates this ritualised leave-taking of the body and gazes on her husband's body. (Here Mishima indulges himself in lovingly describing a male body from a woman's – and of course, his own – point of view. Even Shinji's armpit hair makes it into Reiko's journey from his head to his toes.)

As they make love, in a truly absurd line, Shinji's laboured breathing at his exertions is described using military symbols: 'The lieutenant panted like the regimental standard bearer on a route march.' They rise to greater passions still, over and over, joined as one.

Shinji stops making love to his wife, not from exhaustion or satiety but from a desire to reserve some strength for his suicide – and also from the sense that the sweetness of their love-making should not be diminished by excess. A measured approach, continent even to the last. Rousing himself, Shinji says: Let's prepare. To underscore the tenderness he feels for Reiko he helps with putting away the bedding – something he has never done before.

Shinji and Reiko recall the drinking parties that have taken place in the upstairs room – which is clean and neat as if prepared for guests. Drinking with colleagues who will be met again in the next world and who will be sure to tease him for bringing his wife with him. Preparations go on. As Shinji washes and dresses in a clean loincloth and dons his uniform, Reiko sets out paper for their final letters and grinds ink on an ink stone. Reiko goes to wash and dress and Shinji writes: 'Long Live the Imperial Forces – Army Lieutenant Takayama Shinji.' Reiko reappears wearing a white kimono. The couple stand before the God shelf, the *kamiza*, and pray bowing. They go upstairs, placing their letters – no details of Reiko's are given – in the *tokonoma* alcove, leaving the scroll hanging there in place. It reads 'Sincerity'.

For the lieutenant his death is an exhibition of his military self to set before the eyes of his wife – a side to him she has never seen before. He regards his seppuku as 'a death of no less degree and quality than death in the front line'. Reflecting, Shinji considers this situation as the 'very pinnacle of good fortune'. Reiko notices how beautiful Shinji is in uniform, even more handsome today than normal, perhaps caused by his contemplating his own death.

Shinji will cut open his stomach using his *guntō*, his military sword. To make this possible, he must handle the blade, so he winds a bandage around it, leaving only five or six inches of the point exposed.

There follows an eight-page blow-by-blow account of the act of cutting, from the first incision, to how it feels, to gushing blood and guts, to Shinji's end as he uses the last vestige of his strength to thrust the blade through his throat, so that it protrudes through the nape of his neck. Is this the most gruesome description of its kind in all literature?

Reiko goes downstairs, her white kimono stained scarlet with her husband's blood. She extinguishes the charcoal brazier and puzzles over whether or not to unbolt the front door, deciding to do so and leaving it slightly ajar. The streets at midnight beyond are empty.

She makes up her face, not with her usual restraint, designed to please her husband, but with bolder lines, her aspect to the world. Returning upstairs to the room where Shinji lies dead, she lifts his head, wipes his face and kisses his dead lips for the last time. Having felt that as he died Shinji separated from her, going ahead into another realm, she now intends to join him. Taking out her knife she tastes the metal on her tongue and then quickly stabs herself in the throat. The cut is shallow and she has to do it again, to sever an artery, dying in a red haze.

He read himself into insanity.
NABOKOV on DON QUIXOTE

It had taken me over an hour to read through this harrowing and blood-soaked story. The cup of coffee on the table was only half consumed, but had gone cold and I no longer wanted to drink it. Customers had come and gone, mostly in small groups, but there were also one or two solitary coffee-drinkers like me. At the next table was a nondescript man in a salaryman's blue suit smoking his way through a pack of Mild 7. Exhaled smoke was wafted towards my face by the draught from the automatic doors opening and closing as people entered and left. I noticed out of the corner of my eye that he was reading the title of the book I had just placed cover up on the table.

Unlike most Japanese I never bothered with a paper book cover to deny just such curious impulses in public places. Our eyes made contact and he smiled in a crooked way. 'You like Mishima?' he asked me in English. 'Yes I do,' I replied in Japanese. He seemed relieved he would not have to struggle in a foreign language and then shook his head. 'Eyaaa . . . Mishima is the past. Not now. Not today. Not tomorrow either. I think his work is . . . eetoo . . . dangerous. Yes dangerous. Anyone who says they like Mishima usually regrets it before long.' I wondered if he was drunk. Didn't feel like defending myself, explaining anything to a stranger in a coffee shop, and decided to go. 'Thanks,' I said nodding. 'Thanks for the warning.' It was my turn to smile enigmatically. 'OK,' said the salaryman blowing out a final cloud of smoke before stubbing out the half-smoked cigarette and adding it to the pile of butts in the ashtray. 'See you,' he said as I walked away. I didn't like the way he said it. He'd used a casual form of farewell reserved for close friends, and I felt agitated by this and excluded from the laughter and energy of Shibuya on a Saturday night as I walked back to Ken's.

About ten days before the designated day of his death Mishima telephoned Mitsuaki Owada, a famous tattooist, more formally known as Horikin. He had an urgent commission for him. Would he tattoo a lion dog and peony design on Mishima's back and shoulders? Mishima explained that it had to be completed by the 24th of November, in a mere nine days' time, money no object, but was told that this could not be done. There was a need for rest days between visits, and the design Mishima was requesting would take more than two weeks to achieve. Reluctantly Mishima gave up on the idea of a tattoo, but why did he want one in the first place?

In the mid-1960s a series of yakuza gangster movies was made under the general title *Showa Zankyō-den*, directed by Kiyoshi Saeki. The plotlines were formulaic – a good gangster, always a loner, perhaps newly released from prison, struggles to follow an ethical code of conduct – something like a modern-day variant of bushidō. He will, inevitably, be frustrated by bad gangsters who have long since abandoned any idea of an ethical code and are acting in a lawless, crazed and almost Western manner. By the end of the movie the good gangster is always forced to take bloody revenge against the bad guys – always armed only with a sword, and sometimes backed up by a single friend fated to die in a demonstration of loyalty.

The 1966 offering, *Karajishi Botan* (The Lion Dog and the Peony), cast Takakura Ken, sometimes referred to as Japan's Clint Eastwood, in the starring role. His back is heavily tattooed. As he calmly walks towards the final showdown, sword in hand, we hear him singing a sentimental song – about lion dogs and peonies and tattoos for valour and masculine courage in a failing, fading world.

Last Day *10.40 a.m.*

The white Toyota Corona, registration Tama 5 – ひ – 36 – 86, newly washed earlier that morning, gleams in the November sunshine as it speeds up the Expressway. Mishima tells Koga to take the Gaien exit and then looks at his watch. They are too early, too early for an appointment to die! It won't do, they must be precisely on time. He tells Koga to circuit the Jingū Gaien a few times, and as the white saloon drives round and round Mishima breaks into song to maintain everyone's spirits.

> *Giri to Ninjyō o hakari ni kakerya*
> *Giri ga omotai otoko no sekai*
> *Osana-najimi no Kannon-sama nya*
> *Ore no kokoro wa omitōshi*
> *Sena de hoeteru, Karajishi-botan.*

'Barking from my back, a lion dog and a peony . . .'

Mishima sings this popular *enka*, taken from the movie of the same name: *Karajishi Botan*. The others join in on the chorus of each verse. The symbolism is clear to everyone – the lion dog with its superhuman valour and strength; the peony, most noble of flowers, a spring bloom symbolising purity and a female sensitivity necessary to balance the complete man. Cruelty must be restrained by *bushi no nasake*, the samurai virtue of compassion for the weak.

After a few more circuits, the clean white car filled with uniformed singing men drives on. Mishima decides to pass by his daughter's school, Peers School Elementary, and after this diversion they resume the journey to Ichigaya, on schedule once again for their appointment with the General.

Last Day   10.55 *a.m.*

Tiny Koga pulls up in front of the entrance to the Ichigaya SDF Headquarters, winding down a window. Armed sentries are stationed at the gate, but on seeing Mishima seated in the back of the car they simply salute and wave his vehicle through. He is known to be a VIP. There is no question of asking for passes or permits and he is expected at this time: the appointment with General Mashita has been logged. The white saloon car drives on up the hill and then is lost in the screening treeline as it turns left towards the General's office.

Thirty years later I am milling around at the same gate at the base of Ichigaya Hill. I have arranged to join a 90-minute tour

of the SDF base. Since the 9/11 attack on New York, security
has been stepped up, and I have had to fax my passport in
advance and provide other credentials. I am the only non-
Japanese waiting to be escorted on the tour. All the others are
elderly, in their seventies or even eighties. From their accents
many have travelled here from other parts of Japan. The real
attraction of this visit, I have read, is the hall where the Tokyo
War Crimes Tribunal was held. War veterans all, wanting to
see this place before they die – but why? A pool of elderly
men that must be shrinking as the years pass, but right now is
managing to provide 150 visitors every day.

We are badged, marshalled and directed by two ladies with
loudhailers dressed in bright red coats and black hats, like
department store staff. Some of us clamber up a series of large
paved stairwells arrayed like the seats in a Roman amphitheatre,
intent on reaching the plateau of the steep hill, where the main
buildings are located. Others, perhaps frailer, ride up a covered
escalator. Turning to the left we are decanted into a large courtyard that fronts on to three large buildings of extraordinary
ugliness. The guide begins to tell us how many floors and rooms
each building contains, that the largest has two helicopter land-
ing pads. At the base of each block a roofed gallery makes a
half-hearted attempt to add architectural flavour to the dull
concrete cubes. My fellow tourists snap away with their cameras,
like paparazzi feeding, although there is nothing worth recording. These buildings had been put up to replace a demolished
older building of some grandeur, which had incorporated the
balcony where Mishima stood to address the assembled garrison.
However, this site was not completely lost. It had been rebuilt
nearby, in miniature, complete with balcony and using original
internal features.

We moved on to stare at the communications mast – 'It is
220 metres tall, projecting 175 metres above the roof of the
building,' droned the guide through a bullhorn. I had little
interest in how many tons of concrete were poured to fashion
these monsters. I wanted to move on to the reconstructed hall,
and perhaps to observe something of the day-to-day life of SDF
soldiers. An odd thing was that apart from the sentries at the

gate, so far I had not spotted a single man or woman in uniform, as if they had all been instructed to hide during the public tour. This was the least military military base I had ever visited: no guns, no tanks or military vehicles.

The hall was a two-storey building, with a sort of central turret that added a storey or two. The building it was modelled on had been considerably larger, but the proportions of the frontal balcony were more or less unchanged, except for its depth, which had been foreshortened. I wandered inside and turned into the Grand Auditorium. The flooring, clearly old, had a patina suggesting the shuffling of generations of shoeless feet, and was comprised of a large number of pieces of wood, like parquet. 'The floor is boarded by 7,200 pieces of Japanese oak, each 30 cm square, all are original except for 399 pieces which had been warped beyond use,' said the guide. We were told that this was where the War Crimes Tribunal had convened, where General Tōjō and his six co-accused had been sentenced to death. The onslaught of flash intensified. A number of chairs had been set out and we took our places to watch an SDF recruitment video.

Watching this unconvincing promo I am reminded of a poster campaign adopted by the Ground Self Defence Forces in the 1970s to try to reverse falling recruitment. Their initial effort showed a gloved hand saluting, with the caption 'Come young men for the defence of your country.' It failed utterly. A rethink led to a far more effective poster, showing a rugby scrum in close-up focus on straining shiny muscular thighs, with the shout line: 'Hot sweat! How refreshing! Kindle your passion together with your fellows.'

After the video we were ushered towards the second floor, passing some stairs that led, I supposed, on to the stage. The guide solemnly pointed out that the right-hand set of stairs was reserved for the exclusive use of the Emperor. As the party moved to the next floor I lingered and then quickly doubled back. Some devil compelled me to dash up the Emperor's stairs, something I doubted any older-generation Japanese would do. I managed this without being spotted and hurried to join the others. We were in a room which had been reconstructed to

represent the one used by the commanding General of the
Eastern Army: 'the very room where Mishima committed seppuku,' said the guide, only it wasn't. The transported door frame
was chipped in three places and the guide declared that these
marks had been made by Mishima's sword. I ran my fingertip
across the notches. The guide's brief comments included the
claim that Mishima had smuggled his sword into the base, without SDF permission. That is not true, but is now the official
version to excuse the lapse in security. General Mashita, in due
course, had been scapegoated. He resigned from the army and
spent the few remaining years of his life as director of Haneda
airport.

We were now free to visit the base shop, which was filled
with kitsch SDF souvenirs. I was tempted to buy an army uniform, but relented and instead bought two large bottles of sake
bearing pictures of the original balcony where Mishima
addressed the assembled garrison before his suicide. On my way
out I encountered a small group of men practising *jūken-dō*,
bayonet training using wooden and bamboo weapons, and wearing kendō masks and light padded body armour. After the
Mishima incident one of the journalists leaving the base wrote
that he too passed a group of SDF soldiers, not training in
martial arts but excitedly playing volleyball. They must have
started to play soon after Mishima's balcony appeal. They were
still playing when Mishima's body was not yet cold.

Late one night, after a few drinks, I had convinced myself that
no one was going to talk to me. I was beginning to wonder if I
was just unlucky in my choice of people to approach or whether
it was something more fundamental. Was I kissing the wrong
frogs or kissing frogs wrongly? That no one really wanted to
talk about Mishima was entirely clear. There was a collective

embarrassment or conspiracy of silence surounding the ugly themes that met in Mishima's decision to kill himself. I had by now failed to talk to: Mishima's surviving son; his daughter, who did not live in Japan but in Switzerland; and his wife and parents, who were already dead, as was his brother; Atsuyuki Sasa, the police officer who had investigated the incident and who was now retired, had declined to meet me. The Tate no Kai cadets had formally indicated that they would never comment publicly to anyone on the events of 25 November. I had also been rebuffed by the former Prime Minister and kendōka Ryūtarō Hashimoto; the Governor of Tokyo, Shintarō Ishihara, and the cross-dressing torch singer, stylist and female impersonator Akihiro Miwa. The organiser of the Yūkokuki memorial which took place each year had been distinctly unfriendly and unforthcoming despite a formal introduction. Had someone been getting ahead of me and poisoning the well?

I had no idea why I had met with so little success, but I felt like someone trying to scramble over an enormous wall without ropes or any idea of how to climb even a little way up. So I went behind the bar at Ken's, opened a new bottle of Suntory whiskey, and poured myself an outsize glass to help me deal with the darkening mood.

Arriving back at Ken's tired out after spending the day on a futile trail, I switch on the light and find an envelope lying just inside the door. I open it to find that it is a brief reply to the letter I sent to Funasaka, but written by his son, Yoshio. In it he apologises on behalf of his father, but tells me that it would not be worth while to speak to him because he is in an advanced stage of Alzheimer's disease and is quite unable to remember the events surrounding his gift to Mishima of the Seki no Magoroku sword.

'Damn,' I thought, another witness unable to tell me anything. I was sorry that Mr Funasaka was ill, but also frustrated at one more door closing. But sometimes another door opens. In the last line of the letter, written on another sheet of paper, Yoshio Funasaka informed me: 'I taught Mishima *iaidō*. Perhaps I can help you. If you would like to talk please let me know.'

Browsing in Kinokuniya Bookshop I find a new paperback edition of Henry's biography of Mishima. The jacket is illustrated with a photograph of Mishima practising *iaidō*, kneeling in *seiza* about to draw his sword, dressed all in white, in a white *uwagi* and white *hakama*. I find the book not in the biography section but on a shelf devoted to martial arts. Mishima would have liked that, I thought, and as I already owned a copy of the book carefully placed it back where I found it.

I am standing in a white space, quite alone. In the distance a solitary white-clad figure is visible, walking towards me. He stands in front of me and begins to speak. His words are clear and meaningful. As I am listening another similarly dressed figure with an androgynous face – is it a man or a woman? – joins the first and also starts to talk. My attention switches between them and I can feel the beginnings of a struggle to maintain understanding. A third figure, this time female, then a fourth join the first two and one by one begin to talk, each speaking of something profound, each equally important to me.

More speakers arrive, thronging the white space around me. Soon there is a multitude, their voices overwhelming, and I can no longer make out a single word.

Waking from what seems to have been a dream, I move to write down the details of this vision, which seemed so profound. I write the word 'language' on a sheet of paper. The letters I have formed begin to thicken and grow in front of my eyes. Am I still asleep, dreaming that I have woken? The black ink of the letters bleeds slowly across the flat white surface, until the page is entirely black and nothing remains to be read or written.

Mishima describes his world-view as a child as composed of three equally real parts of experience: the world outside – the eruption of a volcano or the insurrection of an army would fall into this category – what we might today call the news, in his case perhaps overheard in the conversations of parents and other adults; his domestic situation – say the arguments of his truculent grandmother, bedtimes and bath times, the day-to-day events in his household; and finally the world of the imagination, deriving at the time of Mishima's boyhood from fairy stories and other flights of fancy in written and spoken forms – his grandmother's narratives of the myths and legends of Japan and the plots of Noh and Kabuki plays she was fond of.

Mishima points out in *Confessions of a Mask* that he could not credit that either the domestic or the wider world was more real than the vivid and passionate engagement he found for himself in fairy stories. For him the reality of the imagination had at least equal, but perhaps superior, validity in the making of his world-view, forming one of the principal building blocks of his future life. For Mishima, the imaginary *was* real.

Of course, the world of the imagination is a kind of theatre. Inside it you direct the form of reality; you fashion and control it. Why accept the substance and events of the external world? Instead, why not resist, why not direct the most controllable reality: the romantic imagination? Life as you choose it to be. Things meaning no more or less than you want them to mean.

If we adopt a mechanistic view of life then perhaps it might be possible to draw up a spectrum of reality, based for example on how powerfully an experience registers on the five senses. If it engages only a single sense, is the experience less real than one that calls for more than one faculty? Is it more real to eat a sandwich than to listen to a symphony in the dark? Do we find that the six o'clock news with stories about the Middle East, war and violence, or about a missing child, a domestic crisis in the household of someone not personally known to us, is more or less real than our bedside reading about a distant galaxy, fictionalising a world thousands of years in the future?

The solution of the riddle of the world is only possible through the proper connection of outer with inner experience.

SCHOPENHAUER

Mishima had little faith in the real world, hardly any in a world that so differed from the world he desired. Instead of becoming politicised, as were so many of those around him, swept up by the revolutionary spirit of the times – the Sixties, a period of social revolution, characterised by student-led street riots in many parts of the world – he imagined. He staged plays that were miniature worlds, in which he held dominion. If he wanted something, then thinking it so would make it so, or as near as did not matter. Sustaining illusion in the face of reality was an exercise of the will. Mishima's power to command his own will was superhuman. He could invert the world – see death as the goal of life, even when a generation of Darwinians point to the dominance of survival. Sustaining illusion is, of course, the theatrical situation: life as a stage. Consciously choosing illusion is not strictly psychosis, but it seems to me that it is likely to induce it if practised long enough. 'I'm too involved in my dream world' (Mishima wrote in *Spring Snow*.) '. . . They've spilled over into reality. They're a flood that's sweeping me away.'

Public debate is mostly about the unreal. Of the three strands of reality identified by Mishima – the domestic, the outside world of report, and the inner life of the mind, the imagination – only the first and the third are based on experience. The reported world may, in an important sense, be said not to exist. That it is there at all is based on faith and the consistency of accounts. That we can judge very much from reports is practically a religious ideal, an article of faith. The sheer banality and pathos of, say, listening to the radio news declare that 1,500 people have been crushed to death in a North African earthquake and then answering the phone to discuss the details of a party you plan to attend that evening should be overwhelming. That it is not results from you not really caring about the earthquake victims, or caring only for a moment. They are unreal. It is not that you are a monster, or that if you tried to care about all the reported disasters you would soon be overwhelmed. It is because they are unreal. Empathy is possible, but empathy is an interpersonal skill and needs a real connection to be triggered. Hence the charity-driven images of starving children. Photographers have told me that they sometimes have to stalk the starving to catch them in an unsmiling moment. A smiling dying child elicits no gainful sympathy in the wealthy nations where the photos will be seen.

I considered attending the Yūkokuki, the memorial gathering for Mishima and Morita held each year on 25 November, but finally decided that there was little point in attending. Henry had told me of his single attendance, when he had been seated on the stage and deferred to in a manner that made him very uncomfortable. Andrew Rankin, a writer working on what will be the most comprehensive biography of Mishima in English, had a similar experience. I was sure I had little to gain from meeting the typical attendees. I assumed that the Tate no Kai survivors would be there, but as they had already made it clear that they did not want to talk I did not much feel like door-stepping them. Instead I would go to Mishima's grave.

I took the Chuo line to Musashisakai and then the Seibu Tama-gawa line to Tama, the station nearest to Momijigaoka, the small town next to the Tama Cemetery, last resting place for 370,000 souls, and where Mishima is buried. It is perhaps the second most fashionable cemetery in Tokyo after Aoyama Bochi, where Mishima sites the ancestral resting place of the Matsugae family in the *Sea of Fertility* novels. Musashisakai Station is the current record-holder for train suicides, and I also recalled that the last carriage in a Chuo line train is the favourite haunt of train perverts, sometimes operating in groups, where they fondle and harass their sexual targets, mostly young office ladies and schoolgirls. They had even established their own magazine to coordinate 'outings'.

Momijigaoka is a one-street town with a single business: death. There are shops selling the implements required by devout family members in attending to their ancestors' tombs – brushes, small wooden buckets and bamboo scoops for washing the grave, and vessels for flowers and incense. The other commercial activity is that of monumental masons. Gravemarkers may be specially commissioned, or the bereaved can choose from a bewildering array of pre-fashioned headstones, *nishinoya* (stone lanterns) and statuary. Most were tasteful, a few bizarre, such as a 2-foot-high greystone carving of Ultraman about to launch himself into the heavens, or one of Mickey Mouse waving.

I found the entrance to the cemetery, and was given a small map which identified the famous occupants and the location of their graves. General Araki, the leader of the army faction behind the 26 February Incident, was here; so too was Nitobe

Inazō, the Quaker scholar who published an influential if inaccurate work on bushidō in 1899 – a favourite book of President Theodore Roosevelt – and whose image used to grace the ¥5,000 note.

To reach Mishima's grave I had to walk down the main avenue and turn left and then thread a little. The bright sunshine was filtering through the red, gold and orange leaves of the *momiji*, a kind of maple, splendid trees that lined the road for a hundred metres or more. I was so taken with the spectacular colours that I went beneath some overhanging branches and frolicked in the filtering light as it cast multi-hued patterns on my white shirt, like flames of cold fire.

Arriving at Mishima's grave[44] I had expected to find others gathered, but there was no one. Someone must have been there earlier, as a cigarette placed upright had burned down and its ash still lay intact to one side. I peered at it – Caster Mild, not Mishima's preferred brand, which was either Golden Bat or Peace – but if you were a smoker beyond the reach of a tobacconist any brand would do I guessed. Incense had also been offered to comfort his spirit. I had brought some too, not traditional but an avant-garde variety – Comme des Garçons Deux, all I could find at Ken's. I held it in between my palms bowing, then offered it to the *kami* and placed it ends glowing in a burner.

The grave was the Hiraoka family plot. The marker indicated that Mishima's father and mother were here too, and Yōko, his wife's name, also appeared. There were ten bundles of flowers – combinations of lilies and carnations, orchids, roses, irises, gladioli and some flowers whose names I knew in Japanese but not English: *gābera*, *kasumisō*. There were also many chrysanthemums, Japan's favourite flower and the symbol of the imperial family.[45] Behind the four blocks of white rosestone that marked the place were planted three trees, one a tall pine, and three bushes. In the sun-bright sky the moon was still visible, half illuminated, half in shadow – like a yin-yang symbol. It made me think about the continuity of life, despite the inevitability of individual death.

After I had been standing there for a few minutes listening to the birdsong and watching the faint glowing tips of the incense sticks I had lit, a middle-aged woman dressed in a smart grey rose-patterned woollen suit arrived. She was carrying ritual cleaning implements, water in a bucket, a scoop, a small broom. I bowed to her and she smiled and bowed in return. I thought I should stand back, and from a short distance I watched her tidy the already clean grave. After placing some flowers she had brought she walked off into the distance and did not return before I decided to go home.

Waiting on the platform for a Chūo-line train at Musashisakai I looked across towards an Ito Yokado supermarket. There was a branch of a fast food outlet which sold a kind of hot donut – Beard Papa's Pipin' hot cream puffs. Beard Papa, whose giant portrait was visible even at this distance, is a ringer for Ernest Hemingway in a woolly hat. I could also read Est. 1952, and would lay odds that a Hemingway photograph was the source of the drawing. For a few seconds I felt overwhelmed by death. I had just visited a suicide's grave, and now I was staring at a picture of another writer who blew his brains out with a shotgun, while waiting on a platform favoured by those planning to jump.

Although General Mashita is tied to his desk chair using the thin rope taken from Mishima's briefcase, he is not bound in any kind of elegant manner. His wrists are tied and his legs have been attached to the chair, but the knots are simple and improvised. At first the General is gagged with a clean white handkerchief, but this is removed after the outer-office staff have discovered what is happening. The alarm has sounded, and it is clear that the General will not order his men to do anything foolish.

In former times the precise knots used in securing a captive, even the colour of the cord employed to do this, were dictated by feudal rank. A martial art, *hōjō jutsu*, taught how to control and bind a prisoner. It still forms a part of the curriculum of a number of the *koryū*, the ancient schools of martial discipline.

In the twenty-first century the largest residual knowledge of complex tying skills is to be found not in the martial arts but in the sexual specialisation of sado-masochistic bondage. Everyone agrees that real mastery of knotting and tying a human body with a rope is a Japanese skill – indeed the sexually motivated variant of this practice in contemporary Japan is known as *shib-ari*. Certain methods have been developed so that any attempt to struggle ensures progressively escalating discomfort, even asphyxiation – on the battlefield this was a pragmatic consider-ation, for the fetishist a means to heighten erotic excitation.

Shichishō is a contraction of the phrase *shichishō hōkoku*, which means to serve the nation for seven lives. It is often written on a *hachimaki* or headband worn to show passionate resolve – such as those worn by kamikaze pilots on their final flights. Mishima wore a *hachimaki* on 25 November, prominently visible in the famous photograph of him on the Ichigaya barracks balcony remonstrating with the assembled troops below and gesturing with his white-gloved hand. The phrase is over six hundred years old, and is traceable to accounts of the circumstances of the death of two imperial loyalist brothers, Kusunoki Masashige and Kusunoki Masasue. Masashige is the most revered example in all his country's history of a loyal and virtuous hero.

The Hōjō family ruled Japan from Kamakura through the Shogunate, or *bakufu*, and had sought to dilute any political power still attaching to the person of the Emperor in Kyoto by a system of alternate succession: two branches of the imperial family would provide an Emperor who would reign for a fixed period and then be succeeded by the next generation of the other branch. In this way dynastic objectives could be thwarted.

From time to time an Emperor would rebel, either seeking to remain Emperor or to abdicate in favour of his own son, and gather a force to seek to thwart the Shōgun. This usually led to arrest, forced abdication and exile to a remote island.

The ninety-sixth Emperor, Godaigo, acceded to the Imperial Throne at the age of thirty-one. He came to resent the position of the Shōgun and the limits sought over the succession. Dreaming of a camphor tree, he enquired if there were any among his courtiers who were named for such a tree, Kusunoki, and was told that there was such a man, a lieutenant of the Middle Palace Guards whose family traced its ancestry to the Emperor Bidatsu, by name Masashige Tamon Kusunoki.

Kusunoki Masashige was sent for, interviewed by the Emperor and asked for his ideas as to how best to resist the Eastern barbarians – the forces of the Shōgun. This interview took place in 1331, and the struggle for the restoration to power of Godaigo led to a number of battles between 1331 and 1336. In 1336, by the direct orders of the Emperor, Masashige reluctantly faced a much larger force led by Takauji Ashikaga. Masashige had all along counselled the wisdom of avoiding head-on pitched battles with the Shōgun's numerically superior troops, and instead preferred a guerrilla-type campaign, a strategy hitherto successful.

Unsurprisingly, at the battle of Minato River in the summer of 1336, on the shores of the Inland Sea, his army of loyalists was destroyed in a seven-hour battle and Masashige and his brother Masasue and fifty followers retreated into a farmhouse, surrounded on all sides.

Instead of fighting on they all decided to commit seppuku. In a famous exchange between the brothers, Masashige asked Masasue how he would like to be reincarnated in his next life.

'As a man,' he replied, 'as a man for each of seven lives, and in each of them I would fight the Emperor's enemies.'

I have developed a terrible pain in my abdomen. It lurks in the background as I drift awake each morning and grows worse as the day goes on. On bad days it shifts suddenly into the foreground, tearing my attention towards it like a wild beast trying to take a bite out of me, a rabid animal which I must hold off with a chair or a kick to be free from its fangs. I am a very reluctant patient, yet the pain is so alarming that finally I go off to a hospital for a full physical. Tests are conducted. My body is patted and probed, kidneys palpitated and prostate examined – just lie on your side and pull up your knees, this may feel a little strange as the KY-ed finger enters my exit. Samples of blood and urine are collected and studied for likely causes – infection, diabetes, other more alarming things.

All the tests are negative. The doctors have no idea what, if anything, is wrong with me.

I begin to wonder if the pain might be some odd kind of psychosomatic effect: a phantom pain, like a sympathetic pregnancy in a nervous father who so empathises with his wife's condition that he takes it on himself. I know this can happen. Could I, however ridiculous this might seem, have taken on the pain of cutting open my stomach? Could I be experiencing a phantom seppuku?

This morning I have a pounding headache to add to the pain in my belly. I swallow a couple of pills and carry on, assuming it will wear off like other headaches. But it doesn't. After three days I am alarmed. Something odd is happening to my right eye. A cloudy shape seems to be floating about in my eyeball, like the pixillations used in Japanese pornography to censor the genitals, making it hard for me to read. (An excited friend once told me that he had bought a special box in Hong Kong which decoded the pixillations. We rigged it up, popped in a porno video hired from the neighbourhood video store and waited to see what would happen. It certainly worked – the actors' genitals were transformed and now clearly visible. However, everything else in the picture was pixillated. The box unpixillated the pixillated and pixillated the unpixillated. We watched for a few moments as the disembodied genitals floated in a sea of randomised dots.)

I began to feel hot, even feverish. I found I could not concentrate for more than a few minutes, and the struggle to move about in Tokyo was just too much. For days I sat drinking cup after cup of green tea at Ken's, with the lights turned out. The dim light of day in the cave of Ken's bar was soothing and seemed to relieve the occular migraine (if that is what it was) in my right eye.

After a week without change, I called my friend Jun. He sounded alarmed and quickly suggested I return home for Christmas, hinting he might come along to make sure I was all right, telling me he felt like a trip out of Japan. I felt despondent. I was getting nowhere at the moment, and perhaps back home I could sort out my health and work out what to do next. 'OK,' I said, 'let's find a flight.'

It's a beautiful winter morning. Only a few clouds float past on a mild breeze in an otherwise clear blue sky. I gaze out of the window as the bus threads its way through the countryside, tracing the route from the small market town where I live towards Oxford. I always enjoy this journey, no matter how many times I have to make it. The land silently welcomes me. Its shapes and colours whisper to me.

There are not many people on the bus, fewer still in my field of vision. A farmer on a faded red tractor ploughing in the distance, a lone hiker clutching an unfolded map that flaps in the wind as he crosses a square of wheat; a group of old ladies standing cheerfully by the side of the road in warm winter coats, waiting for the bus that will take them shopping. Once on the bus and seated the ladies resume their conversation, as if someone has pushed the 'Play' button on a tape recorder. Two teenage boys who boarded the bus together sit apart, slouching, each occupying two seats, each listening to very similar music over headphones and ignoring the other completely. A techno buzz underpins the hum of female chatter, as the bus winds its way into town.

The land speaks to me, but without words. I think it tells me the truth. Growing things satisfy me in ways I cannot articulate or perhaps that seem secret or at least private. No, they are secrets, these messages from the land, which might dissolve if spoken about or written down, so delicate do they seem.

Oxford is a place I both love and hate. It is a beautiful old space becoming something I don't much care for. No one will be able to stop what it is becoming. The changes are happening in ways we cannot, at first, detect, disguised as convenience or progress. Yet who really needs a dozen outlets for coffee-flavoured steamed milk in an anodyne and standardised setting? I want only the good things to be preserved. By that, of course, I mean the things I like. Beautiful things. None of them have anything to do with buying and selling.

I meander down Broad Street in no particular hurry and step up into Blackwell's main bookshop. I am searching for a re-printed work about Yukio Mishima by Marguerite Yourcenar. Her book should be available by now – the publication date of a new edition was a couple of weeks ago. I move across to the enquiry counter and a sales assistant who looks too young to be legally employed asks if he can help me.

I tell him the title of the book, adding with emphasis: 'You know, Mishima!' He turns to his colleague, silently seeking an answer to my question. 'Mishima,' says the slightly older but still fairly young man sweating in a tweed jacket that hangs from his thin frame, his clothes like hand-me-downs he lacks the energy ever to grow into. 'He killed himself, Mee-shi-ma. Harry carry,' says the thin man and then: 'Wrote *Sea of Fertility.*'

The death before the work, I noticed.

Walking quickly down a rain-soaked St Giles, an Oxford thoroughfare, and like so much else in this market town owned by St John's College, I can see in the distance a thinnish black man swaying and calling out to passers-by. Mostly they are tourists – Taiwanese, Germans, French adolescents with dayglo highlights in their hair, pinks and greens and blues, even streaks of silver. They do not acknowledge the man as they hurry past.

Now I can hear him. 'Beauty, what about beauty,' he shouts, clawing the space in front of him, as if to grasp an answer out of thin air. It is not the usual rant of a drunk seeking attention from the passing crowds. But whatever it is that concerns him, about beauty, no one wants to know. He recites the names of Renaissance artists. His voice, although slurred, is a cultivated one, standard English of the kind perfected in public schools, and once in the great universities. Not the voice of a black drunk in a market street. So I stand and listen.

He notices me and comes over. We talk about some of the beautiful things hoarded in the Ashmolean a few steps from where we stand. He is on his way there now to look at the *Ideal Head*, a bust by Antonio Canova. Inside his jacket I can see a reserve and unopened can of beer in addition to the half-full can in his hand.

We talk of gambling. He plays poker at the Randolph he tells me, and in the past was a habitué of gaming clubs and casinos in London. Used to play poker with the deceased rock star

Michael Hutchence, and once during a game had suggested the name for Hutchence's daughter – Heavenly Hiraani Tiger Lily. More anecdotes bubble forth, of the art world, Derek Jarman, Lucian Freud, the words spilling out in quick succession.

While we were talking something niggled in my brain. This rant seemed familiar, but I could not say how or why – until my drunken friend announced his name. No longer a stranger then and we *had* met before. Fifteen years or more earlier at a party of a very rich friend in London I remembered how he had been thrown out for rowdy drunkenness and insulting the other guests. His background explained to me after he had gone. And so for the second time in my life I was talking to a grandson of the Emperor of Ethiopia, Haile Selassie. An imperial prince drunk on an Oxford street.

As I turned to walk away the prince was returning to his favourite theme, to the subject of beauty: 'Mishima, you know Mishima?'

'Yes,' I said.

'Now there was a man who knew beauty.'

Yes, I thought, smiling. There was a man who knew beauty. So the prince staggered towards the museum in search of the *Ideal Head*, and I in the direction of my bus home.

In the work that many critics, especially Japanese critics, consider his masterpiece, *Kinkakuji*, The Temple of the Golden Pavilion, Mishima has his troubled protagonist Mizoguchi express the suicide problem by reference to the terrifying nature of beauty. The question that he seeks to answer is 'What is beauty for?' Is it simply a means for anyone who is not beautiful to feel that they do not exist?

For some people a beautiful object is just an exaggeration of a nice one. Something very nice. For someone attuned however to the possibilities of beauty it is not simply the end of a sensory spectrum. It is a state quite detached from meaning anything at all. Like staring into the sun, encountering beauty may blind you to ordinary reality.

Yet something beautiful ought to mean something. If it does not, then how can anything less, the ugly and the ordinary, mean anything? To really see into the beauty of an object or a painting, a face or a building, such as the Golden Pavilion in Kyoto, a six-hundred-year-old wooden structure which has endured the calamities of ancient and modern wars, is to perceive the emptiness of things. Mizoguchi declares:

> It is no exaggeration to say that as I gazed on the temple, my legs trembled and my forehead was covered with cold beads of perspiration. On a former occasion when I had returned to the country after seeing the temple, its various parts and its whole structure had resounded with a sort of musical harmony. But what I heard this time was complete silence, complete noiselessness. Nothing flowed there, nothing changed. The Golden Temple stood before me, towered before me, like some terrifying pause in a piece of music, like some resonant silence.

In *The Principles of Psychology* William James comments:

> Whilst part of what we perceive comes through our senses from the object before us, another part (and it may be the larger part) always comes from our own mind.

This very simple idea is worth reflecting on. Mizoguchi's beauty is 'beauty' as perceived by his own mind. If a mind is of a particular composition, sensitive or dull, then this will most significantly affect all the perceptions that arise within it. As Saadi stated, 'To a sick man even sweet water tastes bitter.'

Jorge Luis Borges writes:

> I am not sure that I exist, actually. I am all the writers that I have read, all the people that I have met, all the women that I have loved; all the cities that I have visited, all my ancestors . . . Perhaps I would have liked to be my father, who wrote and had the decency of not publishing. Nothing, nothing, my friend; what I have told you: I am not sure of anything, I know nothing . . . Can you imagine that I not even know the date of my death?

Mishima too may have known nothing had he been honest in his self-evaluation, but he did know the date of his death.

Mishima claimed that he governed his life by an overriding notion – seeking beauty. He certainly thought of all his works as aiming to create beauty, in the form of literary art. His life became a drama, a play, no less carefully scripted than any of his formal staged works. It too had to be beautiful. 'I want to make a poem of my life,' he had written.

Each element must be beautiful according to his own aesthetic judgements: his body, those around him, his suicide companion, the aim of his final sacrifice. He could never accept the idea that he would grow old and gradually slide into the ugly decaying real world, leaving beauty beyond his grasp, no longer within his reach. He once called himself beauty's kamikaze.

Of course, tastes vary. I am sure Mishima saw nothing even faintly ridiculous about the uniforms of the Tate no Kai. Others saw them as theatrical props for part-time would-be soldiers, more useful to stage an opera than a coup.

Perhaps the opinions of others were, for Mishima, irrelevant. At least in deciding what was beautiful. For him beauty was antithetical to ordinary life. The life of the masses could never be beautiful. It was utterly necessary to distinguish yourself from the crowd, to lift your head, to avoid the fate of a lukewarm personality, neither knowing nor chosing a life that suits, but instead accepting it like an ill-fitting jacket made for a man of an earlier generation, a body of quite different dimensions. Made-to-measure living versus off-the-peg conformity. Bespoke is a route, perhaps the only route to a good fit – and a life of beauty requires such an approach.

Walking along in the brightly lit streets of Covent Garden, I feel like whistling. Everyone, not just me, seems to be in a good mood. There are girls in pretty and quite revealing dresses, men with grins, tourists and native Londoners reacting like lizards, acknowledging the change in the weather, soaking up the brilliant light and unseasonal warmth of the day. I am on my way to sign some books in a nearby bookshop, following a route that takes me past the Paul Smith shop in Floral Street, and glancing in at the doorway I decide to go inside. This is a strange thing for me to do: I don't usually window-shop in expensive places. All my current clothes are second-hand, or pre-loved as I have heard someone describe them, bought in the main from charity shops in a process of perpetual scavenging. Yet today something draws me in.

As soon as my eyes have adjusted to the reduced light inside

the shiny shop I notice there is a row of dolls arranged inside
the main counter, a kind of display case made of glass. I see at
once the dolls are Japanese, dressed in period costumes, each
doll nearly a foot tall, and they seem both exotic and strangely
familiar. Of course I realise after only a moment or two, count-
ing them off, left to right, ichi, ni, san, shi, go, roku, shichi, yes
all seven – they are, of course, the seven samurai, modelled on
the title characters from Akira Kurosawa's film, *Shichinin no
samurai – Seven Samurai.*

These were superior dolls in every sense. A full set of all
seven I am told cost an incredible £900. They were fantastically
detailed, as if to justify their price tag. I looked for my favourite
character, Kyūzō the *kengō*, the master swordsman, a taciturn,
silent and serious character possibly intended by Kurosawa to
symbolise *bushidō* itself, the Japanese warrior code. Even the
doll's dead face seemed to possess *heijōshin* – a dignity sought
by all martial artists and signalling a stable inner composure.
Then I thought about it. It is impossible to be more composed
than an inanimate object, a doll, but I was not sure that this was
heijōshin. I examined Kyūzō's clothes, the *hakama* and crested
haori jacket, and then looked even more closely at his sword. I
particularly scrutinised the *tsuka*, the handle of the sword – it
seemed correct in every detail, down to the tiny silk handle
wrapping – every detail except, perhaps, one: the handle-
wrapping ornaments, *menuki*, small metal objects in a myriad of
decorative forms, cranes and diamonds, thunderbolts and irises,
wild boars and dragons flying into heaven, were during the Edo
period placed so that they were on the opposite sides of the
handle, asymmetrically, to the right above and the left below
the position of the gripping hands. The *menuki* nearest the *tsuba*,
the swordguard, was on the left and the other on the right
of the handle. Sword masters always reversed this, preferring
so-called *gyaku-menuki*, saying that the swell of the hand rested
well on the ornaments and improved the grip by avoiding an
unnecessary space. I felt sure that Kyūzō would have adopted
gyaku-menuki. I would look closely the next time I watched the
film to see if the doll-maker had copied the 'reality' of Kurosawa
or had worked from surviving ornamental, non-experts', swords.

Two men face each other, ringed by a gathered crowd. Both hold wooden swords, one in a posture called *seigan no kamae*, the tip of the sword pointing at his opponent's eyes, the other in an attacking posture, *jōdan no kamae*, sword held above his head, the tip of the sword facing heaven. Neither man is moving. No one seems to be breathing, but each is keenly aware of the other's breathing. A long tense pause ensues, neither man moving. The watchers know that each of the fencers is looking for *suki*, gaps in the defence. No gaps and nothing will happen.[46]

Suddenly one of the men, the larger, with the more aggressive posture, screams and charges. The other stands still, turns slightly off-line and cuts down just as the attacker cuts towards him. It is over. The large man blusters that they both cut each other at the same time and that there is no victor. The other man quietly says that he killed the attacker. The large man will not have this and wants a rematch – this time with live blades, real swords. 'Then you will die,' the small man says, trying to walk away, but he is confronted and taunted and finally, reluctantly, agrees to fight again.

There is a similar stand-off, until the large man rushes again, and screams again. The two swords cut down. The large man falls dead. The small man's clothes, but not his body, have been rent, the margin between life and death less than an inch.

This is the famous scene from *Seven Samurai* where the sword master Kyūzō is observed and then recruited by Kanbei. The fictional film scene is based on an account in the life of a real sword master, Jūbei Yagyū, and uses his *sen o toru* technique.[47]

My aikidō teacher, Tsutomu Chida Sensei,[48] is fond of explaining that in budō there are only two things to learn: when to move and when to keep still.

Pascal commented, making more or less the same point in another context, that all mankind's misfortunes stem from the inability to remain quietly in a room.

On the kitchen table in front of me is a newspaper. I am eating breakfast, two slices of toast and some coffee, browsing the paper, a morning routine. A small photograph in the paper catches my attention. It is of an elderly woman, her head inclined to one side as if listening, her face a terrible mess of bruises; both eyes blackened, a panda's face, a dark stain of purple yellowish tint – I imagine the colours, the picture is black and white – on the right-hand side. Her swept-back hair is white, her neck a turkey wattle, and her age is seventy-seven.

'Police hunt killer of widow mugged for a piece of fish,' the headline screams. So she is dead, has been murdered – and for a piece of fish. I cannot help sighing.

The victim, who looks like my eighty-three-year-old mother, or anyone's mother or grandmother, a typical old lady's face, had been walking home from a fish and chip shop in Newcastle when someone attacked her, knocked her to the ground and snatched her handbag, which contained the piece of fish wrapped in paper – no chips, she couldn't manage them, as she had explained to the girl in the fish and chip shop who served her. Apart from the fish – the report didn't say what kind – the contents of the handbag were worth less than £10. Ten pounds and a piece of fish – the price of a life.

'Scum,' I say to myself, like thousands of readers around the country. It didn't seem enough, so I add 'Bastard.' Feeling a deep and visceral reaction to violence against the weak and powerless, I began to daydream an alternative ending to this ugly report.

I am standing in a doorway. An elderly white-haired woman is walking towards me carrying a largish handbag. In the opposite direction ambles a youth in a hooded jacket, his face concealed. Neither can see me. The youth moves suddenly towards the woman and snatches at her bag. Somehow she holds on and struggles, making small noises, half surprise and half defiance. 'Stop!' she pleads.

As I have travelled in time and know how this will end if I do nothing, I feel justified to act. I step out from the doorway, shouting to distract the attacker. 'Heh!' He moves towards me menacingly, transferring his violence from a small defenceless woman to me – an unknown quantity. He doesn't perceive how reckless he is being, doesn't see the sword, not even when I draw it. A fatal mistake. He keeps coming. I correct my distance, pivot to avoid his kick and cut down, *kesa giri*, slicing him across the body from his left shoulder to his right hip. Literally cloven in two, he dies in the gutter. I wipe the blood from the blade on the hood of his sweat top, resheathe it calmly and step over to comfort his would-be victim, whose myopia has saved her from horror at the sight of such an instant and bloody spectacle of justice.

My abdominal pains have grown worse and seem to be building to a crescendo, which is alarming. Pain can be managed if it stays predictable. When it starts to behave in ways you have never encountered before, there is the more worrying question of causation to cope with alongside the pain itself. I had run out of the usual pills I pop from time to time when I find pain hard to ignore and need to concentrate. Rummaging in a medicine cupboard I find a crumpled and forgotten pack of soluble aspirin. I take some, and after perhaps twenty minutes feel a lot more collected and able to get back to work. The aspirin is surprisingly effective for an ordinary pain medicine.

I take the soluble aspirin a couple more times, and Alka-Seltzer, which also contains aspirin, once for a hangover in the next few days and think nothing of it.

The first nosebleed was nothing much. I managed to stop it in a couple of minutes, pinching the fleshy part of the nose, head forward not back, ice – or in this case a bag of frozen peas – applied to the bridge of the nose. I was glad it happened at home and not in the supermarket where I'd been a few minutes before. Reasonably enough, people are skittish about human blood in a food environment.

The second nosebleed came on in the early morning. I woke up and thought my nose was running until I opened my eyes and saw the scarlet trace of blood spots spreading on the white linen pillowcase. Shit! Galvanised by the sight of my own blood I leapt up and ran to the bathroom. This time it took about ten minutes to stop it and I assumed that a blood vessel must have been damaged in one nostril and I would have to be careful – no hard noseblowing, try to sneeze through my mouth. I would do some research on the internet to see if there was anything else I should do.

The third nosebleed preceded a fourth and fifth, and by the sixth it took over an hour to stop the steady gush of salty blood. I had reluctantly called and then cancelled an ambulance, the beginnings of a panic caused by ignorance – how much blood can someone safely lose? – and wondering if I might bleed to death. Death by nosebleed, what a pathetic way to go.

The seventh attack hit on Christmas morning. Just as I woke up I felt the alarming onset of wetness in my nostrils and then the telltale drip drip drip of the blood dribbling on to the latest in my shrinking stock of linen pillowcases. I leapt up. I yelled for Jun to help me – he had been looking forward to the Christmas lunch I had promised to cook for him, and for which we had spent the last few days acquiring provisions and fine wines. He found me naked on the sofa clutching a clump of tissues to my face and ran to fetch a bowl and some ice. After ninety minutes of steady bleeding I gave in and let him summon an ambulance. Shit. Christmas in casualty. I began to feel sorry for myself.

Ten minutes for the ambulance. The paramedics checked that I'd done the right things to end the bleeding, and finding I knew what to do decided to take me to the A & E of the John Radcliffe in Oxford. I bled into my pudding basin as the ambulance wended its way into Oxford. On inquiring I was told that more than three or four pints of blood lost might cause you to pass out. Less if the sight of blood was a problem. For me it was not.

In the A & E department further efforts were made by pinching the fleshy part of my nose and the liberal use of ice to stop the bleeding. As this took some time, while I went on bleeding, I began to notice others. In the next cubicle awaiting treatment was a boy of perhaps eight or nine. His parents were with him and from overheard snatches of conversation I gathered he had punched through a plate-glass window in a rage and had a deep gash that would need stitches. This was complicated by the fact that he seemed to be suffering from Tourette's Syndrome. 'Bubbles in the bath! Bubbles in the bath!' he kept shouting. He managed to get away from his parents, popped his head round the corner and spat at Jun. A gob of spit landed precisely on the toecap of his nicely shined shoe – which was a beautiful thing made by Manolo Blahnik. I was sitting bleeding into a pudding basin, a pint and a half of blood already deposited, while Jun, who had travelled halfway round the world to spend Christmas in England and had been anticipating a first-class lunch, was being spat at by a boy with Tourette's. Merry Christmas.

After nearly two hours in A & E nose-pinching, leaning forward and bleeding into my pudding basin, applying a small bag of slowly melting ice to the bridge of my nose to try to slow down the rate of bleeding, it is decided to transfer me to the Ear, Nose & Throat department of the Radcliffe Infirmary in Walton Street. An ambulance is summoned to take me across and I am pushed in a wheelchair towards the waiting vehicle. Jun walks silently by my side, clearly worried.

Inside the Radcliffe Infirmary we find the ENT department and I wait until a doctor is free. The bleeding, which had stopped for a few moments, begins again and more ice is provided along with a cardboard kidney bowl, like a misshapen relative of an egg carton, to catch the falling blood. After ten minutes or so a doctor pops up, takes me into an examining room and decides to 'pack my nose' on the left side to physically stop the bleeding.

Nose-packing is extremely unpleasant. A nasal pack is a speciality tampon. (Indeed a tampon will serve as a good substitute if you need to stop a nosebleed and don't have access to a hospital with its specialised supplies.) The pack is slid inside the nose to reach where the bleeding is taking place. Up the front of the nostril it goes, and down inside where the nostril slopes back into the sinuses. It can be inserted, as it has a degree of rigidity, and as it is pushed into the nasal cavity feels like a spike being forced through your face. Saline solution squirted onto the protruding part causes the whole thing to expand as it sucks up the liquid and press against the tissue surface so that any blood vessels are physically closed by the pressure.

After a while my right nostril began to bleed and another pack was put in. I now had two tampons up my nose, and as with tampons there were little strings dangling out of the end to enable their removal. They would have to stay in for twenty-four to forty-eight hours, and although I tried hard to persuade them, the men and women in white coats would not let me go home. They wanted me under observation.

I called a friend to bring over a few things from my home and to rescue Jun. He would spend Christmas Day with my friend's family instead of with me. And as he was due to fly back to Tokyo on the afternoon of Boxing Day he promised to look in on me on the way to the airport early the next morning.

I was in a gloomy mood as I sat on the bed in a small ward with perhaps five or six others in varying degrees of consciousness. The bed next to mine was empty. I discovered that its occupant had terminal throat cancer and had been allowed to spend what was probably his last Christmas at home. I began to make the mental adjustments necessary to put a nosebleed, even one which has cost me two pints of blood, into perspective.

Later in the day a festive meal was delivered. I had not been asked to make food choices as my late admission had rendered this impossible, so I received the Christmas lunch selections of 'Bert Wilson' – a small card with his name was on the tray – who was no longer in the ward. Why? Had he died? Was I about to eat a dead man's lunch? After examining Bert's choices I found I didn't much care about his fate, for Bert had elected for the festive option of a cheese and onion sandwich, a packet of plain crisps and a two-finger KitKat. There was a paper hat and a cracker on the tray too, but I left them to one side and silently ate my sandwich.

My nose kept running, like the instant onset of a heavy cold. The packs were causing a massive mucus reaction. I wore an odd contraption made of muslin or cotton gauze, like a tiny beard snood hooked under my nose, but it was soaked through and uncomfortable after only a few minutes. I kept requesting that it be changed, but found it awkward to keep requesting this, and finally located the supplies and was able to do it for myself.

After two days of hospital drudgery and enforced idleness I was allowed home. The packs had been removed and I had been told that if the bleeding recurred I could have cauterisation.

All alone in my house, now that Jun had returned to Japan, I turned my mind to *shindoku*, self-scrutiny, a Confucian exercise.

In performing this you consider how you are, how you act, when utterly alone and beyond the scrutiny of others. This is your real nature: it is not an act as there is no audience. This nature can be improved and must form the basis of self-knowledge. So *shindoku* is the process of stripping away any public persona when alone – a means to see the real self.

Shinjō, a true heart, the aim of all cultivated men as envisaged in Confucian self-training and carried over into Buddhist studies, is achievable only by slaughtering the false selves, facing up to one's mortality and detaching from fear of death, to die before you die. Having done this, the ultimate sanction of the threat of death holds no power to coerce behaviour. Only then may one act in accordance with principles of justice and righteousness. *Shinjō* was a preoccupation of Saigō Takamori.

Walking around the house picking up objects at random I come to realise I am living in a house of dead things. Modern manufactures – a misnomer, as I mean things made by machines – are designed to fail, to wear out, to cease to function after a short time. They have a diminishing 'half-life', are imbued with death. This is a very subtle thing. In the past craft objects carried something of the man or woman whose discipline, skill and patience, even love, were drawn upon to make them. They embodied these traits. No skills, disciplines or love exist in a machine . . . it cannot pass on what it does not have. So my house of dead things.

This may be suspected if not expressed by many who haunt antique shops and charity shops seeking the worn and the crafted; it is not a compulsion to surround oneself with the old, as the idea of antiques suggests, but with the living. These objects live.

For a bookworm a second-hand or antiquarian book fair is an exciting event. Finding myself in Oxford at the time of a very large gathering of booksellers for a fair staged in an annex of the Randolph Hotel, I decided to go along. The space was crammed with shelves and tables groaning with tomes and the rooms thronged with browsers. I rolled up my sleeves and set out to seek for treasure – for that, I am sure, is the motivation of the true bookworm.

After only a short while I began to feel at odds with what I was doing. I dislike browsing whenever anyone else is trying to look at the same shelf. I can scan a large bookshelf very accurately in seconds and become impatient if someone is taking too long in a slot I wish to occupy. I do not like standing too close to a stranger (martial arts training focuses on maintaining a safe distance at all times, a practice known as *ma-ai*) and become indignant if anyone indicates that they resent the way I am behaving, perhaps by trying to block my browsing or in some other way behaving proprietarily towards the books we are both looking at. It is a very mild form of intolerance, even of violence. I sometimes fantasise doing something very nasty to an innocuous bibliophile who is, mercifully, unaware of my growing sense of browser rage.

When I reach a limit in so-called cultural activities – especially browsing-type activities, visiting museums, bookshops, art galleries – I fall into a peculiar habit. I stop browsing the primary subject matter – the pictures, books, exhibits – and begin to browse the browsers. I find gazing at others gazing at something else diverting. If you are satisfied with looking at the back of someone's head, it does not matter that you cannot see the painting. I found myself doing this at the Randolph Hotel book fair, and succumbed to a powerful emotion: I realised that I did not, for some reason, like these people. Not one bit. The booksellers and bookbuyers. The middle-class types who were like me in every outward sense – readers looking for books that might interest them, for something they might buy to justify having paid the small entrance charge. No, I did not like them at all. It was visceral.

I have had the same experience at art house cinemas. What was this emotion and what was its basis? It seemed irrational to me. I did not know anyone in this room, so why did I feel this revulsion so strongly?

Later I came across an anecdote related by Mishima in his autobiographical work *Watakushi no Henreki Jidai – My Wandering Years* (1964). It struck me with the force of an epiphany. We had had exactly the same experience, separated by half a century.

Mishima describes how he had been visiting an exhibition of photographs taken of the mummies of the Chūsonji Temple when he noticed the face of a man near him. He was middle-aged, obviously a scholar, conservatively dressed, thin and pale, an academic or at least an 'intellectual type'. Mishima emphasised how ugly this man was: aged, wrinkled and bent, his skin the colour of someone who stays indoors. So absorbed in what he was examining, the photographs, this was a man utterly unaware of his body. 'His ugliness infuriated me. I thought "what an ugly thing an intellectual face is! What an unseemly spectacle an intellectual being makes!"' Mishima, of course, in saying so realised that he was this man at an earlier stage, that he would become him in time. He was repelled by this idea and resolved to avoid this fate.

I am not sure if I have communicated this insight very well. It is not disgust for the ugly, at least not for me. It is a sense that a bookish individual of whatever age is out of balance. Is living too much within his imagination, in the world of thought.

Has too little regard for his own physicality. That he, or she, is first a body, and only if the body functions properly a mind. Of course, you can also invert this logic. A crazy mind in a healthy body is no good either. But if academic or bookish types have ignored their bodies and on purpose or through heedlessness permit them to slide into dysfunction and disorder, then it might be fair to conclude that something has gone wrong.

Imagine, say, a university faculty where no one may teach if they are unfit in a physical sense: like Athens in its prime, they are obliged to take equal pride in the strength and power of their muscles, their build and posture, as well as their intellect. How very different would such places be from the way they are now. Mishima remarked in *Sun and Steel* how a fat belly signalled spiritual sloth. Is he right about this?, I wonder.

Last Day 11.10 a.m.

Colonel Hara presses his eye against the spyhole into the General's office. He wants to check if he should order tea to be served at once or perhaps wait. Tea is usually served at the start of a meeting, but Mishima made Hara uncertain. Something off-key this morning? He couldn't be sure and thought it best to check.

Inside the General's office, instead of the calm of two men quietly talking, Hara sees a scene of disorder. The General gagged, a rope around his chest, and one cadet standing behind him holding a knife. Mishima pacing the room like a caged cat, holding a drawn sword. In his astonishment Hara can't help saying out loud: 'What are you doing?' – a remark clearly audible on the other side of the thin partition.

Hara and Major Sawamoto now try to force the door. The

furniture piled up against it begins to slide but is pushed back, the door held shut. 'Out! Out!' Mishima screams from the other side of the door. 'We will kill the General if you try to enter. We have demands. Do as we say and no harm will come to the General.' Hara sends a clerk to fetch the next most senior officer on the base after General Mashita – General Yamazaki. Soon a gathering of senior officers has formed within the outer office.

Throughout history societies have been armed. There has never been an unarmed society. From time to time governments have tried to disarm the general populace, reserving for themselves, through armies or police forces, the infliction of violence. Yet equally until the formation of standing professional armies it was necessary to encourage the practice of martial arts, as this was the source of fighting men in times of war. In England archery practice was mandatory. In Japan the military arts became the specialisation of a feudal class, the *bushi* or samurai class, which existed until the late nineteenth century, when it was replaced by a conscript army on a European model.

Currently civil society is unarmed in the UK, armed in parts of the USA, unarmed in Japan, armed in Israel and Switzerland. In New Zealand a man is building a cruise missile in his garage. He estimates it will cost $1,700 and have a range of 60 miles. He bought the giroscope on eBay, the online auction house, for a few dollars. What is interesting about this idiosyncratic hobby – home manufacture of weapons of mass destruction – is that it seems to demonstrate that you don't need state resources to make a modern weapon. The knowledge of how to make an atom bomb used to be expressed in language as if it were a magic formula, something quite occult. Now it is easy theoretically and only a problem in terms of obtaining fissionable materials. An insurmountable problem you might think, until you look into how much enriched uranium and plutonium has gone missing – a great deal from the United States; more still from the former Soviet Union.

The proliferation of so-called weapons of mass destruction is confidentially known by governments to be inevitable. The genie is out of the bottle. In my lifetime the effort required to access hard-core pornography has changed from a trip to Copenhagen to the click of a mouse. It has proliferated to an unbelievable degree, driven by the ubiquity of the necessary technology. Weapons will follow.

Words and the sword can be said, then, to sum up the very basis of the human condition. They define our deepest nature: we are animals with an immensely sophisticated means of signalling and imagining, expressed through language – and at the same time advanced tool-makers whose most ingenious technological breakthroughs have been methods to kill one another.

Words and the sword, opposite ends of a spectrum – or perhaps simply the sound of two hands clapping, clapping quite slowly, a slow handclap, a mockery of applause.

'Life does not tell stories. Life is chaotic, fluid, random. It leaves myriads of ends untied, untidy. Writers can extract a story from life only by strict, close selection, and this must mean falsification. Telling stories really is telling lies.'

B. S. JOHNSON

Writers are liars.[49] They are liars unless they live the truths they write about, and only then. Life is not talking or writing, but living. Life is doing. So any truth that may be spoken of, or reduced to written forms, must have a lived counterpart ... otherwise it is not a truth, it is something else, something not alive but dead. So the realisation that writers are liars and that writing is lying is, for a writer aiming to write the truth, nearly impossible to live with. After this enlightenment there remain for him only two choices and one evasion. The choices are to adjust his life so that it conforms to what he has written, or else to die. The evasion is to lapse back into unawareness as black and bleak as a starless sky at night.

So far I had focused on Mishima, his last years, pursuing those who had known him or were involved with the circumstances surrounding his death. This had yielded very little. I had found out a certain amount from written sources, but felt frustrated that so few of those I approached were willing to talk to me. I was tackling a taboo.

It seemed like a better idea to go back to Japan and to switch away from Mishima, concentrating instead on the sword. To find out about swords in general and about Seki no Magoroku swords in particular. I would compass what was known about Mishima's sword and hope that in doing so I would also find out things about Mishima, about Japan, and even a little more about myself.

SECONDARY

(S)word

*Whensoever any affliction assails me, mee thinks I
have the keyes of my prison in mine owne hand, and
no remedy presents it selfe so soone to my heart, as
mine own sword*

JOHN DONNE

There was no reason for anyone to travel to Seki City in Central Honshu in January. At least not to remain there. You might pass near by on your way to the Japan Alps if you were going skiing or visiting a hotsprings resort in Gero, but no one goes to Seki. Later in the year the sole tourist attraction seemed to be cormorant fishing, *ukai*, a practice imported from China in the ninth century, where teams of glossy birds are used to dive for *ayu* sweetfish that they cannot swallow due to a specially fitted collar. The cormorant fishermen dress in ceremonial robes and a kind of straw skirt. Eight times a year six fishermen fish exclusively for the Imperial Household on the Nagara River. The sweetfish, well iced, are sent to Tokyo by special train as soon as they are caught. I would have liked to see this, having been shown pictures of the boats, the lines of birds on long leads and the burning brands used to attract the fish at night, but it was the wrong time of year. The rivers were frozen over, the fish safe beneath the layers of ice.

To get to Seki was not so hard: a bullet train to Nagoya, then a local to Gifu, and after that what I took to be a tram onward to Seki, which judging from the distances on a map and the published timetable seemed to meander its way at a fast walking pace. It was not hard but nor was it cheap. I knew Japan Railways was hopelessly insolvent and speculated that the high price of long-distance train travel in Japan might be part of some 300-year scheme to recover the mind-boggling sum of money sunk into railway construction. Trains were efficient and clean and comfortable, but part of my mind demanded to know why it cost more to go a few hundred kilometres inside Japan than to fly to Hong Kong or the Philippines.

I bought two tickets at Tokyo Station and waited for my friend Jun to arrive. I was early, but he wouldn't be late, so I could relax for a few moments with the book I was taking with me – *The Craft of the Japanese Sword* by Leon and Hiroko Krapp and Yoshindo Yoshihara, which I had taken to calling the Krapp Book of Swords, though in fact it was superb. This book takes the major crafts employed to manufacture a Japanese sword and subjects them to tremendous scrutiny; it is a model of its kind. I hoped to pick up enough detail so as not to entirely embarrass myself in Seki, where I had arranged to visit working swordsmiths and other craftsmen who made fittings and sword furniture, as well as a sword polisher or two.

Jun tapped me on the shoulder just as the second hand glided to the 12 to signal his arrival at the precise time we had agreed to meet.

'What are you reading?'

'It's Krapp.'

'So why bring it?'

'Well, to be precise, it's Mr & Mrs Krapp and the swordsmith Yoshindo's primer on swordmaking today. Technical but splendid stuff.'

'Oh – Crap is a name?'

'Yes. Look, it's spelled with a "K".'

'I wouldn't want to be saddled with that, especially at school. Heh – are you blind or what? It's not Krapp, it's Kapp.'

He was right. I had been reading without my glasses and had misread the title page.

Seki is currently famous for one thing. It is the centre of razor-blade manufacture in Japan, with more than 90 per cent of domestic output. This, of course, is a secondary or spin-off industry from its cutler traditions. First came swords, then knives and domestic edged appliances such as scissors and bonsai shears, then finally razorblades. The decline and fall of edged steel. Almost every adult male in Japan shaves. Beards and moustaches are uncommon, and razorblades highly necessary – unlike swords.[50]

Only a tiny number of swordsmiths can make a living from laboriously hammering out swords, and only those, *primi inter pares*, who manage to win sword appraisal competitions can make a reasonable living. The co-author of the K(r)app Book of Swords, swordsmith Yoshindo Yoshihara, was a star and did very well indeed, as did his brother Kuniie Yoshihara. Unsurprisingly they came from a swordsmithing family. Traditional crafts in Japan tend to be hereditary, although it is not unusual for apprentices to be adopted to keep a family name going – something which also has a long history.

I came to Seki to do two things: to find and talk to the current Seki no Magoroku and to ask him about Mishima's sword. And also to witness the process of making swords the way they have always been made, and to fix in my mind precisely what is involved. I knew that as well as the smith there is also the polisher, and other craftsmen and women involved in the specialisations which have arisen in hand-making the *koshirae*, the furniture of the sword – everything from the handle and scabbard to handle wrappings and the ornaments bound under the wrappings and the *tsuba* or swordguards and the collar so that the sword fits snugly into the scabbard. Each of these has become a craft and an artform, and as one of the very few places in Japan where swordmaking still occurs, perhaps Seki has the largest concentration of the skilled artisans who together can make a sword from scratch.

As we left Seki station it began to snow. There was snow on the ground and the vistas were vast and flat, with mountains in the distance glazed white like an iced cake. I found the sense of space after the claustrophobia of Tokyo deeply refreshing. Just being here seemed to answer to an urgent need. Cold sharp air and empty landscapes.

We took a taxi to a nearby hotel that overlooked the Nagara River. In the entrance hall there was a suit of Japanese armour. Apart from a solitary clerk behind the reception desk there was no one else in the lobby, nor did we meet anyone on the way to our room. Later, waiting around before meetings and by examining where keys were kept behind the front desk, I began to suspect that we were the only guests in a hotel which had over 200 rooms. At this time of year there really was no reason to come to Seki, or not unless you were interested in swords.

Our room was large and traditionally appointed. The flooring was tatami matting, the bedding futons and quilts hidden away in a recessed cupboard. There was a balcony that provided a good view of the river and a low table that held a lacquered tray with tea-making equipment. All you needed to do was to ask for some hot water to be sent up to make tea, which could then be transferred into a thermos flask. There was also some instant miso soup, next to the tea bags on the tray. On the frozen river I could see a lone cormorant ice-skating close to the bank, as collected snow rained down its power from the branches of an overhanging pine tree.

I had met Igarashi two months earlier in Tokyo. He ran what was generally regarded as the best manufacturer of *iaitō* in Japan, called Nōsyūiaidō. He also practised *iaidō* and had come to Tokyo to take part in competition and to exhibit his wares at the gathering. We met in a hotel bar where he had turned up late with a couple of silent employees in train, one of them wearing a jacket with LAPD SWAT TEAM written on the back. I had told Igarashi of my intention to travel to Seki and asked if he might introduce me to craftsmen and swordsmiths, and in particular to the current Kanemoto, the lineal descendant of Seki no Magoroku. He was friendly and happy to oblige, but as he was going to China, where some of his edged-steel *iaito* were made, he suggested that I visit after Christmas. January or February would be best.

After we had installed ourselves Jun and I called Igarashi to tell him we had arrived. He sounded glad to hear from us, as if we had livened up a slow day, and said he would drop round in an hour. Would we like to see the shrine dedicated to sword-making?

First we stopped at a Buddhist temple called Miroku-ji to see the wooden Buddhas, by *Enku*. This had nothing to do with swordmaking, but Igarashi had fallen into tour-guide mode and the empty temple looked pretty against the snowy landscape. Next we drove to the Zenkōji Temple. In front of it was a large rock set up as a memorial to Motoshige, the first smith to establish swordmaking in Seki during the Kamakura period. After we had stared at the rock for a while we drove on to the Kasuga Shrine, dedicated to swordmaking and established by swordsmiths in the fourteenth and fifteenth centuries to help their craft businesses prosper. The *kami* were invited from the main Kasuga Shrine at Nara. Kanemoto I, the first Seki no Magoroku, had been responsible for renovating the shrine in 1433. I walked up the steps, rang the bell to summon the *kami* and clapped and bowed, praying for success in my quest to find Mishima's sword.

We decided to see some swords and drove over to the exhibition at the Seki Industrial Promotion Centre, which has a permanent display of the town's manufactures, including a large range of scissors and knives alongside swords made by traditional swordsmiths.

Outside the exhibition hall was a smith's forge. No one was working it now, but later in the year there would be demonstrations of swordmaking for tourists. In the corner there was a shrine to *Kanayama Hiko*, a fire deity, and wooden name tags indicating the names of all swordsmiths resident in the city. I counted eighteen including the current twenty-seventh Seki no Magoroku.

Inside the exhibition I searched for a Kanemoto I or Kanemoto II. One glass case had two empty sword stands. The caption indicated that a Kanemoto II and a Kanesada sword should be on display. I asked an attendant where the swords were. 'Wish we knew,' he said. 'There was a break-in last month. Those two swords were the only things taken.' So even in Seki there was no Seki no Magoroku for me to see and with luck to handle. The only old swords left in the exhibition were by Kanemasa and a later-generation Kanemoto, this one I noticed unsigned.

After lunch of a Japanese hamburger – bunless and served with grated *daikon* radish and a soy-based sauce – we went to call on a swordsmith. Ikuo Kojima was in his mid-thirties I guessed, and worked in what at first seemed like a small factory or garage. There was a forge, but the room was cold, as he was not working that day. He made swords as Kanemichi, and had taken over from his father, who had retired. He said his forge was the same as his father's except that he now used a power hammer and a belt hammer. His father and Kaneko Magoroku had gone to school together and had both studied at the Tanren Juku under Kanenaga Watanabe, who revived swordsmithing in Seki before the Second World War and was responsible for swords that were presented to Hitler and Mussolini as gifts from Japan.

Kojima-san confirmed the oral transmission about forging temperatures being the colour of the August moon,[51] which he said was around 720 degrees C. The charcoal used in his forge was made from pine, but in the past chestnut wood had been used. I asked him about secrets and he said that different combinations existed for the slurry used to coat the blade, and some smiths used antique iron to make steel, sometimes sourced from exhumed swords or old nails taken from castle doors. He too had a shrine to Kanayama Hiko.

Kojima-san had no *deshi*, apprentices, but was a third-generation smith, following his father and grandfather into the craft. His grandfather had had seven *deshi*, all of whom lived with his family. His hands were dirty and there were bits of metal and tools scattered around the room. It reminded me of a garage, rather than an artist's studio.

During the ban on swordmaking under the American occupation his father had made Western fencing swords and metal farming tools. Kojima-san told me he was unconcerned with changing traditions: the spirit of the samurai was of no concern to him. He did however try to make swords that would not chip or bend or break, and which would cut well.

We walked round the corner to a private house to visit a sword polisher, Isagi-san. He was working when we arrived, crouched on the floor with one foot bent under him and one foot standing on a frame on which a sword rested. The position was similar to an extremely uncomfortable position in *iaidō* called *iai-goshi*, which I knew took some getting used to. He was finishing a blade using tiny polishing stones. 'The *bōshi* [the temper line at the point of the blade] is the trickiest part,' he said without looking up.

We sat watching for a while, and during a tea break I asked if sword-polishing techniques had changed since ancient times. 'Yes,' he said, 'they have. The change occurred in the Edo

Period when samurai no longer went to war. Before that time the polish was pragmatic – the blade wouldn't shine as it does now and the edge would be sharpened so that a kind of wave was visible if you stared at it edge-on . . . serrations, like teeth. This was designed to tear flesh when the sword was used to cut. As samurai wore armour, a fine razor-sharp edge would chip.' I thought about this, a kind of dumdum bullet equivalent for swords, and realised that fighting men will always modify their weapons to make them more effective.

Isagi-san also had no disciples, but said his son would follow him into the craft. 'It's hard to make a living,' he said as we said goodbye.

Our next stop was a *sayashi*, a scabbard maker – Mr Mori. His workshop was tiny and included a rarity, a woman who specialised in handle wrapping, *tsukamaki*. She was working on a handle as we arrived, and for a few moments we stood and watched. I asked how long it took to wrap a handle. 'About a day for a standard wrap,' she said, and for a katana you used up about 12 feet of *ito*, the wrapping material. The handle she was working on had been covered in a single piece of *same* or ray skin, the grain of which fixes the handle wrap and prevents it slipping when gripped. I watched her insert and glue in place tiny paper wedges, *hishi-gami*, over which a knot was tied. The lady, whose name I forgot to write down, worked quickly, each winding movement precise and identical to the last. I asked what materials were used to wrap a handle. 'Cotton, silk and . . .' I struggled with the word she used, and had to discuss it to understand, 'whale whiskers.'

Mr Mori explained that there was no licensing system for the ancillary crafts, only for swordsmiths. He worked closely with smiths, as every blade made needed at least a *shirasaya*, a plain unvarnished wooden storage scabbard and handle. The scabbards and handles for Japanese swords were always custom-made from *hō* wood, a kind of magnolia, most of which came from Northern Honshu, but the best grade from a place called Hida, 30 kilometres from Seki. The wood needed to be at least five to ten years old to have dried completely. *Hō* heartwood, after sufficient seasoning, is nearly sapless, free of resinous oils, and is ideal for a scabbard because of its non-reactive properties.

Finding wood with a suitable grain was getting more and more difficult. Mr Mori said he only made plain *saya* and did not decorate them with lacquer, another specialised craft. I asked if there was anything different in the way he made *saya* from the past. 'Only for *iaitō saya* – I use bond glue instead of the traditional glue made of rice paste, for safety, so it doesn't break when the sword is drawn suddenly. Everything else is as it always has been – buffalo horn for the *koiguchi*, the entrance to the scabbard. Bamboo to fix the blade to the handle with a small pin or *mekugi*. The bamboo is flexible, you know, and is good at absorbing shocks when a sword cuts a target.'

Back at the hotel there was a small package addressed to me. Inside was a card, signed 'Your Friends in Seki', explaining that the enclosed item was a souvenir of my visit. It was an 8-inch chef's knife of the Seki no Magoroku brand, the name inscribed boldly on the blade.

Every murderer loves the knife.
NIETZSCHE, *Thus Spake Zarathustra*

On 30 December 2000, around 11.30 p.m., forcing the locks on the door with a Swiss Army knife, someone breaks into the house of Mikio Miyazawa, a business consultant, in the quiet residential neighbourhood of Kami Soshigaya, in Tokyo's Setagaya ward. Miyazawa, aged forty-four, is working in his ground-floor study. The intruder, or perhaps there is more than one, nobody knows, enters the study brandishing a 24-cm chef's knife. Miyazawa, startled, tries to fight but in the struggle is stabbed through the neck and quickly bleeds to death. The knife is particularly sharp, has been manufactured in Seki City. A famous and widely used brand name is etched onto the blade: Seki no Magoroku.

Despite the excellence of the cutler's traditions in this renowned centre of blade production, in cutting Mr Miyazawa's throat the Seki knife is damaged, chips in several places. Another sharp knife is found in the Miyazawas' kitchen to take its place, for there is more killing to do.

The intruder walks upstairs to the next storey of the house and enters a bedroom where Miyazawa's forty-one-year-old wife Yasuko and his eight-year-old daughter Nīna are sleeping. They are murdered without waking, stabbed repeatedly. Many of the terrible wounds are inflicted after death. It is a frenzied attack on the utterly defenceless. Their bodies are then thrown down the stairs.

The last surviving member of the family is Rei, a speech-impaired boy of six. He is not stabbed but instead is strangled with a black Muji handkerchief.

The Miyazawa family has been slaughtered in only a few minutes, and yet the intruder does not flee, but instead settles down to remain in the blood-washed house for the night, not leaving until some time before 10.30 the next morning, when the carnage is discovered by Yasuko's mother. Her horror can hardly be imagined. At this point the behaviour of the murderer or murderers becomes bizarre:

This much has been ascertained by a forensic investigation. The house was ransacked and all cupboards and drawers were opened. Around ¥200,000 was stolen from Mikio's wallet. Two litres of cold tea, a melon, and three ice creams were consumed. At least one attacker had been injured in the struggle with Mikio Miyazawa and had been cut, as his blood and fingerprints were everywhere. Clothes belonging to the murderer were abandoned at the scene: a Uniqlo Air-Tech parka coat, a chequered scarf, a pair of black leather gloves and a waist pack.

Inside the pockets of the parka there was sand, later identified as originating in Nevada, USA. Inside the waist pack there was a quantity of barium titanate, a toxic substance not available on the general market and used in hi-tech applications such as manufacturing capacitors, pyroelectric devices and in non-linear optics. Also found in the waist pack was a specialised film. Latex gum was used to try to stop the injured attacker bleeding, as a kind of improvised tourniquet. There was evidence that amphetamines had been taken, possibly as a pain-killer. Household documents were scattered in the bathroom.

While in the house the murderer or murderers used a computer to access the internet. Most of the websites visited related to scientific and technological subjects, some of them highly specialised. The final piece of evidence was two sets of footprints not belonging to any member of the Miyazawa family – one was made by a sneaker, manufactured in Korea, size 28 cm, and the other was an imprint of an army boot. According to the time/date stamp of the last website accessed on the Miyazawa computer the murderer or murderers were in the house until at least 10.05 a.m. on 31 December.

Two years later, after a police investigation force of up to two hundred officers had failed to find any significant leads, a Miyazawa relative decided to offer a reward of ¥2 million for any information leading to the arrest of a suspect. As I write this a further two years have passed and the Seki no Magoroku kitchen-knife killer is still at liberty. The brutal murders of a young family remain unpunished, the crime unsolved.

Mishima liked to encourage myths about himself, or at least did nothing to dispel them. Writers are storytellers and frequently cannot resist applying their creative capacities to embroidering their own stories. Among the dubious beliefs which have grown up around Mishima's public persona are: that he was a samurai, a warrior, a master of the martial arts, a happily married man.

Mishima was not a samurai. His descent on his father's side was from peasant stock. Mishima's paternal grandfather Jōtaro Hiraoka married Natsuko Nagai, who claimed descent from the Matsudaira, a noble family related to the Tokugawa ruling house. Irrespective of this connection the feudal samurai class had been abolished in 1876, and by 1925, when Mishima was born, there were few former samurai left alive. A samurai is a feudal retainer. No samurai can exist after the end of feudalism.

To aspire to samurai values is another thing, but this brings up the question of what those values were. One samurai ideal that Mishima certainly supported and practised is *sogai* – the idea of standing aloof from the mainstream culture, espousing a strong belief in one's own elite status. Mishima set about this in a manner no samurai would have endorsed – by becoming an exhibitionist and an artist. The *Hagakure*, Mishima's favourite book, admonishes: 'A samurai who practises an art is an artist not a samurai.' This, however, is an extremist position and there are many historical examples of the joint mastery of sword and pen.

Mishima said of himself that he was perhaps 40 per cent cut out to be a soldier. He trained hard with the SDF and with his own Tate no Kai militia. Long years of body-building had prepared him for the physical pain that goes with military training. But his body was no longer that of a young man. In the end he simply devoted too little time to military training to be taken seriously as a soldier.

By the time of his death Mishima held a fifth dan in kendō, a second dan in *iaidō* and a first dan in Shōtōkan karate. None of these ranks stands for mastery. The highest rank, in kendō, was rapidly earned and may have owed something to his celebrity status. Everyone comments on his kendō skills in the same way: not physically gifted, even gawky, yet displaying intense concentration and a serious spirit. Makes extreme efforts in tests. His inflexible wrists were a problem. Henry Scott Stokes, who also studied kendō, told me Mishima never learned how to hold the *shinai*, the bamboo sword, properly. One senior karate man described Mishima's karate as 'simply awful', and all the pictures I have seen of him practising karate show a beginner's poor posture.

Mishima said in his twenties that he was interested in women for their psychology, but was not physically attracted to them – he had no interest in having sex with a woman. Perhaps he changed his mind later in life. In *Confessions of a Mask*, the narrator remarks that for him the word 'woman' holds no more erotic charge than 'pencil' or 'broom'. In 1957, when he was thirty-two, Mishima phoned a friend[52] excitedly to tell him he had at last managed a successful sex act with a woman. One year later he had married, mostly to please his mother, who might have misleadingly given the impression that she was terminally ill, and because in Japan being gay was not an available lifestyle to anyone with a career that turned on wide social acceptance. Most gay men married and somehow managed. In his novel *Forbidden Colours* Mishima claims there is no contradiction in gay men marrying, indeed that they make the best husbands:

> Yuichi did not know the common truth that a multitude of men who love only men marry and become fathers. He did not know the truth that, though at some cost, they use their peculiar qualities in the interest of their marital welfare. Fed to satiety with the overflowing bounty of a woman in a single wife, they don't so much as lay a hand on another woman. Among the world's devoted husbands men of this kind are not few ... Women who have known the pain of being married to philanderers find it wise, should they marry again, to seek out such men.[53]

Mishima was not a typical Japanese husband and seemed genuinely to like his wife,[54] asking her advice on many things and allowing her considerable freedoms. He objected to one or two of Yōko's public displays of independence – such as her desire to learn to drive racing cars – and told friends she was entirely devoid of imagination.[55] According to John Nathan, who witnessed it at a party in 1963, the Nobel laureate Kenzaburo Oe called Yōko a 'total cunt', employing an English expression he had picked up from reading Norman Mailer. Presumably Yōko failed to understand what was being said about and to her – and no elaboration is given as to why Oe might have wanted to say such a thing. As Mishima's parties tended to be gatherings of the glitterati, perhaps he was reacting to visible scenes of social snobbery.

Mishima was a writer, not a samurai or a warrior, a martial arts hobbyist, not a master. He was also a homosexual husband with two children and a string of male lovers.

Igarashi patted his stomach as he spoke the ominous word so dreaded in Japan – *gan*, cancer. The twenty-seventh Seki no Magoroku was ill, reputedly with stomach cancer. I hesitated then asked: 'But will he see us? Is he able to talk?' Igarashi said he thought so. He would try to arrange a meeting.

We pulled up in the four-wheel-drive in front of a number of low-rise buildings, one of them a house, another some kind of workshop. I read a plaque fixed to the entrance of the building while Igarashi went to find the swordsmith: *Seki no Magoroku Nihontō Tanren Dōjō*, 'Seki no Magoroku Japanese Sword Forging Dōjō', it declared.

Igarashi returned after a minute or two with a short elderly man wearing a pale blue track suit. He had grey slicked-back hair and wore a large framed pair of spectacles. I noticed he had large fleshy ears, with dangling lobes like a Buddha, which I wanted to touch, something I remember doing to my father, who has nice earlobes, when seated on his lap as a small boy.

We all went into a kind of outbuilding made of corrugated iron and used as an office. There were desks and cardboard boxes and some chairs gathered around a gas heater. It was a cold day and I was glad of the source of warmth but kept my coat on anyway. On the wall there was a calendar with a picture of a sword for the month of January. Apart from the calendar, nothing suggested that a swordsmith used this room.

'I am retired now,' said Kaneko Magoroku, handing me a small handwritten *meishi* made of *washi*, handmade paper. It seemed like an appropriate visiting card for a craftsman.

'Can you explain about the fact that you are the twenty-seventh Kanemoto? Were there twenty-six smiths in a line of succession in your family before you?'

'I am the twenty-seventh generation. Not every generation was a smith. There have been, in fact, only thirteen smiths in twenty-seven generations. Only the smiths used the title

Kanemoto. Magoroku became a family name and my personal name is Kaneko.'

'As you know I am interested in the sword used in Mishima's seppuku. It was described by Mishima as Seki no Magoroku, yet evidence in court during the trial of the cadets who survived the incident stated it was *mumei* [unsigned] and that the *hamon* was *gunome midare* [a wave pattern] not *sanbonsugi*.[56] This suggests it was not Kanemoto I or Kanemoto II.'

'I went to Tokyo after the incident. I met Funasaka, the man who owns Taiseidō Bookshop, who gave Mishima the sword, and then went to the police station in Meguro where the investigation was being conducted. They showed me the sword. It was chipped in several places and a little bent. The length was 2.1 *shaku* and there was no signature. I told them it was a Kodai Kanemoto, perhaps the fourth or fifth generation. There was evidence of the sword having been shortened at some time. The signature may have been removed then – all genuine Kanemoto swords are signed.'

I was watching the smith as he gestured. I noticed he had lost part of one of his fingers. He followed the direction of my gaze.

'Yes I have lost a finger. But not in making swords.' He didn't elaborate to say how he was reduced to nine and a half fingers.

'Neither I nor my son, who is also a smith, work at the moment. Let me show you something.'

He moved to a desk and returned with a catalogue. A picture of a sword was visible where he held the book open for me. 'This is one of mine.' A rather beautiful sword was illustrated, but I thought it odd to be looking at a picture and wondered if there were no swords in the house.

'Do you know what happened to the sword? Mishima's sword?'

'After the trial I believe the police tried to return it to the family. Mishima's wife was horrified by the idea and refused to have it in the house. Some say Azusa, Mishima's father took it, but frankly I don't know. The blade was damaged and rusted and caked in blood. Why would anyone want it?'

'What do you think of Mishima's seppuku?'

'I do not approve. I do not make swords to be used in such a way. In my view he was wrong to do what he did.'

A friend telephones to tell me about a wedding he has reluctantly attended. Weddings and funerals are always expensive in Japan, as you need to buy gifts and make cash donations. To slightly soften the sting, the bride and groom give presents to those attending, usually a dinner plate that no one wants. If the couple depart from the plate formula they sometimes distribute presents via a game of bingo or a raffle draw, only winners receiving a gift. My friend won a DVD of the Hollywood movie *Pearl Harbor*. All the guests were Japanese and no one seemed to think this an odd choice.

Igarashi arrived at the hotel in the dimming light of the early evening in his Mitsubishi Shogun. It had been snowing during the day and the roads were blanketed in white. We had arranged to visit Wakasa Sensei, a leading local expert on Seki swords and a contributor to the 1995 encyclopedia *Seki Kaji no Kigen o Saguru* (Looking for the Origins of the Seki-den Swordsmiths), on the sword-manufacturing tradition of this area, which I had bought the day before at the Sword Exhibition. 'We need to make one stop on the way,' Igarashi said, and I realised it would involve acquiring some kind of gift for Wakasa Sensei. No one arrives empty-handed when meeting someone for the first time, but in this case, it seemed that the duty had shifted to Igarashi as our sponsor.

Our gift turned out to be two crates of Japanese beer, forty-eight 500-ml cans of Kirin Ichiban Shibori. We might have some drinking to do.

As we entered the *genkan* of the large house a bird began to chirrup loudly somewhere near my right ear. Looking to my right I saw a bamboo perch hanging from the ceiling, on which sat an artificial bird I did not recognise – some kind of local thrush? This avian automaton had been activated by a hidden infrared beam to indicate by its song that someone had entered the house, and in this way operated as a sort of secondary door bell, useful in a part of the country where no one thinks seriously about locking doors. Wakasa Sensei's wife came shuffling out to greet us, and we were conducted into a traditionally furnished room complete with an impressive suit of armour. Other weapons and helmets were mounted on the walls, as were a number of scroll hangings. There was some porcelain in a small cabinet in one corner. In the centre of the room was a low central table, and near by a pile of cushions scattered on the tatami. Soon Wakasa Sensei came in wearing a quilted jacket over what looked like pyjamas. He said he had just finished dinner. His face was a little flushed, perhaps from a beer or some sake with his meal. Igarashi introduced Jun and then me and gestured towards the beer with a nervous-sounding laugh. We all sat down.

Some tea and savoury snacks were brought in by Mrs Wakasa, who as she knelt to serve us was referred to by Wakasa Sensei as 'my stupid wife' – a usage I had read about but had never heard practised before. I knew it was very old-fashioned courtesy to a guest to denigrate your wife and children. 'Stupid wife and, *tonji*, pig son,' was the standard formula.

For a few moments the conversation was quite formal. How did we find the town, our hotel? Then Wakasa Sensei pointed to a small bowl and asked if I knew what it was. I told him: 'It's a *kinrade*, or gold brocade, bowl by Wazen, perhaps late nineteenth-century.' Then he asked me about one of the snacks we were served – some thin slices of *wagyu* beef, beautifully marbled with fat from the cow's pampered existence. It was clear I was being tested to see what, if anything, I knew of Japanese culture. Was I as sincerely interested in Japan as had been indicated through Igarashi, or just a dilettante? I must have passed, as soon after that the first beers were extracted from the crate, and everyone, except for Jun, who did not drink, began to drain the beer enthusiastically.

Wakasa Sensei described the history of swordmaking in Seki, explaining which geographical features had been decisive in establishing the city as a centre of production. He also told me about Japanese sword manufacture more generally – how in the Muromachi Period up to 700,000 swords were exported to China in exchange for various goods, such as silk used in making Noh theatre costumes. None of these swords exists today, as the knowledge of sword preservation, storage, cleaning, repolishing and so on was not transmitted and the Chinese neglected the swords they acquired.

I popped the ringpull on my fifteenth beer in unison with Wakasa Sensei and Igarashi. We had been matching Wakasa Sensei beer for beer, but it was not easy, as he was clearly involved in yet another test, this time of my tolerance for alcohol. '*Kampai*' – Bottoms up! – we all shouted. By this time Wakasa Sensei's face was an alarming shade of red, shiny with sweat, but his speech was coherent and he was clearly enjoying himself.

'*Nansensu!*' shouted Wakasa Sensei. We had somehow got into a discussion of the Nanjing massacres in China in December 1937 and January 1938, when the invading Japanese army captured the city and ran riot against the civilian population. I had been asking about the *Nichinichi Shinbun*'s account of two young officers competing with each other to see who could cut down 100 Chinese using only their Japanese swords. One officer had a Seki no Magoroku sword. '*Nansensu!*' repeated Wakasa Sensei, slamming his palm down on the table top for emphasis. My beer can bounced a little and the small, now empty, dishes rattled then settled. 'Propaganda!'

Wakasa Sensei had just finished telling me that the massacres at Nanjing were massively inflated figures. The usual number of 300,000 killed in a few days was unsustainable. The Chinese had made them up, he said, after the final numbers had been published of those killed and injured by the atom bombs dropped on Hiroshima and Nagasaki, as a kind of parity of criminal scale. I didn't want to argue about Nanjing, for want of detailed knowledge, and also because I was a guest, forbidden by protocol to challenge an albeit controversial position of my host. I shifted tack and asked about the armour in the corner of the room.

'It belonged to my great-grandfather. He was Prime Minister and a senior retainer of the Kuroda family in Fukuoka. He was against the policy of opening the country to the West, and due to failing to prevent an attack on foreign ships was ordered to commit seppuku. He did so in front of nearly 1,000 witnesses. Can you imagine that?'

(I could indeed. It sounded like something reality television makers would love, if they could get away with it. An exotic spectacle on the grand scale – snuffvision.)

Earlier he had told me that his wife was related to a general in the Kōdō-ha faction implicated in the 26 February incident and that a cousin was one of the participating young officers.

'Seki swords were not art swords, they were never especially pretty, but they were appreciated by the *bushi* for their utility. Soshū swords, which had dominated during the best production period of the Kamakura era, were quite weak, as too high a heat had been used in their forging for too long. As a result, although sharp, Soshū swords often bent in combat.'

Wakasa Sensei was defensive about the swords of his adopted home, but I had heard similar remarks all over town. There was a belief that even today smiths working in a Bizen or Soshū style tended to win competitions and that the functional aspects of swordmaking were being sidelined. No one lives or dies by the sword any more and their manufacture had become an exercise in the mastery of metal to produce pleasing effects on the visible surface of a length of carefully shaped and polished steel.

Wakasa Sensei disappeared, and I assumed that all that beer required unloading. In fact he had gone to fetch a sword. It was kept in a *shirasaya*, and he first removed the bag then drew the blade. He passed the sword to me, turning the cutting edge towards himself as sword-handling etiquette dictated. I looked at it carefully. The *hamon* was flat, and at its top edge something strange was visible, what looked like a misty cloud moving along the blade. This was *utsuri*, I was told, a reflection of the *hamon* temper line, an effect one or two modern smiths had only recently managed to produce. The sword was a Kanesada, the second generation of smiths of this line, known as Nosada. This sword had been made for a domain ruler and was of museum quality. I felt glad I had at last been able to hold a great sword.

After we had returned the sword to its scabbard, Wakasa Sensei told me to grasp his wrists, as he wanted to demonstrate his family jujutsu style. Kneeling in *seiza*, facing each other, the grasp is used to feel and then break the attacker's balance. This exercise develops *kokyū-rokyu*, breath power. I did as I was asked, allowing myself to be thrown to the floor and pinned a couple of times by the laughing Wakasa Sensei. I secretly felt that I could have resisted but that might have been the effects of too much beer.

Seppuku, another term for hara-kiri, is the notorious method of formal suicide of the samurai. The term seppuku is written in Japanese using two *kanji*: *setsu*, to cut or slice through, and *fuku*, stomach or belly, the compound word pronounced when elided as seppuku. Mishima, who was fastidious with language, preferred the term hara-kiri over seppuku despite its perceived vulgarity.

Hara, belly, carries a range of associations in Japanese which overlap into other cultures and languages. The idea that the belly or guts is the seat of courage obviously derives from having felt the stomach-churning effects of fear. That it is the site of the mind and the location of true intentions, however, is a uniquely Japanese notion. By cutting open the belly, then, not only do you willingly suffer terrible agonies as a means to demonstrate courage or expiate sins, but in exposing the *hara* you provide a visible proof of your sincerity.

Mishima claimed that Japanese culture had uniquely evolved

seppuku as a physical demonstration of sincerity without explaining how the exposed intestines of an insincere man might appear. Perhaps that was his point, that in all such cases there would be no need to discriminate: the act of exposure through cutting the stomach renders the insincere sincere.

Hara-kiri, often distorted into Harry Carry in English mispronunciation, has, alongside kamikaze and only a few other terms (most of then martial), entered English from Japanese to describe self-destruction of the most fervent kind. The word suicide hardly seems adequate. Within Western cultures, among the better-informed, it is often thought that hara-kiri was the only means available for a Japanese to apologise adequately for various types of offence and in this way expunge any shame attaching to himself and his family. But is this so? The answer is yes and no – there is indeed an expiatory form of seppuku, but there were a number of other varieties.

Seppuku is written using the same two *kanji* used for hara-kiri, the order reversed, and pronounced with the Chinese reading or *On-yomi*. It is commonly pointed out that hara-kiri is a vulgarism, but this is a misunderstanding. Hara-kiri is a Japanese reading or *Kun-yomi* of the characters, and as it became customary to prefer Chinese readings in official announcements only the term seppuku was ever used in writing. So hara-kiri is a spoken term and seppuku a written term for the same act.

The history of seppuku mirrors precisely the rise to power of the samurai class, and no reliable example can be found before the twelfth century. The first instance of seppuku, described in the *Hogen Monogatari* (Tales of the Hogen Civil War), is usually attributed to Minamoto no Tametomo, who fell on his sword in 1156 to avoid ignominious capture, and more to the point, to thwart his certain torture before execution. Degrading your enemy through vicious and contemptuous treatment was, at the time, quite normal. The origin of battlefield suicide was quite clearly a pragmatic one, intended to deny the enemy the glory of having killed you and taken your head by superior combat, whilst avoiding a slower and probably more painful death.

And at first there was no formal method. Cutting your own

throat would do. Later, the Japanese genius for formalisation developed a complex ritual of seppuku, part aesthetic performance, part prayer, part living emblem of valour and heroism. A fusion of poetry, sangfroid and blood-letting sufficient to revolt any modern observer – but for some comprising the essence of Japanese culture, fusing both the Harsh and the Benign gods, the male and the female aesthetic.

Following a shift from government by noblemen at the court of the Emperor in Kyoto to a Shōgunate or *bakufu* based at Kamakura, the arts and high culture were militarised. Emphasis was placed on battlefield virtues, the highest of which was physical courage underpinned by loyalty to your lord. Loyalty was a Confucian virtue, expressed in feudal terms as a relationship between samurai retainers and their princely rulers, later termed daimyō – literally big name – in theory all benevolence, descending from the lord to his vassal retainers. The role of the retainer, who received his income as a rice stipend, was to perform unswerving service according to his rank and station and whenever necessary to fight and die on the battlefield. As this relationship was counted as the source of his livelihood and of all things good, a form of seppuku developed to enable close retainers to 'join their lord' on his death. *Junshi* was seppuku committed shortly before or shortly after the death of a daimyō to express loyalty and distress at his death. It was a romantic gesture, not a practical one, as it frequently weakened the domain, lowering the chances of a stable succession to the daimyō when the best warriors of the land had just killed themselves.

Logically *junshi* was an extension of choosing to die following the death of your lord on the battlefield, but in times of peace, and where the cause of death was illness or old age, there was no collateral gain in enhancing martial valour or reputation. *Junshi* was also a hangover from the practice of immolating the household of the Emperor in ancient times upon his death. He would be buried with servants, concubines and even horses and other animals, all alive at the time, to ensure his comfort in the next life. Eventually this was opposed, and the use of clay figures of men and animals replaced it. There is a condemnation of this form of immolation as early as AD 3! Yet a taste for dramatic suicide has lingered in Japanese culture until the present, a period of 2,000 years.

In the modern period *junshi* was last noted on the death of the Meiji Emperor in 1912 with the double seppuku of General and Countess Nogi.[57] After assisting his wife to kill herself by the severing of the carotid artery (alternative accounts claim she managed this herself by plunging the dagger into her own heart),[58] the general performed *jūmonji*, the most painful form of seppuku, involving both a horizontal and a vertical cut and symbolising the purification of the soul, before buttoning up his white naval uniform jacket and expiring. He wrote a dullish death poem:

> *The Master of the World*
> *has passed away –*
> *and after him,*
> *eager to serve my lord*
> *go I.*

Nogi's suicide attracted both praise and criticism. His Zen master, Nantenbō, sent a three-word telegram to his funeral reading simply 'Banzai! Banzai! Banzai!'[59] Yet the *Asahi Shimbun* newspaper declared Nogi's suicide to contain no lessons for Japan, and others condemned it as thoughtless, meaningless, illegal – *junshi* had been outlawed since 1663 – and anachronistic. Japan's most popular author, Natsume Soseki, wrote: 'I had almost forgotten that there was such a thing as *junshi*.'

The outlawing of *junshi* under the Tokugawa Shogunate in the seventeenth century included the ironic sanction that the heirs of a man who performed it would be ordered to commit seppuku, suggesting that self-execution was in fact a mere contrivance to save the honour of the samurai class, allowing them the dignity of seeming volition in their act of dying.

Distinctions between execution by decapitation and seppuku are worth describing. The practice of employing a second to assist the principal by cutting off his head after he had cut his stomach, killing him and ending his suffering, known as *kaishaku* from the verb for assisting, meant that cutting the stomach was never the cause of death. It was, of course, extremely painful, and if performed without flinching was certainly a fine opportunity to demonstrate self-mastery and composure. *Kaishaku* was most often performed by a friend or retainer, hopefully a good swordsman who would not make a hash of it or lose his nerve. There would usually be a back-up *kaishaku* as a failsafe, and other assistants assigned to kill the principal performing the seppuku if he lost his nerve and attempted to escape. There is a handful of accounts of escapee samurai condemned to commit seppuku who successfully resisted, seizing their *kaishaku*'s sword and fighting their way out.

In the case of an execution the prisoner would most usually be bound. The colour of the cord and the selection of the knots used to restrain the captive were a gauge of social rank. The site of the execution was also selected to convey contempt – usually a desolate place – and its most extreme form would involve burying the body still bound and without ceremony by simply kicking it into a pit dug next to the site. No care was taken: beheading was simply a means to dispatch a criminal.

By way of contrast seppuku followed an elaborate ritual, including the positioning of the seppuku according to rank, inside a building or in the grounds, the clothing worn – a white *hakama* and a white *haori* jacket without family crests or *mon* collectively known as *shini shozoku* or death costume – the seating arrangements of the witnesses, the type of last meal eaten, the writing of a death poem, and where a skilled *kaishaku* was involved, the cutting of the head using a 'soft' stroke and leaving a flap of skin at the throat unsevered so that the head remained attached to the body, technically known as *kakae kubi*, also as *daki kubi*. This last feature was most significant, if extremely difficult in practice, as it distinguished seppuku from mere beheading of a criminal.

Seppuku had a number of variations. So far we have considered *junshi* – suicide to follow your lord into death – and self-execution, which became the means by which samurai were condemned on committing a breach of etiquette or for some real or imagined crime against the central government or the rule of the daimyō in their own realm. There were other forms.

Kanshi was seppuku designed to express admonition or to

remonstrate with a superior. The most notable case was the seppuku of a senior retainer of Nobunaga Oda who had endeavoured to protest against the dissolute lifestyle and attitudes of his master. When Oda ignored him he wrote a sternly worded letter and committed seppuku to indicate his sincerity. It had the desired effect and Oda went on to conquer Japan.

Funshi is seppuku to express indignation, a protest, as at injustice. This is perhaps the term that best describes the action of Mishima. He was indignant at the social direction of Japan, its 'emasculated' state under the peace constitution and the illegal status of the Self Defence Forces. This is where you back up your words with that which is most valuable to you, your own life. In this way is sincerity formally demonstrated. When the tea master Sen no Rikyu was ordered to commit seppuku, unjustly in his view, he did so, but sent the Shōgun a slice of his intestines to 'convert' the self-execution into a protest or *funshi* seppuku.

The final significant category of seppuku is expiation for an act adjudged to be a mistake or having led to some unwholesome outcome. This form of seppuku is designed to take responsibility for an action or omission – the polar opposite of passing the buck – and in paying such a price to wipe the slate clean for the benefit of family and reputation: this is called *sokotsu-shi*, or in modern times *inseki-jisatsu*.

During the Pax Tokugawa the samurai class evolved from battlefield warriors into administrators and policemen. The chances to show valour in battle and to die 'under the hoofs of the horse of their lord' were severely limited. A shift in thought occurred to rate seppuku as the best opportunity to demonstrate martial courage, the best available means to satisfy the death mania of peacetime soldiers. Hence the desire to destroy an enemy on the battlefield was turned against oneself – the samurai became both victor and vanquished, and an obsession with a fine death in battle converted into considering opportunities for a good suicide.

In the late nineteenth century, before seppuku was abandoned as a sanction available to the government, Western envoys were sometimes obliged to witness 'executions' by seppuku following the murder of their countrymen during the *shishi* assassinations of the *sōnno jōi* movement. Lord Redesdale, on the staff of the British Minister in Japan, Sir Harry Parkes, was obliged to witness the seppuku of a retainer of the daimyō of Bizen, a samurai by the name of Zezaburō Taki who had ordered an attack on a procession of foreigners on the Osaka road outside Hyogo (modern-day Kobe). He expressed his admiration for the courage displayed by Taki, but was disgusted by the event itself:

> When he drew out the dirk, he leaned forward and stretched out his neck; an expression of pain for the first time crossed his face, but he uttered no sound. At that moment the kaishaku, who, still crouching by his side, had been keenly watching his every moment, sprang to his feet, poised his sword for a second in the air; there was a flash, a heavy, ugly thud, a crashing fall; with one blow the head had been severed from the body.
>
> A dead silence followed, broken only by the hideous noise of the blood throbbing out of the inert heap before us, which but a moment before had been a brave and chivalrous man. It was horrible.

In 1993 a book was published in Japan titled *The Complete Manual of Suicide*, by Wataru Tsurumi. It digested a mass of information for the would-be suicide, detailing the most effective, cleanest and least painful ways to kill yourself. It also went into bizarre digressions, such as how to ensure that your body will look its best when found. Despite the encyclopedic approach of this deathstyle handbook not one word was included on the most notorious form of suicide, unique to Japanese culture – seppuku or hara-kiri. The author in an interview commented: 'I don't think this sort of tradition has been continued amongst young people in Japan. The Japanese way of suicide these days is just like the European way.' To drive the point home, when questioned about Mishima's seppuku – certainly the most famous recent example – Tsurumi, then in his thirties, was emphatic: 'For our generation, I think his way of suicide is trivial, even irrelevant, even for people who like his books ... It has no great meaning or importance. I know this is all part of our history, but our generation has not carried this sort of thing on.' So even contemporary suicide in Japan is a Western import – the easy-living, pain-avoiding, scientific culture of Europe and America.

In Japan there is such a thing as the revenge suicide, committed to impose the maximum financial burden on the surviving members of the man's (it is nearly always a man) family after his death. The method is always the same: death by train.

I have witnessed or nearly witnessed three train suicides. In one case I saw a man get splattered by a high-speed train flashing past the platform. His head was cut off and the rest of his body shattered. The other two cases were less spectacular, as they had chosen slower-moving trains to end their lives. Another time when I arrived a few minutes after the final leap the body was lying on the tracks covered by a sheet. I might not have known what it was had I not spotted a shoe 30 feet away and then noticed the shoeless foot protruding from under the sheet.

The motivation here is that the railway company will charge the dead man's relatives for the hold-up and clean-up costs. This varies, but might be as much as $100,000. 'I'll make you pay' is no empty threat in such cases.

Whenever someone commits suicide and an inquest is held it is common for a verdict to be recorded in terms such as 'death whilst the balance of mind was disturbed'. So suicidal insanity may be said to indicate a lack of balance in the mind, and presumably sanity involves the opposite, balance, so that a balanced mind is a sane mind.

If this is correct it may be worth while to point out that art seems to call for imbalance, and in this context is immediately allied against life, with the risk of 'premature' death significantly elevated. In this sense a balanced mind is content in itself, at rest, unproductive. A mind in imbalance seeks to right itself, to escape the pain that such an awkward posture is likely to provoke, and this process has often led to creativity and to what we have decided to call artistic expression. This is what produces remarks such as that all art proceeds from neurosis.

Like the shaman who has mastered the ability to enter into a state of temporary madness, many artists create whilst mad, then, spent, drained of these dangerous impulses, return to the sane world of balance and dinner parties and mundane chores and banal details (must remember to buy more toilet paper), to the drear and grey of everyday life. The 'unsuccessful' artist may get trapped on the other side of the mirror, be unable to get back and feel obliged to disappear into the invisible realm, to choose by choosing death over life.

One way of thinking about the balance of the mind is to acknowledge that human life is a drama between an invisible interior mindscape and a visible, more measurable, exterior frame of reference that we have come to call the real world. Two sides of the coin: what happens inside our heads and what happens 'out there' in the real world. Art then may be said to be about bringing the interior world into the exterior world in some concrete if not always permanent form. An artist is by this definition someone who dwells, out of balance, in the interior world of his own mind and as he lives in the real world is forced to reconcile the differences of these varieties of experience in some way. If I imagine myself in all sorts of heroic scenarios in my daydreaming, yet in the real world I am a post office clerk, a form of stress is likely to build up. My real life is not at all heroic, yet in my mind I am constantly proved to be a hero. Subjectively speaking, I might easily be convinced that I am living a lie.

We are all in both 'worlds', the inner and the outer, simultaneously. Yet the dominance of each form of experience waxes and wanes according to the degree of self-consciousness we feel. The permanently self-conscious type is closer to the artistic temperament, never able to silence the inner critic. The life-in-the-fast-lane man of action who is absorbed by some challenging activity or adventure, so-called flow states, is hardly ever self-conscious; he does not experience the problem that some philosophers have labelled 'individuation', or more simply the awareness of being alone and beyond anyone else's reach.

To know if a person is balanced, examine their shoes. If one heel is more worn down than the other, the wearer is unbalanced. This method was advocated as a foolproof means to gauge the skills of visiting challengers prior to *shiai*, kendō matches, in the Edo Period at the suggestion of Tesshū Yamaoka, poet, calligrapher, swordmaster and bodyguard to the Meiji Emperor.

Mishima's shoes were quite small. He had tiny feet. The heel of the right shoe was always more worn than the left, perhaps from his habit of cocking his left hip while standing.

Back in Tokyo I had arranged to meet a famous craftsman. Now in his early fifties, the Sword Polisher had reached a mature and respected position in his elite craft. The outstanding student of a Living National Treasure,[60] he had himself been designated *mukansa*, beyond judgement. In competition *mukansa* craftsmen only compete against each other. Theirs is the highest attainment short of elevation into craft heaven, National Treasure status, a status likely to await both the death of their own teacher and possibly of others – since a kind of quota seems to operate – as well as the passing of another twenty years of life. There are no middle-aged Living National Treasures. Perhaps 'Soon to Die National Treasure' would be a more accurate description. Is this another example of a Japanese aesthetic applied to ranking, something wonderful fated to expire at its most beautiful, *mono no aware*, the pathos of transitory things? More likely, it is nothing more than plain Confucianism.

The Sword Polisher had lived in England. He spoke fondly of the green swathes of the southern English countryside and had, whilst resident, restored Japanese swords from the British royal collection. Back home he had received imperial commissions. A heavyweight, and I was delighted that he had agreed to talk to me.

Travelling on a JR line I had last used when I lived in this part of Tokyo five years before, I made sure to turn up early at the station where I had been told I would be met. Beyond the wicket gate the Sword Polisher himself awaited my arrival. He was easy to recognise from his photographs. A tall man, conservatively dressed, and wearing, I noticed, nicely polished shoes, he had come early out of courtesy. For a few minutes I lurked at a distance, remaining out of sight, although he probably didn't know what I looked like and there were other foreigners in the station. I passed through the gate so as to reach him at precisely the time we had arranged to meet, down to the second.

The Sword Polisher lived in a large Japanese-style house. Like Mishima's, his parents lived in a separate dwelling within the grounds. He told me that he had returned to Japan to look after them, his traditional duty as an elder son. He didn't complain, but something gave me the impression that he would have preferred to stay abroad.

We sat down in a Western-style room, elegantly furnished and comfortably appointed, and the Sword Polisher's wife brought in some coffee and two varieties of cake. I had handed over a carefully selected bottle of sake on arrival – a nice one from Niigata in an understated box labelled in strong grass-hand calligraphy that I couldn't quite read and then neatly wrapped in the paper of a well-known department store – with conventional phrases apologising for the insignificance of the gift. We sipped our coffee for a moment and then he started to answer some of the questions I had already sent on to him.

'There are only a few things I can tell you about the sword,' he told me. 'But first I should like to explain a little of my own background. When the Mishima incident took place I was a student. I attended the same university as one of Mishima's Tate no Kai cadets, one of the ones involved in the incident in General Mashita's office and afterwards arrested. The investigating police were, perhaps unsurprisingly, anxious to establish if others sympathetic to Mishima's ideas existed amongst the general student body. It was natural they would look first at the institutions attended by Mishima's young revolutionaries.

'So a few days after the suicide the police were conducting searches of students' rooms. I was saved by my – what do you call it?' He paused and rubbed his chin. 'Yes that's it, saved by my landlady. A most formidable woman. I say "saved" because at that time I had recently begun my interest in Japanese swords and had a live blade, an edged sword, in my room. It was not registered with the police – which as I'm sure you know is a legal requirement – and I would have been in some trouble and might possibly have been mistaken as a neo-nationalist, something I most certainly was not. Far from it.

'She wouldn't let the police inside. "He's a nice young boy," she kept saying in the *genkan* to the house where I had rented a room. "Quietly studying all the time he is, and has absolutely nothing to do with this terrible business." They believed her, apologised and went away. So, as you can see, I was saved by my landlady.'

We both started to nibble at the slices of cake.

'You have to understand how we were educated at the time. All of our teachers at school and most of the professors in the universities had more or less left-wing political leanings. They were determined that we should feel nothing but shame about Japan's wartime military adventures. You could call it a balancing obsessive commitment to peace – Japan was now, they felt certain, an exceptional and worthy example of a peace-loving nation. They held this view as the battles raged on all around them. The late 1960s, as you know, were a time of unrest. During my studies many universities, mine included, were closed for months at a time. The students took to the streets. There were riots. There was a climate of violence and it seemed a watershed in retrospect – but at the time it felt like revolution was possible, even likely. It was all about the US security treaty. And about Vietnam. Really I suppose it was about perceived American imperialism. It was happening all over the world, of course. When you are a student you take sides. Some, a fairly small number I think, reacted against the prevailing pro-Leftist student orthodoxy and joined nationalist groups. They were mostly from the countryside, farmboys. They were all for imperialism – but Japanese imperialism rather than its American version.

'Some of the rightist groups were recruiting grounds for yakuza gangsters, who professed to be protecting our cultural heritage as they pimped and bullied and gambled. Mishima's people were very low-key, next to invisible. And anyway there were hardly any of them – about a hundred at the time of his death I think. Hardly a private army. There were tens of thousands of leftist students. If they had ever chosen to fight in the streets it wouldn't have lasted too long.

'So I am the same generation as Mishima's men. And was a neighbour of Ogawa, and because of this feel slightly connected. But not at all sympathetic. I didn't read Mishima then and haven't found reason to start in the years between. His themes don't relate to anything in my life.

'I don't know why I became a sword polisher's apprentice. I just did, and as you may know the old system involved living with your master, living in his house and eating with the family, being a part of the family really. You were not paid, apart from a small pocket money-type allowance. But you were housed and fed and expected to do chores and to work hard. Not real work, as it was impossible for you to be much help for several years – you were not allowed to work on anything important, the chances of you ruining a valuable blade were simply too great. But practical exercises were set and the need for careful observation of the master absorbed many hours each day. There was quite a turnover in *deshi* at that time. Many found it was not what they expected and even more simply had no talent for the work.

'I don't have live-in disciples. It's just too much trouble. Yet as I am quite well known in the West I am always receiving requests from earnest Americans and Europeans who are always quite sure I am looking for *deshi*, for them in particular, and will I let them know by return email if they can come and live with me and learn sword polishing, which they feel so so drawn to. I have even been asked once whether I might be able to send an airline ticket! About twenty a day on a bad day. If I want *deshi* there is no shortage of Japanese willing to try – and with a better chance of understanding how much effort is required.

'For me the Japanese sword combines three areas. As a work of art, a beautiful object. As a cultural and historical craft skill it is a bridge into our past. And finally there is a hard-to-describe aspect which I feel is best labelled "spiritual". For me swords are spiritual objects; they contain or express something of a non-material kind. I do not think so-called art swords have chosen to ignore the pragmatics of traditional swordmaking. Or put more simply are all show and would not function as weapons.[61] Anyway we live in the age of the gun and the bomb and the missile – what is the practical value of a short-bladed weapon?

'You asked me about bushidō. You have read the *Hagakure*?

Professor Nitobe's book? Well the short answer is there was more than one bushidō. *Hagakure* was written by a Nabeshima samurai, a Kyūshū clansman. I come from Aizu in the north-east of Honshu and have a less than good feeling about the Nabeshima. They have a reputation, you know, as calculating. They were the first *han* to adopt guns and their behaviour was decisive in the overthrow of the Tokugawa shogunate. This was all later than *Hagakure*, which was, as you know, dictated in the early eighteenth century and, to use a modern expression, not intended for publication – but the point is still valid. Bushidō was not a universal and unvarying nationwide code of practice or a written legal system. There were state-sponsored regulations on the correct conduct of samurai issued and enforced by the Shōgunal authority, some of which modified traditional practices, like *junshi* seppuku after the death of your lord – and later, after the Meiji Restoration, there were imperial rescripts to soldiers and sailors which attempted to codify some aspects of bushidō. *Hagakure* is, anyway, usually misunderstood. It's quite long, rather illogical and inconsistent, and most people can only quote its famous opening line – "The way of the samurai is to be found in death." There is much more to it than that – and a lot of it is quite ironic, quite intentionally funny.

'Yamamoto had a sense of humour. So did Mishima, but probably it did not quite overlap.

'I believe that the traditions and crafts of swordmaking will survive. The reason is economic. Top-quality swords sell for the equivalent of tens of thousands of dollars. It's true that only a small number of craftsmen (and it is mostly men) can make a living in this field. Perhaps the top twenty or thirty smiths and their circles of polishers and *koshirae* makers. Everyone else is obliged to find another source of livelihood. But it is enough to keep things alive – and the next generation is coming through. This is a craft and the principle is that of attrition – perhaps as many as 99 per cent of those who try to become swordsmiths or polishers fail to make the grade. Some do succeed, however, and they are sufficient. It is other traditional crafts – where the value of what they make is low – that are threatened and will, I feel, die out. It is a sad fact. After all in London there are no longer any lamplighters – or if there are, there is nothing for them to do.

'Japanese culture is not threatened, although I understand why you ask. Although on the surface there have been many changes in the way we live since my childhood, I also find many things, fundamental things, have remained the same. Perhaps this is rooted in language, I don't know.

'You asked me if I have come across the sword used by the *kaishaku* in Mishima's seppuku. Well I have not seen it, but one of my students has. He was asked to polish and evaluate it in the early 1960s, well before he became my student. He told me the sword was not Seki no Magoroku, not Kanemoto I or Kanemoto II, but was a later-generation Kanemoto sword. The later-generation Kanemoto swords represented a decline in quality and are not so valuable or collectible.

'Mishima was not a sword collector. He knew little about swords and did not attend any sword appraisal meetings as far as I am aware. He studied kendō. I'm not sure of his rank.'

'He was *godan* at the time of his death.'

'Oh, fifth degree eh? Well, that is advanced, but the subject of swords is in a sense independent of kendō. There are kendō masters who know a great deal about swords and a few who do not.'

As he was showing me out the Sword Polisher started to talk about seppuku.

'I am occasionally asked by the police about cases where some-one has attempted to cut their stomachs with a kitchen knife and the like. There was a sad case near here a couple of years ago. Can this be said to be seppuku? I don't think so. Seppuku belongs to the feudal practices of the samurai. It is a closed chapter of history.'

I took leave of the Sword Polisher, thanking his wife, who had reappeared to say goodbye, and returned to the station on foot, passing on my way a McDonald's and a KFC, but also a small shop that sold hand-made wooden and bamboo imple-ments for use in *o-furo* and *sento*, traditional Japanese baths.

One of the gimmicks of Ken's snack bar was his insistence that all his customers pose for a photograph on leaving the premises after their drink or meal. The photographs were rapidly developed and filed in date-ordered albums, which were stored on shelves near the door. Customers came back out of curiosity just to look at the pictures, so I suppose it was a good commercial practice, not just the indulgence of Ken's photographic hobby.

I was thumbing through the albums for the months immediately before my arrival in Tokyo in October last year. I sat there speculating about the faces of unknown individuals. A group of men, who were always photographed together, featured day after day. They looked like gangsters.

Iron is full of impurities that weaken it; through forging it becomes steel and is transformed into a razor-sharp sword. Human beings develop in the same fashion.

MORIHEI UESHIBA O-SENSEI, founder of aikidō

Iron is simply too soft to make a useful weapon, especially an edged weapon. Steel, a combination of iron and carbon, being harder is more suitable for making swords and knives, but very hard, high-carbon, steel is brittle, and if used to make a sword will often break or chip on impact. The problem for swordsmiths has always been how to make a cutting edge hard enough, whilst retaining ductile qualities in the sword as a whole. Japanese swordsmiths characterise the objectives they have for their swords with the slogan: *orenai, magaranai, yoku kireru* – doesn't break, doesn't bend, cuts well.

A Japanese sword begins its life as a form of ferrous oxide, an iron sand called *satetsu*, which is gathered and then heated in a traditional smelter, or *tatara*, using pine charcoal as a direct fuel. The charcoal is the source of the carbon required to transform the iron sand into small pieces of carbon steel called *tamahagane*. The resulting *tamahagane* is not homogeneous, and the usable steel produced this way has a carbon content ranging from 0.5 to 1.7 per cent. Each piece of *tamahagane* is assessed and further refined by the swordsmith, who adjusts the carbon levels by moving it around in his forge, which is also charcoal-fuelled – a process known as *oroshigane*. To reduce the carbon content the *tamahagane* is heated without contact with the forge charcoal and by directing air using a bellows to raise the temperature. In this way carbon is burned off as carbon monoxide. To increase the carbon in the *tamahagane*, ingots are moved into the top of the forge and surrounded by charcoal. The steel is then hammered and folded whilst hot to even out the carbon distribution. The extent of hammering and folding depends on the type of steel being worked. Low-carbon steel is folded only about a dozen times. Higher-carbon steel, destined to take the edge of the blade, is folded dozens of times. The process of hammering and folding in this way gives rise to certain visible features in the steel, which are brought out when the blade is polished, and such grain features are known as *jihada*.

The essential technical problem in making swords is therefore how to achieve two opposed qualities: to make the steel hard enough to take and retain a very sharp edge, but soft enough not to bend or break when enduring the shocks which are cutting and parrying in battle. The two main factors affecting the hardness of steel are the carbon content and how it is heated and cooled, the tempering process.

A Japanese sword is not usually made of a single type of steel but instead combines at least two kinds. In the simplest form of construction, called *kobuse*, low-carbon steel is used as a core around which a jacket of higher-carbon steel is wrapped. The hard jacket will hold an edge and the inner softer core helps to provide the necessary ductility.

Alternative and more complex methods exist for combining

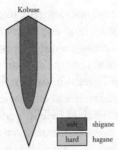

softer and more ductile forms of steel with harder steel. This is sometimes referred to as laminating, but Japanese swords are not laminated. The softer and harder forms of steel, sometimes with an intermediate form – medium-hardness steel – are combined in the forge and hammered into a weld; they are forge-welded, and the various steels combine into a single piece of metal with different qualities at its core, edge, back and sides. It is disastrous if any air pockets or imperfections enter the weld, as this will significantly weaken the blade and may cause it to break or crack when heated and cooled in the tempering.

Seki swords use four types of steel in a forge-weld pattern called *shihōzume*. Masamune swords were more complex still, using five kinds of steel applied in seven layers – *Soshū kitae*.

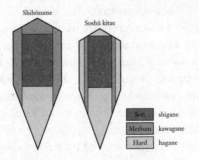

Once the various kinds of steel have been forge-welded and hammered into shape it is necessary to adopt a heating and cooling process to change the properties of the metal. When steel is heated to a critical temperature a so-called austenite state occurs – a crystalline state where carbon and iron molecules combine – and when it is suddenly cooled the austenite becomes the hardest form of steel, a crystal structure with a locked-in carbon atom called martensite. When steel is heated to a critical temperature but is cooled slowly the austenite does not become martensite but instead breaks down into ferrite (pure iron) and a hybrid of ferrite and carbon called pearlite. By controlling the rate of cooling of parts of the blade it is possible to cause different parts of the same piece of metal to have different degrees of hardness.

This is achieved as follows: a slurry of clay, charcoal powder and pulverised sandstone called *omura* is applied in a thick layer to the sides and back of the blade. It is applied in a much thinner layer to the edge, and a brush pattern is made which will be visible when the blade is polished, forming a temper line or *hamon*. The blade is then heated to its critical temperature, around 1,300 degrees Fahrenheit, in a process always conducted at night. This is because the temperature of the metal is judged exclusively by its colour. Oral transmissions used poetic references to recognise this critical temperature: like the moon on an August evening – which is a bright red-orange colour. Once the metal has reached the critical temperature it is plunged into water. The edge cools quickly and forms martensite and the rest of the blade cools at different rates becoming ferrite and pearlite embedded with martensite crystals. This differential cooling process also causes a curvature of the blade or *sori*. More than half of all blades crack during this process and are rejected.

The next stage is a further heating and cooling to relieve some of the stresses in the metal. The temperature is much lower this time, around 300 degrees F, and this process does not change the structure of the steel. Finally some gentle reheating and hammering may be required to adjust the curvature of the blade. This is followed by a rough polish before the blade can be sent to the polisher.

Mishima, I knew, very much admired the work of the Italian poet and nationalist patriotic activist, Gabriele D'Annunzio, expending time and effort translating his verse play *The Martyrdom of St Sebastian* into Japanese. An Oxford professor once calmly told me over a small sherry, eyes glinting donnishly, that D'Annunzio had had a rib removed, surgically, to enable him to bend forward just that little bit further in his irresistible desire to perform acts of autofellatio.

This sort of anecdote is one of those killer 'facts' that for ever after alter the way you feel about some historical character. Like the story of Evelyn Waugh's banana – said to have been made up by his son Auberon as an act of filial revenge, but none the less potent in an it-should-be-true kind of way. Waugh, so the story went, whose young children had never tasted a banana due to wartime rationing, ate the first one he obtained after the war was over, all by himself and in front of his children, without letting them try even a bite – the bastard!

Or Camille Saint-Saëns, the French composer of *The Carnival of Animals*, confessing in his confidential journal to sexually experimenting by forcing a live mouse up his arse. Since learning this 'fact' – and why lie in a confidential journal? – I can never hear *The Swan* without this nugget popping unbidden into my mind.

What facts of this kind – killer facts as I am calling them – might I discover about Mishima? They are often, but not always, sexual peccadilloes. Oddities. The things people do to themselves and those they lust after. That everything has already been tried may well be true – but you never know, and one cannot deny the power of Mishima's imagination. Mishima was hardly conventional sexually, so I might get lucky and add to my stock of anecdotes. Sexual rumours are the easiest to keep alive, I have found, however implausible. That Mishima was Kawabata's lover kept on popping up, but I seriously doubted it. I was told this by unsmiling individuals on more than one occasion, and wondered if they had any idea that Mishima was revolted by old men's bodies.[62]

Until recently Yukio Mishima was the best-known Japanese writer in the English-speaking world, even though in Japan a foreigner interested in Mishima is often greeted with expressions of surprise – 'Why are you so interested in Mishima? No one reads him any more.' Yet while trying to unearth some facts in a country where every statistic must be taken with a large grain of salt, I found that as recently as 2000 a 41-volume edition of his collected works sold 8,000 sets in ten days, something quite unprecedented for a literary author. In Japan the interest in Mishima is, however, a covert one, a private vice. It involves the examination of something dark and troubling, an activity best done in private and plausibly denied. Like masturbation.

Authors with one eye on a life of action, such as Henry Miller, are unquestionably impressed when a writer uses his life to back up his work. Walking the talk, as it were; more war than jaw. But it is a grudging admiration only, as the subtext seems to be an act of criticism: are we then a watered-down version of the REAL THING, unlike Mishima? Norman Mailer may have stabbed his wife, but is this enough to consider oneself a warrior, to escape into the reality of life as opposed to the created, unreal, arena of figurative art, including writing?

Mishima has been described as a 'gorgeous mosaic', but might just as well be called a collage of contemporary taboos. In a single individual, we find overlays of homosexuality, Emperor-centred political radicalism, and a belief in the need for a return to full sovereignty by revising the Peace constitution to acknowl-edge the real status of the army – described by Mishima as possessing the last vestige of the true Japanese spirit. Each of these topics taken alone might provoke an embarrassed silence. Added together you have a recipe for positive denial as the only viable means to ignore something deeply unpleasant in the Japanese national psyche.

For a number of years following Mishima's suicide in 1970 there seemed to be an orchestrated campaign to rubbish his reputation. *Kichigai*, crazy, said Prime Minister Satō – a friend of Mishima, and arguably under an obligation of loyalty to restrain his language in public. The same goes for Nakasone, then in charge of the Defence Agency and a future prime minister. The compliant press joined in, as it always does when prompted in the Press Club lobby briefings.

In Japan there is a concept called *wa*. This word means harmony, but is better understood as the avoidance of conflict. The prescription to avoid argument and dissent is practically interpreted as rendering any form of direct criticism a hostile act. Famously, Japanese is sometimes said to contain no word for 'No'. Although this is not correct, it is true that normal speech negates using a verb – *chigaimasu* – which literally means 'It is different.' A head-on clash of ideas is considered socially unacceptable.

I had just poured a beer when I answered a knock at the door. Standing in the street were two men, one tall, wearing dark glasses and a black suit, the other short and heavy-set, with a shaved head and pockmarked face.

'Good evening, can I help you?' I said.

'Where is Ken?'

'He's away. I am a friend, staying here for a while.'

'When will he be back?'

'I don't know. I'm sorry, but he didn't say.'

Then they turned and walked away.

After I had closed the door and was sipping my beer I realised that this might have been the most abrupt conversation I had ever had in Japan. No pleases or thank yous or even hello or goodbye. I found the album for August and flipped back to a picture of the group of gangsters. My latest visitors were on the far left, standing behind a middle-aged man in an expensive jacket smoking a cigar. It looked like a movie still from something violent starring Takeshi Kitano.

Ryūtarō called me early one morning. I could hear laughter, not his, and the sound of someone stacking chairs in the background and immediately guessed that he was not an early riser, but had yet to go to bed after a night out. His Japanese had an Osaka accent. He explained who had given him my number and asked me if it was true that I wanted to talk about Mishima to anyone who had known him.

Yes, I said.

He told me he had known Mishima, that they had met in a bar in Ni-Chōme, Tokyo's gay ghetto in Shinjuku, in the early 1960s. He agreed to meet me in a place called Club Akashiro where he'd be that evening, briefly explaining how to get there and suggesting a time. The laughter in the background suddenly got much louder as if someone had just finished telling a joke as he hung up the phone.

Akashiro means Red and White, and I wondered what kind of a place it was. In England red and white traditionally symbolises the Wars of the Roses, the houses of York and Lancaster, or for the less historically minded they conjure up the kit of a number of football teams – Arsenal or Manchester United. In Japan the historical association is also with warring princes and their dynastic houses, the Genpei wars, the epic struggle between the Taira and the Minamoto, chronicled in the thirteenth-century *Tales of the Heike*. Perhaps this club was an historically themed bar decorated with woodblock prints of Prince Genji?

After examining a map I found the block number for the Red and White Club and worked out how to get there from the station. It wasn't far from the place where Ryutaro had met Mishima, a small second-floor bar called Sazae, which although no longer fashionable still exists, in Shinjuku Ni-Chōme, a cluster of perhaps 200 or so small bars, clubs and shops. As I came out of Shinjuku Station, the world's busiest, it had begun to rain and the lights of a number of noisy electrical and camera shops and a row of *rāmen* (Chinese noodles) restaurants sparkled on the wet roads and pavements, glittering as my wave of the human sea flowed east, as if draining downhill. Having memorised the route I found the block containing the club quite easily, and after a couple of minutes spotted a sign below my knees leading into a basement area. The word Akashiro was in *kanji* but Club was in English and there was a drawing of what looked like a cage which had faded and was now hard to make out. I climbed down nine slippery metal stairs, opened the door and went inside.

After my eyes had adjusted to the low lighting of the entrance area I could make out a small booth, and beyond it a row of lockers like a gym changing room – was this a sauna? I dropped my head to the level of the window and stared into a cubbyhole where a middle-aged man sat reading a paper and drinking a steaming cup of tea, in sole charge of those entering. Without looking up from the sports paper – the headline referred to a star baseball pitcher's earnings in the US major leagues – he asked for ¥10,000, about £50, and then said: 'Red or white?' 'White,' I replied, without knowing why or what it might mean, and was handed what I first took for a towel and then realised was the wrong shape, even in Japan, too long and thin. It was the material used for a *fundoshi*, a Japanese loincloth. 'You can change over there,' he said, passing me a key to a locker and gesturing with his still bowed head.

Well, Ryūtarō was inside and I couldn't go to look for him unless I stripped and put on the *fundoshi*. Luckily I had once been shown how to tie this mysterious undergarment and I struggled to remember the sequence of moves. There was no one else about and I managed on the third attempt, although I could have done with some help in pulling it tight before the final wrap and knotting.

Beyond the locker area was a nondescript door, and just past it a set of metal bars, exactly like those in a town jail in a Western. There was a further door into the caged area leading onto a dim corridor. I strolled down the semi-lit passage and glanced left and right into the recessed rooms. It took only a few sideways glances at a couple of *tableaux vivants* to explain where I was. This was a sado-masochist club. There were wooden frames, stocks and benches, some with manacles and leather thongs and whips and flickering lit candles and spikes and paddles and more obvious sex toys shaped like the hypertrophic genitalia found in *shunga* woodblock prints. One man, reclining in a leather sling which divided his legs like a woman on a gynaecologist's examining table, was enjoying the attentions of another man who was dripping hot wax onto his nipples. I hoped this was not Ryūtarō, as he seemed busy and, having his eyes shut in deep concentration (or pain), unlikely to notice me. I also saw that the man being burned was wearing a red *fundoshi*, his torturer a white one like mine. I was I reasoned a sadist; instinct had enabled me to make a more or less correct choice.

Moving away into a small unoccupied enclave I sat down on a stool, after unscrewing and removing the detachable dildo. If I just waited here for a while I hoped Ryūtarō would find me. I was the only gaijin in the place, and waiting seemed somehow less hazardous than approaching people at random. After what seemed a long time but was perhaps five minutes, and having refused one man who wanted me to piss on him in a bath – I honestly told him I didn't need to go – a bald middle-aged man in a red *fundoshi* smiled at me and introduced himself as the person I was waiting for.

'Hope you don't mind meeting here? I don't want to be recorded' – he patted his body as if searching for a tape recorder – 'and I was intending to come here tonight anyway.'

'No, it's fine. I've never been to an S&M club, or indeed anywhere in a *fundoshi* before.'

'You managed to get it on. Looks good.'

'Yes, I was once shown how to tie it by an elderly taxi-driver at my dōjō. He said he had never felt right in Western under-wear.' I paused, wondering how to begin my questions. 'Mishima once wrote a list of the things that were for him essentially Japanese. He included the *fundoshi*. He is often wear-ing one in many of the photos of him I have seen.'

'Yes. He liked *fundoshi*. At school they used to swim in them, red ones, called a Cat Fundoshi, they used less material than these. I don't know why it's called cat though. But Mishima didn't swim at school. He told me he learned much later at the YMCA where they swam naked. Even better for him perhaps.'

'How long did you know Mishima?'

'I met him in a bar. He had slept with a friend of mine and I knew both who he was and what he might want to do with me if I decided to go with him. I felt attracted to his fame. I knew he was a star but didn't really fancy him. Not my type. Not at first. But he bought me drinks and made me laugh. He was very funny. Good at jokes. He seemed intense, but confident and in control. I noticed he didn't drink his drink, but made sure I finished mine.'

'How old were you then? When was this?'

'I was twenty and a student. It was in 1965.'

Ryūtarō nodded at a man who had just walked past trailing another man on his hands and knees, his neck attached to a lead by a studded collar, like those worn by a larger breed of dog.

'How shall I put this?' said Ryūtarō, sucking in a long breath through his teeth – a Japanese habit indicating hesitation. 'Well, Mishima liked what nowadays would be called role play. He wanted me to wear my high-school uniform the second time we met. Luckily I still had it, although we no longer wore them at university. That was OK but I got bored by the hara-kiri stuff.'

'What do you mean, hara-kiri stuff?'

'Mishima liked to pretend he was committing seppuku. I had to watch, and eventually he brought along a sword and showed me how to stand behind him as his *kaishaku*. He also had other props. He would write out a death poem. Can't remember any of it though, poetry's not my thing. And oddest of all, he pulled a huge length of red cloth from his briefcase. What's that? I asked him before we started. "Blood," he said. "Blood and guts."

'I was impressed the first time we did this. Mishima got hard at once and as he died he came. Without touching himself at all. I had never seen anyone do that before. I didn't find the role-playing at all arousing and wanted him to fuck me, but he didn't want to – I think I was just a witness to something he wanted to do in front of an audience – and after we had re-enacted his bloody death on three "dates" in a row I decided not to see him any more. I wasn't surprised when he did himself in later. I think he'd spent a long time thinking about it.'

'Did Mishima mind being recognised? Did he ask you not to tell anyone what you had been up to?'

'No. He did not. He was very polite. Everyone in the bar seemed to treat him with respect. The master called him "Sensei".'

'Did you ever meet again after you had stopped "dating"?'

'I saw him in a couple of places. But he didn't seem to notice me. We had both moved on. I don't know if my refusal to keep meeting had upset him. Probably. Who knows? I was cute then and never short of guys chasing me.'

We talked a bit more and it became clear both that there was no more to learn about Mishima and that Ryūtarō wanted to carry on with his evening's entertainment. He asked if I wanted to join in. I said I had to get going. Perhaps another time.

All his life he had dodged things fundamental and artless: white silk, clear cold water, the zigzag white paper of the exorcist's staff fluttering in the breeze, the sacred precinct marked by a torii, the gods' dwelling in the sea, the mountains, the vast ocean, the Japanese sword with its glistening blade so pure and sharp. Not only Honda, but the vast majority of Westernized Japanese could no longer stand such intensely native elements.

YUKIO MISHIMA, *The Temple of Dawn*

In his difficult essay *Bunka Bōei Ron*, 'In Defence of Culture', published in 1968, Mishima lists a number of things he identifies as typically Japanese:

> ... like a transparent crystal containing the national
> spirit: a Noh kata; dying soldiers in New Guinea bathed
> in moonlight holding Japanese swords; the willingness
> to die of the Special Attack Forces of WWII; literature

from the *Tale of Genji* to modern novels; poetry from
the *Manyōshū* to avant-garde tanka; sculpture of the
Buddha in Chuusonji to modern works of sculpture;
ikebana; the Tea Ceremony; kendō and judō; kabuki;
yakuza gangster movies; fundoshi, the spirit of the
army, navy and airforce of today; everything from the
Chrysanthemum to the Sword.

Perhaps the most unlikely item on this list is the *fundoshi*
or loincloth. Underwear researchers have proposed that this
garment is Polynesian in origin but acknowledge that, as with
everything else absorbed into Japanese culture, it underwent
significant development through the ages. There are several
variations of the *fundoshi*, but the most common is the *rokushaku
fundoshi*, referring to its length – upwards of six feet of cotton
cloth. A diagram showing how to put it on is overleaf.

In claiming that the *fundoshi* contained the 'national spirit'
I wonder if Mishima knew the poem 'A Man's Root', by
the fifteenth-century wandering Zen poet and later abbot of
Daitokuji in Kyoto, Ikkyū:

> Eight inches strong, it is my favourite thing;
> If I am alone at night, I embrace it fully –
> A beautiful woman hasn't touched it for ages.
> Within my *fundoshi* there is an entire universe!

I had mislaid my mobile and was conducting a search when
there was a knock at the door. Recently tradesmen had been
calling to ask why Ken had not put in his usual order for food
and drink supplies, so I expected it would be another delivery
man. It was nearly 11 a.m.

I opened the door to find a policeman.

'Good morning. I am Officer Kawakubo from the *kōban* of

How to tie a Fundoshi

① Double the cloth then drape the folded end over your left shoulder.

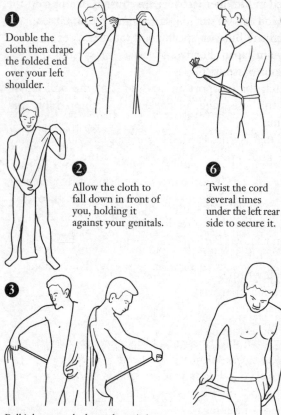

② Allow the cloth to fall down in front of you, holding it against your genitals.

③ Pull it between the buttocks, twisting the cloth to form a more cord-like shape and pull it around to the right.

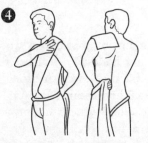

④ Wrap it all the way around your waist at the front and then around behind.

⑤ Loop the cord under the right rear side cord and pull back towards the left so a 'T' shape is made. Pull tight.

⑥ Twist the cord several times under the left rear side to secure it.

⑦ Drop the part of the *fundoshi* resting on your shoulder forward and pull it tight between buttocks to form another covering layer.

⑧ Twist to make a cord shape and loop under the existing cords to the left so as to form a clear 'T' shape, avoiding a 'Y' shape, then pull across to the right and twist the cord several times under the right rear side to secure it.

Note: Your penis should not hang down, as when wearing boxer shorts, but be held in place vertically pressed against the body.

this neighbourhood. I understand you have been living here for several months.'

'Yes, I arrived in October last year. I returned to England for the Christmas and New Year holiday and then came back.'

'You are English? But you speak good Japanese.'

'I used to live in Japan. For five years.'

'May I see your passport please?'

I went to fetch the passport and passed it to the policeman. He examined the visa page, glanced at my photograph and returned it to me.

'Thank you, that is fine. Is Mr Hiramatsu here now please?'

'No. He has gone away and lent the bar to me as a place to stay.'

'When will he be back?'

'I don't know. He left me a note but it didn't say.'

'When are you planning to return home?'

'Again, I don't know. Perhaps in a couple of months. I am a writer.'

'What are you writing?'

'A book about another writer.'

'Not about gangsters?'

'No, not about gangsters.'

'Well, enjoy your stay Ross-san. Please let me know if you have any problems. You know where the *kōban* is?'

'Yes I do, thank you. Thank you very much.'

After saluting he turned and walked down the alleyway towards the chaos of Sentagai.

Donald Richie, sometimes described as the dean of Western-born Japan-resident art critics, is the leading Western authority on Japanese cinema. He has written over thirty books, including a number of classic works, such as the travel book *The Inland*

Sea, *Some People*, a selection of biographical vignettes, and with Ian Buruma *The Japanese Tattoo*.

In the late 1950s he shared a house called the Senri-an, a reconstructed *minka* or farmhouse taken piece by piece from Chichibu in Saitama and reassembled in Roppongi in central Tokyo, with publisher and translator Meredith Weatherby and his Japanese boyfriend, the photographer and actor Yato. Mishima knew Weatherby, who translated *Confessions of a Mask* into English in 1954, and later *The Sound of Waves*, and through him became Richie's friend.

Richie agreed to meet me for a chat in the FCCJ canteen. I sat waiting and examined the lunch menu, which, it declared with a traditionalistic pride, was unchanged since 1983. Today was Wednesday and the 'Correspondent's Lunch' offered A. Canelloni. B. Fried Seafood. If you were hungry you could start your meal with a choice of cream of pumpkin soup or cauliflower and olive salad.

Richie arrived on time. He was a slim man in his mid- to late seventies, dressed conservatively in a jacket and tie. He wore large confidence-inducing spectacles and was relaxed and easy to talk to, instantly at his ease the moment he sat down, asking for some coffee. I told him what I was doing, why I was in Japan, and invited him to tell me whatever he liked about Mishima.

'Well Mishima liked to compartmentalise his life. Those in one box almost never met those in another. Mishima liked to talk to me about sex. He had placed me in a box marked "sexual confessor" and almost never discussed his writing. Once, I recall commenting that it must be nice to have a private army of healthy boys so available to him. He looked at me and said: You are quite wrong. He seemed shocked that I would fail to see that his militia had nothing to do with his sex life – at least not in any direct way.'

'Some critics, Japanese critics, persist in saying Mishima was not gay. That *Confessions of a Mask* is not autobiographical, but is pure fiction. What do you think?'

'Well they are wrong. Mishima's taste in men ran to two main types. Willowy Peers School boys studying literature or French, essentially himself at that age. He often had one in tow. Or meaty butch types, sometimes foreigners, whom he liked to be rough with him. Mishima was not secretive about his sex life, but he was discreet. He made his own arrangements. Anyone who was unaware of this side to him probably occupied another box, where the homosexuality had no role and was never mentioned.

'He liked to hold salons at his house. They were formal occasions. Many famous people from various walks of life were invited. I remember meeting Issey Miyake for the first time at a Mishima party. But the thing to realise is that he collected celebrities for just one reason – to provide a glittering background to exhibit the star item: himself.

'In a way he was postmodern even before the idea of postmodernism had been articulated. He believed there was nothing fixed about a human personality. That you might, by exercising your will, make yourself into nearly anything. This was the only reality. The reality you make for yourself. You needed to fashion a mask, one which would fit. Mishima struggled hard to find a persona in which he felt comfortable – like a man in search of a perfect suit of clothes. He tried various things, boxing, dancing, singing, Kabuki, Noh. He decided that bodybuilding and martial arts suited him. We used to train at the same gym, Kōrakuen. He had worked hard on his upper body but had thin, underdeveloped legs. He wasn't comfortable about his legs and preferred to be photographed above the cock, as it were.

'Meredith used to host gatherings and Mishima was often invited. He would always telephone in advance to announce he was near by, on his way somewhere else, and then he might drop by for a limited time. He always prepared an exit for himself and seemed ill at ease in someone else's home. I think this was a control thing. He felt nervous if he couldn't control everything. He always followed up such visits with an elegant note of thanks. He had superb manners.

'I remember when we were filming *Rites of Love and Death*, you know, *Yūkoku*. Have you seen it?'

'Not yet. I have arranged to get a copy.'

'Well Mishima was insisting that the seppuku be utterly realistic. We needed blood, buckets of it – and guts. We approached the local butchers and eventually had pig guts delivered in paper sacks. And buckets of blood, just as requested. When the film was shown women fainted. They fainted in Tokyo and even in Paris. I also suggested the *Liebestod* as suitable music, found the right recording, Stokowski's 1939 version on 78s, and Mishima used it in his film.'

'Do you think Mishima believed in reincarnation? Literally believed?'

'No, I don't think he did. He was always going on about purity. Whenever the subject came up I thought, oh God, here he goes, we will be harangued on this for hours now. I tended to tune out and wait for the all-clear or suddenly remember I had to be somewhere else.

'Mishima died just as Japan was starting to accelerate its adoption of Western culture. To abandon the more obvious separations of the sexes and to adopt a more androgynous society. He would have hated what Japan has become. He was, I suppose, a traditional fundamentalist. He stood for a beautiful imaginary past as a bulwark against a literally ugly present.

'Coppola was the producer of the Schrader film,[63] you know. He paid Yōko to cooperate and then she reneged on the deal. There was a scene showing Mishima in a gay bar and Yōko told him that when her daughter had seen the rushes she fainted – that it couldn't be included.

'Mishima's best novel, in my view, was his first – *Confessions of a Mask*. He was at his best writing about himself. Nothing he produced after that book came close to it.'

We finished our coffee and Richie left me to ponder with a firm American-style handshake.

I first came across Mishima in Paris. I was broke and bored and needing something to read as a source of cheap entertainment found my way to Shakespeare & Co, the delightful American-owned second-hand bookstore on the left bank in sight of Notre Dame. On a small freestanding bookcase outside the main entrance were rows of books for 10 francs or less. I was poor, but in Paris, which is a different kind of poverty and somehow more bearable than being poor anywhere else. And the sun was shining! Often hungry or thirsty, and certainly regarding myself as a struggling student, I saved money by sleeping on a friend's floor. Only a few weeks remained of my summer vacation and I had calculated by budgeting I could manage the cost of a book – if I skipped lunch. Right then in the summer sunshine I felt I needed to read more than I needed to eat and so I carried the book inside and bought it.

Examining the book jacket later that afternoon sitting on a bench in the Jardin du Luxembourg and before beginning to read, I wondered what *Confessions of a Mask* by Yukio Mishima might be about. On the cover of this UK paperback edition was an oriental man, stocky rather than muscled, stripped to the waist – not Mishima himself, who adorned the back cover and was also stripped to the waist, his muscles clearly defined and bulging, and holding a sword. The man on the front jacket I decided was a model, his arms raised above his head, bound at the wrists in a pose invoking the martyrdom of St Sebastian. He was wearing only a white loincloth. Instead of arrows three samurai swords menaced the body from different directions. Had one just sliced into the exposed flesh? – a line of too-red fake blood traced a path across the right breast. We can see the black bush of his exposed left armpit. Was this man being tortured? I knew nothing much about the martyrdom of St Sebastian. Or about the author Mishima. It wasn't clear if this book was a memoir or a novel – although the word 'Fiction' which appeared on the back suggested the latter. The critical quotes praised the honesty of the writing, and as it had cost only 6 francs it was honesty I could afford.

Another envelope was lying on the floor as I sleepily groped my way towards the coffee-making equipment one morning. I slit open the letter as I munched on some toast and glanced at the headlines in the *Japan Times*.

The letter was from Yoshio Funasaka. He was, he said, happy to meet me, suggesting a date a week from today, 3 p.m., at his office in the Taiseidō bookstore. I was to ask for him on the third floor.

So did Mishima hanker for the chaos of a wartime emergency? Many who lived through the most recent large-scale conflagration, the Second World War, look back on this time with a sense of nostalgia. They were most alive, paradoxically, when faced with the prospect of their own imminent deaths. The small things could be set aside. There were pragmatic reasons to appreciate the wisdom of seizing the day. No one lacked for an example of someone for whom tomorrow did not come. So it was not the fact that opportunities for heroism might arise in some distant field or patch of sea or sky, but that the proximity of death rendered trivial the things which in a time of peace obsess us all. Can I afford this bauble? Will I look good in this dress? Nonsense, and seen to be nonsense when viewed up close and with the fact of one's own mortality brought daily to mind.

Was Mishima nostalgic for the war? Not from his own experiences. But perhaps he was nostalgic for the seriousness of living that such emergencies provoke. People were having to cope daily with death, privation, the elimination of hope and ambition. They were forced into a shortened timeframe, and as a survival strategy had to live in the present moment. There was no future. Tomorrow really never comes.

Is Mishima concerned with decadence and if so is he a hypocrite? He lived in considerable luxury, but nevertheless seemed above the adverse effects one might expect such an environment to engender. He was, above all, a man of discipline and judged the world around him by his own impossible standards. He found that youth and contemporary society had degenerated into soft living and self-indulgence in the pursuit of the staggeringly trivial. Discipline is forcing yourself to do what you do not want to do. I am typing this passage at past midnight, having resolved to write my two thousand words today even though I don't feel at all like doing them. The mind, especially a creative mind, will find endless excuses for avoiding an unpleasant task. One solution to this is to ignore all excuses – a very Japanese approach. Just focus on the outcome. What anyone says, given the mannered and circuitous forms of ordinary Japanese polite speech, is far less relevant in seeking to know what may be happening in front of your own eyes.

In the violence of overcoming, in the disorder of my laughter and sobbing, in the excess of raptures that shatter me, I seize on the similarity between a horror and a voluptuousness that goes beyond me, between an ultimate pain and an unbearable joy.

GEORGES BATAILLE, *The Tears of Eros*

Kamen no Kokuhaku, translated as *Confessions of a Mask*, was published to critical acclaim and with gratifying sales in 1949. It was a breakthrough work for Mishima, and had it failed might well have sunk the depressed young writer in his resolve to keep going.[64] The topic – a novelised account of homosexual alienation – was controversial and unprecedented in Japan or anywhere else at that time – Gore Vidal was about to publish *The City and the Pillar*. But there was nothing new about an author choosing to shock the public as the means to raise his head above the crowd, guaranteeing otherwise hard-won attention.

The household into which Kimi-chan,[65] the narrator, is born comprises ten adults – his parents, his (paternal) grandparents and six maids – all living on top of each other in a rented house. The family fortunes are in serious decline and grandmother, the dominant family member, is both ill and filled with hate for her financially inept husband, perhaps blaming her semi-invalid status on syphilis contracted from his hinted sexual infidelities. Kimi-chan is taken from his parents' care and moved into his grandmother's sick room at only forty-five days old to preserve him from the perhaps imaginary dangers of life on the second story of the house where his parents have their quarters. He will stay in this odd situation until the age of twelve.

This excess of grandmotherly care is partly due to a perception that the boy is weak and sickly and might easily die. He suffers a fall at one, then contracts 'auto-intoxication', a kind of digestive disorder, at four. He soon becomes resigned to the idea of being permanently excluded from the physically tumultuous life of a boy. He encounters a nightsoil man, hinting at a precocious eroticism directed towards an inappropriate object of excitement, a young man's thighs and the 'soil' and its source. He retreats into the third reality, his burgeoning imagination.

Kimi-chan accounts for his interior development by referring to the power of fairy stories, consumed eagerly in picture books. He regrets that Joan of Arc is not a man, and designates this as 'life taking revenge' by imposing an undesirable reality, something that can only really be a source of disappointment to a romantic fantasist. Outside in the 'real word' soldiers march by, offering up their male scents of sweat and handing over empty cartridge cases to the watching children. They are tragic figures fated to go far away to die.

Kimi-chan concludes that his life is subject to Augustinian predetermination, that in these early experiences reside all the clues to his future, to how he must live.

He is taken to the theatre and instantly feels an overwhelming empathy for a famous actress, Shōkyokusai Tenkatsu. He dresses up in his mother's clothes and realises that he has no capacity for accepting the love of others – in this case his mother's, which seems dependent on his conformity. He is too wilful ever to yield to another. In his ongoing reading he retreats into the limitless landscape of the imagination – a world of princes and princesses, the princes fated to be killed, handsome young men who die young. He particularly likes Andersen's tale 'The Rose-Elf', where a youth is stabbed and decapitated by a villain with a big knife. He finds in this his own fascinations, a lust for Death, the Night and Blood, an urge he is unaware is perverse and which will prove irresistible.

In a revealing comment, when playing at war with two female cousins, Kimi-chan realises that his true nature is considered a pose – as when he dressed in his mother's kimono in imitation of the actress – whereas his pose, playing war as a boy, is accepted instead as his real nature. Things are upside down.

Aged twelve, Kimi-chan is troubled by spontaneous erections and his awakening sexuality and sexual curiosity. Nowhere can he find answers to the questions he wishes to ask. He discovers that what he had hitherto taken to be a poetic impulse, an aesthetic interest in male bodies, is in fact an erotic urge. He also discovers that this urge is stimulated by other darker things, by 'death and pools of blood and muscular flesh'.

The household living arrangements suddenly change. Kimi-chan is reclaimed to live with his mother and father, joining his younger brother and sister. His grandmother, distraught at this development, can only be consoled by a kind of custody visit for one night each week – at twelve, Kimi-chan realises, he has a true love sweetheart, a woman aged sixty.

Left alone at home with a cold he finds a concealed book belonging to his father. It includes a painting by Guido Reni of the martyrdom of St Sebastian, a muscular young man, his hands held aloft, his body tied to a tree and shot full of arrows. Kimi-chan unconsciously begins to masturbate and experiences his first ejaculation whilst lost in this, for him, intensely erotic image.

Kimi-chan's prose poem to St Sebastian, written in his teens, describes the outsider and would-be artistic genius, using martyrdom as a metaphor of his situation – 'this brand [i.e. martyrdom] which fate had set upon him was precisely the token of his apartness from all the ordinary men of earth.'

At Middle School, as a day boy – Kimi-chan is not allowed to board, as would be normal for a year or two, due to his delicate health – Kimi-chan forms an obsessive interest in another day boy, Ōmi. Ōmi is rumoured to have sexual experience with girls and to have a big thing – *mono*, thing, is a common euphemism for penis – and delights in breaking the school uniform code, wearing flashy socks and a white muffler. Ōmi stands for the spirit of individual rebellion against authority, but is finally shown to suffer from extreme loneliness despite his bravado.

One morning Kimi-chan literally follows in Ōmi's footsteps, walking in marks left in the snow. Finding the older boy alone scratching his name in the drifts in Roman letters he realises quite how alone Ōmi is, that his confident behaviour is a persona, a pose, and perhaps identifying with this falls in love with him. It is Kimi-chan's first love at the age of fourteen – not a pure love, but bound up with lust for Ōmi's muscular physique and big thing.

Ōmi becomes a model for the future erotic character and desires of Kimi-chan, who identifies his initial attraction as a revolt against reason, then without further explanation claims that for him – a rational intellectual – such a revolt is absolutely impossible.

There is a highly symbolic fight between Kimi-chan and Ōmi on a swinging log. Kimi-chan struggles between hanging back, an instinct for self-preservation, and hazarding its suicidal opposite – risking all. Both boys fall down together as Ōmi realises he is loved, and they walk away, to assembly, arm in arm, an experience Kimi-chan wants to go on for ever.

Kimi-chan watches Ōmi exercising on the horizontal bar in gym class, and identifies a Nietzschean quality of abundant life. Ōmi is so utterly vibrant and alive that it seems like a challenge to anyone who is less alive:

> . . . the feeling he gave of having too much life, by the feeling of purposeless violence that can be explained

only as life existing for its own sake, by his type of
ill-humoured, unconcerned exuberance.

Kimi-chan no longer senses his own vulnerability in Ōmi, his
abject loneliness. Instead he sees Ōmi's power and feeling jealous of this trait, instantly 'falls out of love'.

Kimi-chan sets out to achieve a transformation of his will,
devising Spartan exercises, focused on a single idea: Be strong!
He stares at people on trolley cars until they look away, as a
corrective exercise to counter his natural shyness. At the same
time he is mocked by a friend for his poor health and told he
will surely die before he is twenty.

During summer vacation Kimi-chan's family visit the seaside.
He is fascinated with the power of the sea, yet unable to swim.
He stretches out alone on the beach, and gazing at the nascent
hairs growing in his own armpit begins to masturbate, for the
first time in the open air. He allows his sperm to merge with
the invisible microscopic teeming life of the sea.

On returning to school Kimi-chan finds Ōmi has been
expelled, for unspecified reasons. He develops anaemia, is taken
to see a doctor. The doctor silently examines a textbook, whilst
Kimi-chan reads over his shoulder that self-pollution is one
possible diagnosis. He feels his guilt growing and analyses his
own situation as a deficiency of blood – contrasting Ōmi's abun-
dance of blood.

His thoughts turn towards blood in a more literal sense. He
begins to imagine a theatre of murder. He prefers ancient bladed
weapons to modern explosive ones. And, in order to prolong a
victim's agony, the target for any cutting must be the belly. Such
blood lust progresses to its ultimate conclusion – the basest
dream possible: cannibalism of a living person.

In his dream a classmate with a nice body is lured into a
chamber and strangled into unconsciousness by a burly cook.
The body is stripped naked and placed face-up on a huge customised platter with five holes to enable the arms, legs and head
to be tied down. The body is hefted into the dining hall, where
a gathering, all faceless, only rows of hands visible, clamours to
be served this diabolical meal. Kimi-chan stabs the victim with

a fork, is sprayed with his blood, and then begins to slice up his chest.

Kimi-chan decides he must somehow begin to live, to live a true life – but this sentence is in the form of a question. What is a true life? Even pure masquerade will do, at least as a beginning – it is time to leave the waiting room, get on the train and find out where it is bound.

Life is chaos, a conglomeration of falsehoods. Stefan Zweig is quoted in support of the idea that what we call evil is just a portion of the original chaos out of which man was born.

Lacking any interest in women, Kimi-chan is free of the inherent shyness natural to adolescent boys of that time. His lack of erotic interest means that for Kimi-chan both the idea 'woman' and the reality, and the ideas and objects 'pencil', 'automobile', 'broom', have the same essential quality. They invoke a more or less indifferent reaction. Is it in fact the case that when we lack any erotic connection to someone they begin to fade back into the vast category of things about which one is aware but mostly indifferent? Spark plugs. Knitting needles. Computer games. The population of Luxembourg.

Kimi-chan fails to find reassurance in the fact that his classmates have taken up his 'bad habit' with single-minded enthusiasm. It provides no evidence of his being 'normal' – not other – as although the physical actions are the same, the mental landscape is quite different. They are utterly focused on women, and he on a much more bizarre erotic scenario of homosexual sadism.

Kimi-chan wonders if his failure to follow the path of normal sexual development is simply laziness. Perhaps he just cannot be bothered to understand the alien nature and culture of the opposite gender, and instead falls back on what he knows well – his own kind, males. Yet the fact that most males are fascinated with females makes his very preference a paradox, for theirs is a fascination he can only understand by approximation and metaphor.

He reads in novels about how a boy of his age should feel. He is researching in the same way an actor might try to enter into character. He reviews his feelings towards the women he

has encountered in his life. His cousin Sumiko, who affection-
ately rested her head on his lap. A woman who seems to be
suffering from anaemia glimpsed on a bus. What is love? he asks
himself, but can make no connection between his ideas on love
and his feelings of sexual desire. Why should they be connected?
His erotic feelings seem to have arisen without any linkage to
notions of love. For him, love is a pure emotion so delicate that
to express it is to endanger it. The idea of sexual love is an
obvious contradiction in terms. He finds that his feelings for
males and females have separated into discrete categories, that
they do not compete, as they are so distinct.

Kimi-chan subjects himself to an extraordinary degree of scrutiny, dissecting himself alive, confessing what any ordinary
person of that time (and in some reaches of any time) might
regard with shame and horror: autoeroticism, homosexuality, a
desire to murder, sexual excitement at the sight of blood and
another's slow death. Cannibalism.

Kimi-chan experiments with inducing feelings of love towards
the sister of a school friend. These feelings are seen as artificial.
At the same time he finds he has widened his homoerotic long-
ings to include boys younger than himself. 'To my love of the
savage there had now been added a love for the graceful and
gentle ... along with my natural growth there was developing
in me something like a guardian's love, something akin to boy-
love.' Although the word love is used, he means desire.

The subject shifts from love to death. The war is the background to this account and the prospect of death, of a life
foreshortened, is taken as the one certainty by Kimi-chan's generation. He claims he is looking forward to death 'impatiently'.
The notion of a glorious death in battle seems like an ironic
joke waiting to ambush him as he notes his fear of air raids.

Kimi-chan claims he has no particular desire for friendship,
no wish for friends, and is willing to take risks with the relation-
ships he has. Is this a form of self-justification for a lonely boy
with no particular talent for friendship?

He is forced to explore how he will live in a conventional
society, although why this matters for someone convinced he is
shortly to die in the war is not explained. He argues that he can

love a girl without feeling the slightest desire for her – then labels this conviction 'probably the most foolhardy undertaking since the beginning of human history'.

The notion of purity is, for Kimi-chan, a seductive one. A pure form of love, a love of purity itself.

Kimi-chan is put to work in support of the total war effort. He is assigned to work in an enormous factory manufacturing Tokko,[66] kamikaze planes. Manufacturing death itself.

Now old enough to be drafted, he is called up for a medical examination. He is misdiagnosed as having TB, whilst suffering from a severe cold and because he is abnormally thin and weedy – a swot, with skin so translucent that his veins seem purple against the pallor of his skin. He feels relief at having cheated death. So then is his professed desire to die nothing more than mere acceptance of the inevitable, a form of resignation to the plight of a nation at war?

Despite these inconsistent feelings, Kimi-chan expresses a disgust for the notion of 'death in ordinary life', its mere tawdriness. He desires something more for himself, an heroic end. Not exactly a meaningful death, but not a mundane one. 'What I wanted was to die among strangers, untroubled, beneath a cloudless sky.'

An insignificant death is one of the characteristics of an insignificant life. Death is not merely something that happens, like a battery running out of power, a gradual fading and then nothing. Rather, it is an event itself. And for the ambitious man, the nature of his own death should equal his ambitions for his life. To expire in bed at home, or worse still in a hospital bed: how banal for a man of destiny, a man marked for glory. Something so dull and ordinary can have no part in the story of a great man. We remember beginnings and endings. Endings are so often our epitaph.

There is a sense of anticlimax as Kimi-chan realises that nothing in the rest of his life will yield an experience equal to his sense of relief at having escaped death in the army. Life already over at eighteen. The time to come a downhill slide, a living death.

How might a sadist react to the idea that his own desire to

die has been frustrated by a mistake? He imagines scenarios where someone who desires above all things to die is repeatedly refused by Death, his suffering equalling the pleasure such scenes bring to Kimi-chan. How baroque an idea. How perverse. It recalls the joke about the masochist asking the sadist to hurt him, and the sadist, keen to deny the seeker's pleasure, refusing.

Sonoko, Kimi-chan's first girlfriend, evokes something like real love and utterly amazes him. She has a round, childlike face and provokes 'endless circles of introspection' in Kimi-chan. He wonders how his feelings compare with those of a normal boy of his age. Layer upon layer. Is his desire to believe only in counterfeit emotions a means to escape from the idea that he is truly in love with Sonoko and to that extent has become normal? Is his desire for uniqueness – even at the price of being a freak – his greatest, if unspoken, ambition?

Kimi-chan eventually concludes that 'love and soul' are illusions, employed to mask the ugly facts that man is driven by primitive lusts – virility, a superabundance of vitality as exhibited in an ejaculation, the desire to kill, the letting of blood. He is running his colours up the mast as a nihilist, encamped on the Dionysian side of the divide. He discovers his real life's aim. It is death.

The theme of this novel is Kimi-chan's attempt to be normal. He tries on the roles of an ordinary young man like garments, and finds that they simply do not fit. He cannot hush the voice in the background which is harping on a more exotic fate, a sense of being special – special yet alien.

> As part of my self discipline, dating from childhood, I constantly told myself it would be better to die than become a lukewarm person, an unmanly person, a person who does not clearly know his likes and dislikes, a person who wants only to be loved without knowing how to love.

When Sonoko moves away, the pain it provokes is intense. Kimi-chan contemplates suicide, but rejects it as absurd when there are so many other likely causes of death at the time. When a letter arrives from Sonoko declaring her love for him he feels jealous of her, of her capacity to love him, seeing his love for her as a cultured pearl set beside a real one. How absurd – a man jealous of a girl for the love she feels for him!

Japan surrenders in 1945. The solution to the problem of everyday life, a certainty that he will die, evaporates. A condition of peace is for Kimi-chan a terrifying situation, as it isolates him once again, forcing him into a category comprising but a single member. He is alone with his life and faces choices of which he knows nothing.

'The measure of a woman's power is the degree of suffering with which she can punish her lover,' Kimi-chan quotes approvingly from an unnamed French writer. He attempts to manufacture desire for women – summoning provocative images while masturbating. Aged twenty-two he is still a virgin, a condition that he faces as an urgent problem to be solved. The options of the day are to visit a prostitute or to marry. Stark choices: wife or whore. A friend who is already familiar with the world of brothels offers to take him along, and with some reluctance he agrees. He fails to perform, but this fact is known only to him and the prostitute – 'Ten minutes later there was no doubt of my incapacity. My knees were shaking with shame.' This terrible fact, were it to be guessed at by his friend, would let the cat out of the bag and reveal his secret nature.

Kimi-chan's image of himself falls to a new low, echoing the despairing themes and existential angst of Osamu Dazai novels – an author Mishima claimed to despise. He now regards himself as having become 'not human . . . a being who is incapable of social intercourse . . . nothing but a creature, non-human and strangely pathetic'. The issue of sex suggests a wider problem – the idea of potency, of being effectual, able to act on the world rather than just passively receiving whatever may happen, simply reacting. To be an actor, not a reactor. Kimi-chan meditates on the absurdities of passions – if we can employ passion to rise above life's absurdities, why not rise above the absurdity of passion itself?

Bookish by nature, Kimi-chan researches into homosexuality and concludes that his situation is not, in fact, uncommon. He reads the German sexologist pioneer Magnus Hirschfeld;[67]

learns about the adventures of Count Von Platen in Venice in the early nineteenth century, and of an even earlier figure, the art historian Johann Joachim Winckelmann, whose adventurous sex life led to his being stabbed and strangled to death in a tavern in Trieste in 1768. And, of course, the poems of Michelangelo. But even these discoveries, an intellectual grasp of the widespread nature of homosexual desire, do nothing to solve his emotional problems: he feels no better for knowing that his plight is not unique.

Kimi-chan realises that his feelings towards other men and boys are limited to sexual desire. He is not seeking any kind of relationship, just sex. A Teflon-coated sex, satiety without strings. He offers the idea that he has given his soul to Sonoko, and thus it is unavailable to anyone else – a male lover, for example. He cleaves himself, somewhat neatly, into two parts – spirit and flesh – and allocates the former to Sonoko – the normal world, 'my love of normality itself, my love of things of the spirit, my love of everlasting things' – and the latter to his homosexual desires. This is, of course, a means by which love can remain pure, a classical courtly love – frustrated and denied it must remain, as its gratification will sully it.

Sonoko marries, and when Kimi-chan encounters her some years later by accident they arrange to meet up from time to time. They have coffee and talk. Innocent encounters. Finally he takes her to a dance hall. Inside it is hot as hell, and the atmosphere sleazy – not the place to bring a woman like Sonoko. She asks him if he has yet lost his virginity, and lying, he tells her yes.

In the hall couples are dancing. The dance of life itself, 'a dance without end'. Kimi-chan watches a group which includes a young tough, a gangster whose upper body is naked and muscled. He is rewinding a belly band and has a peony tattoo on his chest. His is a rough and savage beauty. This image wholly absorbs Kimi-chan's attention until he realises he has forgotten Sonoko's existence. It is a moment of self-realisation. As they leave the dance hall Kimi-chan looks again for the young man, seeking a final glimpse. But he has gone. A presentiment of his future? Fleeting encounters with men who love women, for ever just out of reach, in sleazy places.

Before he established his own small militia, the Shield Society, Tate no Kai, Mishima had a far grander vision. He planned to form and finance up to 100,000 men in something akin to a National Guard, an organisation he called Sokoku Bōei Tai, or Homeland Defence Group. This more ambitious scheme was abandoned when Mishima decided that financing it would compromise his aims – he would need help, and the conditions attaching to any such assistance would be unacceptable. Instead, with two university students he met while training with the Ground Self Defence Forces, Nakatsuji and Mochimaru, he recruited the first volunteers into a new society, one which had as its primary declared purpose the simple defence of the Emperor and the upholding of Japan's traditional culture, something they all believed was under attack. The Shield Society formally came into existence on 5 October 1968.

Earlier that year, on the significant date of 26 February, Mishima had met with several students he had told about his goal of forming a militia, and they had joined him in signing a document, writing their names in their own blood – a *keppan*, a type of blood-oath which is a traditional means to indicate the seriousness of an undertaking and is still used in some martial arts systems on the admission of a new member to the school. The blood from each pricked finger dripped into a teacup. Once the signatures had been written, the left-over blood was sipped by each man present. 'I hope no one has syphilis,' Mishima joked.

Perhaps fearing ridicule, and as part of the process of tidying up his life before his suicide, in January 1970 Mishima arranged to have the *keppan* document stolen and destroyed. None of the original signatories remained connected to him. They were no longer members of the Tate no Kai, despite their commitment to die for each other and for their aims.

In the eyes of others, the man who donned a uniform became
thereby, quite simply, a combatant.

Yukio Mishima, *Sun and Steel*

A new militia needs something to identify its members, a uniform. Mishima consulted a leading designer, Tsukumo Igarashi, who had designed military uniforms for General de Gaulle. Two designs, one for winter – a sand-coloured double-breasted tunic with two rows of brass buttons and green cuff and collar flashes, with tightly cut trousers, a belt and a peaked cap adorned with a distinctive badge taken from a samurai helmet design – and a summer uniform in white. They would cost ¥30,000 each. Mishima ordered one hundred sets, the maximum number of members he would accept in his elite corps.

The Japanese press was quick to react to a first sighting of Mishima in uniform and his public statements about what he was up to, about his militia and its aims. 'Captain Mishima's Toy Army,' read one headline. The uniforms may have resembled those of a Hollywood costume drama, but the young men so oddly garbed were deadly serious.

Mishima told his cadets that the rioting leftist students were sure to attempt a revolution, to attack the Imperial Palace, and in such circumstances the Tate no Kai, armed only with Japanese swords, would rush to the Palace gates and die in defence of the Emperor, certain to be overwhelmed by the sheer numbers of their enemies. Mishima had selected nine young men of the Tate no Kai and armed each of them with a sword. Three of the final four who would accompany him on the Last Day were included – Morita among them. By this time he had become the cadet captain and was among the most zealous in insisting on a death stand in the streets.

In the event the rioting leftist students were subdued by the newly formed Tokyo riot police and no attempt was ever made by them on the Imperial Palace. The Tate no Kai were denied their moment of glory, and nearly two years would pass before Mishima decided to manufacture a crisis where he could demonstrate his acquisition of all the attributes of a warrior, his means to a hero's death.

I had taken about five steps beyond Ken's door when I realised that the two men walking on either side of me were my gangster visitors of the week before. They nodded, a tiny acknowledging bow. I stopped and asked if I could help them.

Now they bowed more formally.

'Please come with us.'

I bowed back.

'Where are we going?'

'Our boss would like to talk to you. Please, follow us. We have a car near by. It will not take long and then we shall bring you back.'

In the seven days since we had last seen each other these two men had apparently learned manners. Their tone and language were super-polite. On the spur of the moment I decided it would be better to cooperate than be stalked by gangsters.

A few streets away there was a large car with darkened windows, a Lexus of some sort, with leather seats. I was seated sandwiched between the tall and the wide man while a man I had never seen before drove. In about twenty minutes we had arrived. A downtown location by the look of it, somewhere in

Shitamachi, from the couple of landmarks I had noticed on the way. I was led into an ordinary office building.

The room of the yakuza boss could have been the office of any moderately prosperous businessman. There was a large rosewood desk, a leather sofa and several leather easy chairs. Gangsters liked leather, I concluded. One of the goons sent to fetch me was wearing a black leather sports jacket of extremely high quality, which I suspected was Hermès. I had tried on a similar jacket in Paris a few months before, and knew they cost £3,000.

I was given tea, and after perhaps five minutes the middle-aged man in Ken's photographs appeared. He bowed and offered me a card, which I swapped for one of mine. My cards had only my name, the word writer and a mobile telephone number. The boss's card was more impressive. I recognised the name of his gang, which was openly stated on the card. It was a large organisation whose leaders tended to die unnaturally and was, in general, very dangerous.

'Thank you for coming Mr Ross. I am sorry to take up your time when you are a guest in our country and I am sure are busy. I would like, if you don't mind, to ask you about our mutual friend Mr Hiramatsu. My associates tell me he is not at his bar and has gone away. That you are currently living in his apartment and that you do not know when he will return.'

'Yes, that is all correct. I am sorry but Hiramatsu-san likes to vanish sometimes. If you know him well you will know that.'

'Yes. I do know him well. We like to drink at his bar. Are you quite sure you do not know where he is right now?'

'Yes. Quite sure. I think he will come back after I have left.'

'When, if I might ask, will that be?'

'That depends.'

'Depends? On what exactly?'

'I am looking for the sword used by the writer Yukio Mishima in committing seppuku in 1970. So far I have not found it or much trace of it. It is important to me, I am writing a book about it.'

'Hmmm. The sword used by Mishima? A book? And if you find it you will return home?'

'Yes. Yes I will.'

He paused, swivelled round on his chair to stare out of the window for a minute or two, and then turned back to me.

'I see. Thank you Mr Ross. Please call me if you do hear from Mr Hiramatsu. I would like to see him as soon as possible. Thank you for coming here. I will have you driven back to Shibuya.'

The meeting was over, and less than half an hour later I was standing opposite Shibuya Station wondering what was happening. Was I in any danger? Was Ken? I knew almost everyone in the *mizu shōbai*[68] had dealings with gangsters, but usually that was routine. Protection payments. Unlikely to involve the boss of a yakuza gang.

The Swordmaster was nearly ninety years old. In fact it was his ninetieth birthday in two days' time. To meet him I had to pass through a number of layers of scrutiny. He was a kind and forthcoming man, and those around him were determined he should not be exploited in some way. After some unsavoury past encounters, they were suspicious of the motives of writers and journalists.

I had taken care to approach in a formally correct manner, submitting an introduction from one of the Swordmaster's senior students whom I had travelled to meet in England, and mentioning my connection to a highly regarded aikidō dōjō in Tokyo. The founder of our school had been the head of the aikidō division of the International Budo Organisation and the Swordmaster headed the *battō-dō* section. By some means of reckoning, the Swordmaster was the greatest living *kenshi*, swordsman, in Japan.

We had arranged to meet in a restaurant near the Swordmaster's house, in a suburb of Yokohama. Apart from the kindness of wanting to give me lunch, I thought one reason for this was that the Swordmaster probably lived in modest circumstances. This was quite normal for authentic teachers of budō – they never got rich from a lifetime of practising and teaching the martial arts and usually managed to keep going only with the backing of business sponsors or wealthy individuals ready to support traditional culture.

In addition to wanting to ask about various controversial ideas in budō and the technical possibilities of a Japanese sword, I was interested in the Swordmaster for one very specific reason: he had formerly owned Mishima's sword, and had sold it to his kendō student Hiroshi Funasaka.

At the appointed time I was met by Roberto, a Brazilian *deshi* of the Swordmaster. He too was an interesting man. He had travelled to Europe and worked on a stud farm in England, employed for his skill in breaking horses, having been a kind of South American cowboy, although not a gaucho. He journeyed on, and ended up in Japan, intending to study swordsmithing, and apprenticing himself to a smith who made swords in the Soshū tradition. In the course of his studies he became interested in learning how to wield a sword, as well as to manufacture one, and took up *iaidō* and later *battō-dō*. Now he was a *deshi*, or disciple, of the Swordmaster. His Japanese was good. When we first met I used an interpreter, as a device to give me time to frame my replies. He spoke in Japanese, and was then translated, I spoke in English, and was similarly translated. It soon became obvious that each of us understood the other's replies before they were translated – that I spoke Japanese and he English. Later we spoke to each other in English without referring to the oddness of our earlier conversation.

The Swordmaster's legs were no longer strong, and he was helped to walk into the restaurant by Roberto, who had gone downstairs to meet the arriving taxi. The Swordmaster had brought along his daughter, who wanted to monitor what was taking place. We all sat round a low table with a sunken well for your legs, avoiding the need to fold them beneath you. The Swordmaster was a little deaf, and his daughter positioned herself on his right side to relay my comments and questions if she sensed he had failed to hear or understand what I said. He was dressed in Western clothes, a suit and tie – the tie kept in place, I noticed, not by a tiepin but by a paper clip. In the buttonhole of his jacket was a golden Chrysanthemum pin, signifying the receipt of an imperial order.

I handed over my bottle of good sake, as custom dictated, and thanked the Swordmaster for agreeing to see me. For a few moments we spoke about mutual friends, and then I asked him about the sword.

'It was not Seki no Magoroku. It looked like the second Kanemoto, but was not by him. If it had been I would never have sold it. I bought it in the early 1960s from a sword shop near here, next to the police station in Tobe. I remember paying ¥40,000. I sold it in 1965 to Funasaka, the man who owns Taiseidō bookshop, for ¥50,000, having used it for around five years. The blade was slightly damaged, a couple of chips, from cutting hard bamboo. The papers with the sword attributed it to a later-generation Kanemoto, but there was no signature on the *nakago*.'

Lunch arrived. Large lacquered boxes with a variety of foods, some mysterious and unidentifiable, including large cold prawns, hard to eat.

'After the Mishima incident a shrine in Kumamoto tried to buy the sword for over ¥3,000,000. They didn't get it though. I would have heard about it. I was called to identify the sword by the police and went to see it. It was covered in dried blood and there were more chips and it was slightly bent.

'Mishima was a very polite man. He washed my back in the bath. He was famous yet he understood how to behave. I taught him a few times. Kendō at the Shibuya Police dōjō. I never taught him *iaidō*. His kendō was OK, but not especially good. He started too late in life and had stiff wrists. He trained hard and had good concentration.

'You asked me about cutting a machine-gun barrel. No, I do not think a Japanese sword can cut a machine-gun barrel. The article I think you are referring to appeared during the war and was propaganda. I was a fencing instructor during the war and the standard of swordsmanship was very poor. We were trying to train people in too short a time and focused on instantly effective techniques. A sword is not a weapon to employ against many opponents. It will chip or break or bend. The other story you mentioned about cutting down one hundred men is simply impossible unless you kept changing swords. I do not believe this ever happened.[69] After the war I went to see a former officer who had killed in battle using a sword. He had been sentenced to imprisonment as a war criminal, but once he got out I was interested to ask him technical questions and so went to see him. I have never killed a man with a sword. I was once asked to kill some cows for food and did succeed in cutting off the heads of two cows with a single cut in each case.

'I do not think there is a *kami*, or spirit, in the blade of a sword. But a sword is worthy of respect, for what it represents. It is a symbol of our cultural history. It is made with great skill and to use it requires sincere efforts over a long period. All this taken together is worthy of respect. Once I saw an advertisement for an exhibition of a photographer's work at a gallery in the Ginza. One picture showed a Japanese sword between the naked buttocks of a woman. I dressed in a kimono and took my sword and went to visit the gallery. I told them this was an abuse of a national symbol. The photographer looked very frightened. Well, I am a small man but I have a serious face sometimes. He apologised, and satisfied with this I left.

'I think *budō* is dying. It takes so long to achieve anything genuine, I feel young Japanese cannot now devote the time to learn. They are busy with speeded-up lives. I have excellent students from other parts of the world. Never mind *yamato damashii* [Japanese spirit], I found excellent *doitsu-damashii* [German spirit] in Germany. In Korea too there are good students.

'I agree with you about modern swords. Many are beautiful, but never having been tested against targets would not function as swords. In short they are works of art, not weapons.

'Mishima's *kaishaku* messed it up. But Mishima was spiritually very strong. His cutting was accomplished in *seiza* and he cut very deep. I respect his spirit and have attended the Yūkokuki and demonstrated *battō-dō* at the event held for Mishima at the Yasukuni Shrine.

'I gave the former prime minister Hashimoto a sword. He is a kendōka and knows a good deal about *budō*. Here are some photographs of the memorial of me paid for by this municipality. And this is for you.'

The Swordmaster, who was also a nationally famous calligrapher, handed me a verse he had written on a scrap of paper before leaving home to join me at this lunch.

After we had finished eating and had had some tea the Swordmaster told his daughter they needed to see about getting him a new driving licence. I thought I wouldn't want to drive with this ninety-year-old man, but put a sword in his hand and you would feel, justly, entirely safe.

In Japanese there is a number of quite ordinary expressions that use the language and terminology of swordsmanship. In English, the equivalent is perhaps nautical terms, which abound in proverbial and ordinary expression. In Japan it is not ships and the sea but swords and the men who wielded them, the samurai. One such term, *shinken shōbu*, literally means a fight to the death using live blades, real swords. Figuratively it is now used to refer to making a renewed and serious effort, or challenging someone in a serious manner.

We were sitting in the back office on the third floor of the Taiseidō building. Although Yoshio Funasaka was Shachō, the boss, in typical Japanese style there was nothing to indicate this in the room he used as an office. Ordinary metal desks, filing cabinets, clutter and piles of paper. On the wall above his desk was a signed photograph of the Kyōkushinkai karate founder Masutatsu Ōyama, the man who smashed the horns off live bulls and started his career as an enforcer for Korean gangsters in Kobe. Funasaka had practised martial arts all his life, kendō as a boy and young man, then *iaidō* as an extension of his kendō training, then karate.

Yoshio Funasaka is a small man with a nice round-featured face. I tried to imagine what he looked like at nineteen, his age when he taught Mishima *iaidō* forms, including how to assist at a seppuku. Mishima had a thing about round faces, in women as in men. It was one of his conditions in the search for a suitable wife. Yes, Funasaka was his type, or one of his types. I hoped this train of thought was invisible to the smiling middle-aged man in a jacket and tie sitting across from me and sipping his tea.

'In those days we used *shinken*, real swords, for *iaidō*. Even a beginner. It made things intense and I remember how much concentration we were able to muster to avoid cutting off our fingers. Mishima studied kendō at Shibuya Police Station when I first met him. He had started kendō under Yoshikawa Sensei at the Himonya Police Station in Meguro. When Yoshikawa moved to teach at Shibuya, Mishima followed him. We studied what is now called Ōmori Ryū, but we called it Hasegawa Eishin Ryū – one of the styles of *iaidō*. Mishima was friendly to me. My father had got to know him and had given Mishima's son a sword on his fifth birthday.[70] I used to wash his back in the bath after training. He also washed mine, which was polite of him.

'One day he asked me to teach him the form *kaishaku*, and I suggested someone more senior, but he insisted he would like me to teach him. After these lessons he sent me some cloth to make a suit as a thank you. I went to his house to visit him. He was cheerful and polite and didn't talk about himself at all, or about writing. He asked me about my studies and life at university. It was a friendly and relaxed conversation. He was wearing a very smart suit, but I noticed he had holes in his socks. I sent him three pairs of socks to thank him for his interest in me. Mishima always dressed well. He told me he had once asked a taxi-driver what kind of work he thought his passenger did – and had been told "rock star".

'After he formed his militia, the Tate no Kai, his mood in the dōjō changed. He was serious all the time. And then he stopped coming.

'In my opinion his kendō was OK. My father has said he deserved his kendō ranking, that it was not an honorary award. In my opinion though, he was not really a physical man. He had good concentration powers and was good at tests, but his wrists were stiff – maybe from all that writing – and his body was inflexible.

'My father no longer has any swords. I remember we had two Seki no Magoroku katana. One was given to Mishima, as you know. My father says he regrets the gift. Perhaps, he thinks, had he not given the sword to Mishima, he would still be alive.'

I am standing outside the Mishima family home in Magome. The name board on the wall still reads 'Mishima'. It is raining, but I am sheltering under an umbrella made of clear plastic bought for a few coins at the station. There are lights on in a number of the adjacent buildings, but no sign of life in the large house beyond the wall.

I thought I had to come here to see where Mishima had lived and where many of his works had been written, although I had no idea when I set out whether the house had been sold or even demolished since Yōko's death in 1995. I could not bring myself to ring the bell or try to gain access. It was enough to wait and watch.

The house beyond the gates was a large Mediterranean-style villa, sometimes described as Spanish Baroque, of several storeys. I had leafed through a photo book called *Mishima's House* by Kishin Shinoyama, showing the garden and interior as they were at the time of Mishima's suicide. Apart from the Japanese books in Mishima's library it would have been difficult to guess that this was the house of a Japanese author. The ground floor was furnished entirely with 18th-century French antiques and the upper storeys with modern European pieces. In 1968 a French TV crew filming an interview at his home asked Mishima about this, the absence of Japanese art, his exclusive choice of European style and decoration, and he explained, 'Here, only what you cannot see is Japanese.'

More than thirty years beforehand, on another wet evening, a high-school boy had stood where I am now standing, but unlike me he had first rung the bell, asking to talk to Mishima. He was told the famous author was busy. Undaunted, the boy quietly crossed the street and waited outside in the rain. Waiting for hours or days for someone to agree to see you has a long tradition in Japan and is regarded as a demonstration of sincerity. After some hours Mishima appeared at the gates of the house, beckoned the boy over and told him, 'You may ask me one question only.' The boy hesitated, then said, 'When are you going to kill yourself?'

It was a place I had walked past hundreds of times. A small alley with an entrance you had to cross going from Ikebukuro Station to Kimi – Kimi Ryokan or Kimi Information Centre, an employment and property bureau with facilities for receiving and sending mail, much used by the gaijin community. Many gaijin spend their initial couple of weeks in Tokyo at the Kimi Ryokan, which although a traditional inn is both inexpensive and foreigner-friendly. But the alley was nondescript, and I was not surprised I had never noticed it.

Down the alley led to the entrance of Sasashū, a restaurant and sake-ya owned and run by an ex-kamikaze pilot. I had heard there was a restaurant somewhere in Ikebukuro famous for the range and excellence of its sake and notably run by a former kamikaze, but I had never tried very hard to find the place before.

I thought it would be interesting to ask Mr Sasakawa, the kamikaze pilot turned restaurateur, about his wartime experiences. Indeed his very survival seemed to pose a question. But most of all I wanted to know if he would turn out to hold nationalistic sentiments, would be right-wing, still loyal to an ideal of dying for the Emperor. Was he ever? I wondered.

I received a long and detailed reply to my letter of enquiry, and was moved by the care and attention to detail which a line or two from me had provoked. The letter went on for seven pages. I telephoned to thank Mr Sasakawa for his letter and realised on being put through that I had received a reply from his son. The son told me his father was happy to meet me. He would be happy to come along too, and I arranged to drop round late one morning the following week. The address seemed a bizarre coincidence: the block number for the building was 2–2–6, *niniroku*, the shorthand for the date of the Young Officers uprising on 26 February 1936.

Arriving on time I was met at the entrance by both Sasagawa Shūei, the father, and Sasagawa Shūji, the son. Shūji told me his father was hard of hearing as he was deaf in one ear, but promised to stay with us and help in any way he could. We went up a flight of wooden stairs after passing down a stone-clad corridor. There were alcoves floored with tatami matting and in one corner was a propeller which I later found had come from a Mitsubishi Zero fighter. On the second floor we sat next to an *irori*, a sunken hearth, on which a kettle was heating for tea.

'I joined the navy in the spring of 1944,' Shūei began, 'when I was seventeen, passing fourteenth in my flight-training class. Here, look, you can see me in this photograph. I borrowed the flying jacket to take the picture. At that stage in the war we were short of absolutely everything.

'I joined up because it seemed the right thing to do. It was expected of healthy young boys. The alternative was to do some kind of war work, like charcoal-carrying, which didn't appeal. I thought the navy was the most prestigious service but didn't really know what to expect. Certainly I had no idea of the kind of hell I was descending into.

'The base where I trained was in Ibaraki. Many of my *sempai*, seniors, went on to Tokkō units in Kyūshū, such as the one at Shikaya. By that time due to an extreme shortage of fuel the only use of aircraft was for Tokkō missions and training.

'We were treated very severely by those in charge of us, the NCOs. It was pure boot camp and quite brutal. Many of the day-to-day tasks, such as cleaning floors, which we called decks like on board ship, were conducted harshly, and if you failed in any way you would be beaten. I remember one boy was beaten to death with a stick, and I thought, this is not why I joined the navy – to be beaten to death with a stick while cleaning floors. I think things were out of hand by this stage.

'One of my fellow trainee pilots, after the war, became a yakuza, a gangster. He was eventually arrested for something and sent to prison. He told me, after he'd got out – prison was nothing. After our navy training, he said, anything else was easy.

'I survived simply because the war ended before I could be deployed. That fact combined with the shortages, so that fewer and fewer missions could be flown. There are quite a number of ex-kamikaze, ex-Tokkō, pilots still alive for the same reason. Although they are old now. My war friends come here once a month, the ones who are left, and we drink and talk about the old days.

'In the navy we were not so interested in patriotic ideas like Japanese spirit, *yamato damashī*. We believed in *kaigun damashī*, navy spirit, which was much more akin to the sort of pride in the service found in the British navy. On board ship in the Japanese navy some orders were given in English. We were less insular in our thinking, less fanatical. Except for the brutal NCOs, and I don't know why they behaved like that.

'There was a strong inter-service rivalry. We despised the army. Navy pilots were an elite, and thought themselves a cut above the crass thinking of army factions.

'Another thing. Hardly any of the crashing pilots said "Tennō

Heika Banzai," as they were about to die. The most common "last cry" was "Kā-san" – Mummy! They died for their families. To defend Japan all right, but because it was their home, where their families lived. Not for some imaginary ideal.

'You asked me about Yasukuni.[71] Well you probably know that a common expression when parting from comrades was – see you at Yasukuni. The shrine is for those who died defending the imperial cause, in recent history, in defending Japan. Yasukuni is my Mecca.

'I have no problem with Article 9 of the constitution.[72] I don't care that it is a fuzzy or contradictory law. I like it that way. Only those who have never participated in a war can be hawkish. Those who have fought never cry out for conflict – they keep silent. War is terrible. Anyway Japan has no military leaders capable of waging war.

'I thought Mishima's seppuku was a waste of a life. He should not have taken Morita with him. Mishima never fought in a real battle. For him it was a fantasy.'

Shuji nodded then added: 'Mishima made a number of predictions which have come true. Today people are only after money. No one is interested in the future and everyone is cynical about politics. Teachers used to be respected figures, but now they are just workers. Education has declined. The future is so uncertain it is a worry.'

On the way out I noticed a picture on the wall. It was a photograph of the record producer Quincy Jones, looking very young, who I was told ate at Sasashū in the 1970s. What did he eat? I asked.

'He had *nabe* – a stew made with wild duck we have specially caught with nets in Niigata.'

Later I came across a reference to the early life of Quincy Jones in his home town of Chicago. His family were so poor they caught and ate the neighbourhood rats.

Last Day   11.20 a.m.

Eleven junior officers struggle to push aside the barricade of furniture and get into the office. The gap is narrow and they can enter only one at at time, one by one facing Mishima, wielding his sword. Morita has a *tantō* knife and Ogawa a truncheon. Old Koga is guarding another of the barricaded doors armed with an improvised weapon, an ashtray taken from the General's desk, and Tiny Koga holds the blade of the *yoroidōshi* knife to General Mashita's throat.

One officer swings a *bokken* at Mishima, who parries and breaks it. Mishima thrusts his sword at 'non-lethal' targets, arms and backs. He cuts an officer across the back, and slashes at another man's wrist, nearly severing his left hand, in repelling the first wave.

Another attempt. An officer called Terao jumps in front of Morita and punches him hard in the face. Mishima cuts him on the shoulder, but he manages to wrestle the *tantō* from Morita's stunned grasp and run out of the doorway. As he climbs over the scattered barrier furniture Mishima cuts him again three times, on his back. Lines of blood soak through his shirt in the shape of the *kana ki* – キ.

At around 11.30 the assaults come to a halt and Mishima tells Colonel Yoshimatsu that he will kill Mashita unless the attempts at rescue end. He has demands, he repeats.

In October 2003, Kin, the last Crested Ibis (*Nipponia nippon*) born in the wild, dies from a brain haemorrhage on Sado Island, an outcrop of rock where deposed Japanese emperors were sometimes exiled. After thirty-five years of captivity the much-loved *toki* bird committed suicide by flinging itself repeatedly against the bars of his cage.

I'd arranged to meet the Critic at Mariage Frères. I had never been to this Ginza branch, but liked the Marais-based Maison de Thé so much that it seemed a good choice. The staff were dressed, as in Paris, in white linen, and moved around the rooms like ghosts; the opulent ambience both calming and slightly decadent too, something from a former, grander, age.

The Critic and I arrived at the same time, exchanged bows and visiting cards, and were shown to our table. When I phoned to arrange the meeting, he had stipulated that our discussion was to be off the record. I sighed as I hung up. Another anonymous contribution – I was glad I was not writing a biography.

Large menus, listing dozens of teas, some single varieties, others ingenious blends, were handed to us as we sat down. I cast my eye down the lengthy list until I found an irresistible choice. My guest decided upon Lu Yu, a smoked Chinese tea named after the Tang dynasty tea sage and author of the *Classic of Tea*. The waiter hovered with his pad whilst I delivered myself of my choice with the line: '*Watashi wa samurai desu.*' Literally, 'I am a samurai,' but understood to signify: 'My selection is samouraï-blend tea.' I could think of no other context where I might have been entitled to say this, and spent a few seconds enjoying this unlikely declaration.

After we had been served our tea – my samouraï blend scented with bergamot, like Earl Grey – the Critic considered my main question: Just how good a writer was Mishima? How would you rank him among, say, twentieth-century Japanese novelists? I waited for him to start talking, gazing for a moment out of the window. On the other side of Suzuran Dōri, over the heads of the passing crowds, I could see a Shimizu Pharmacy displaying a flashing green neon sign advertising Virginia Slims. An intermittent green shadow fell across the literary man's face, one moment there, then gone.

'Well, the magazine *Gunzō* asked exactly the same question a few years ago, although they confined themselves to the second half of the twentieth century, considering only postwar authors. They consulted fifty or so leading literary critics, including me, challenging them to name their top books and also to rank authors. As I recall, Mishima's *Confessions of a Mask* was chosen as the third-best book, his *Sea of Fertility* cycle as the fourth-best, along with several other titles. Mishima himself was selected as the most significant literary author of this period, with about 20 per cent of critics voting for him. Oe, our most recent Nobel Laureate, came third.

'You have to realise that Mishima's largest sales came from works he wrote for a magazine-reading female readership. Potboilers. Minor works. They are highly unlikely ever to be translated into foreign languages. His more literary writing was a much more specialised taste. He wrote in a baroque style. He used elaborate language and archaic forms. He was, I think, intoxicated by words, yet he often wrote in a flat style – and famously his creations seem to lack realism. They serve as devices. He populated his novels with representations of certain philosophical values. They are formulaic, if sometimes in surprising ways. Some critics think this is particularly so for his female characters, with perhaps a couple of exceptions.

'I would agree that *Confessions of a Mask* is quite remarkable. It contains some of his best, clearest and most poetic language. It also seems to me to be a truthful work, to possess a special quality that I cannot find anywhere else in his writings. Mishima had not, at the start of his career, learned to conceal himself behind his pen, and he wrote candidly what he best understood, drawing on a precocious insight into his own troubled soul. I believe he referred to this as "dissecting himself alive".

'The other thing that sets him apart is his range. He wrote very good plays. He was the only writer of his generation able to write convincing Kabuki and Noh drama. He wrote essays, poetry and much else besides. The essays, towards the end of his life, became increasingly difficult as they became more political. I doubt whether anyone outside a university faculty is reading them any longer.

'And he was prolific. Unlike Kawabata, who took thirteen years to write *Snow Country*, Mishima was a workaholic. Perhaps after such a spate of publications the public simply could not keep up. It might explain his decline in popularity between the 1950s and the 1960s.

'Mishima was seen by many in the *bundan* [literary establishment] as a buffoon. They thought his publicity stunts undermined his work. That he was a sensationalist. When he killed himself they felt vindicated. One critic said the death made a Roman candle of his work – that the death eclipsed the work to such an extent that no one would bother with it after a while. Well, there is little sign of that. It is true that Mishima's themes have less relevance to today's youngsters. But there remains a strong and steady support for Mishima and he is a consistent seller. His collected works have sold well and there is an ongoing project with further unpublished material – such as letters and diaries – due in a few years' time. I doubt if Mishima as a source of controversy has faded much. He seems to flare up from time to time. Many regard his writing as prescient.'

We had finished our tea. At the next table two women dressed expensively in kimono were talking about a friend's adultery in hushed but still audible tones.

The man who kills a man, kills a man. The man who kills
himself kills all men. As far as he is concerned, he wipes out
the world.

G. K. CHESTERTON

Mishima chose to live as if life itself was comprised solely of his own perceptions, the world nothing more than the sum of his thoughts and sensory impressions. No reality but that which I make for myself. In this schema death operates like a cosmic off switch – throw it and nothing remains. This idea is put into the thoughts of the elderly Honda in *The Decay of the Angel*, the last volume in the *Sea of Fertility* cycle:

> They made their way through the rows of banks and brokerages at fifty miles an hour. Huge, solid, the buildings spread great wings of steel and glass. Honda said to himself: 'The moment I die, they will all go.' The thought came to him as a happy one, a sort of revenge. It would be no trouble at all, tearing this world up by the roots and returning it to the void. All he had to do was to die. He took a certain minor pride in the thought that an old man who would be forgotten still had in death this incomparably destructive weapon.

A man may be hard to persuade by rational argument while he
is easily swayed by a display of passion, even if feigned.

YUKIO MISHIMA, *Spring Snow*

Last Day 12.00 noon

The soldiers assembled below the balcony gaze up, shouting to each other. Explanations of what is taking place – that Mishima is holding General Mashita hostage in his office, that a fight has injured a dozen SDF personnel, that he has a sword. They are told Mishima will soon make a speech. The police arrive. There are helicopters, some police, some press, buzzing overhead. The noise of the men and the sirens and the helicopters is considerable.

A banner written on cloth falls over the edge of the balcony. It orders the men to hear Mishima without interruption, in absolute silence. It warns that any attack will get the General killed and that Mishima will commit seppuku. Mishima, holding his Seki no Magoroku sword, stalks up and down the balcony waiting for the crowd to fall silent. Morita is throwing down copies of a 'Last Appeal', *Gekibun*, which Mishima intends to read out, followed by an improvised plea to the men to rise up and attack parliament, the Diet, where the Emperor is in attendance.

Finding he can wait no longer, Mishima hands his sword to Morita and steps on to the edge of the balcony, raising his hands, his outstretched palms clearly visible from below due to the white gloves he is wearing. He wears a *hachimaki* around his head, as do the others, signalling his deadly resolve. *Seven Lives for the Emperor* is inscribed on either side of a *hinomaru*, the red circle that appears on the Japanese flag, the colour of freshly shed blood. Mishima mentally steadies himself. He has long suffered from vertigo and joked at the last preparatory meeting that his fear of heights would be a greater problem than cutting his stomach.[73]

He starts to read and the crowd quietens slightly. Then the shouting begins. 'Why did you injure our mates?' 'Gangster.' 'Get down and let the General go.' Someone keeps screaming: 'Shoot him.' After he has read the text of his appeal over an increasingly noisy crowd, which takes about five minutes or so, he stops. There is no point going on. No one can hear. No one is listening. He jumps back down and followed by Morita returns to the window to re-enter General Mashita's office.

I had learned many things about Mishima's sword. I knew how it had been made, could identify the characteristics of the Kanemoto line of swordsmiths in the Mino-den tradition. I knew what the signature temper line looked like, that the first and second Kanemoto smiths known as Seki no Magoroku used a signature Sanbonsugi, or Three Cedar Tree, *hamon*. I knew who had owned the sword before Mishima. Had discovered how it became chipped, not on the battlefield as Mishima had imagined, but cutting green bamboo. I knew its value in 1965. I had been told how badly it had been damaged after cutting off Mishima's and Morita's heads and I knew its dimensions, shape and likely state (rusted, chipped and slightly bent). I knew it was *mumei* – without a smith's signature – and had been shortened at some time. And that a shrine in Kumamoto had tried to buy it for 3,000,000 yen. I knew that Yōko Mishima had refused to take it when it was offered to the family following the Tate no Kai trial, a decision that was easy to understand as it was still caked with the dried blood of her dead husband. I now knew all about metallurgy and the crafts employed in manufacturing sword fittings. I had even found the man who taught Mishima how to commit suicide according to the formal rituals of seppuku.

Yet although I now knew a great deal about Mishima's sword I felt I was no closer to finding the sword itself, or even to making a reasonable guess at what had become of it. It had last been seen in public during the trial, when it was in the custody of the police as physical evidence of a crime. Then nothing. The police told me they no longer had it, but did not say what might have happened to it. I had reached a dead end. All the leads had been followed and the trails had led nowhere. I had no idea where to look next.

Shinigurui, a term coined in the *Hagakure*, combines the *kanji* for dying with that for going mad to signify the idea of a death-madness, mania for death. This was, Yamamoto said, necessary to achieve any great deed, and first required a state of mind able to set aside self-interest and the instict for survival.

The *Hagakure* instructed that the prospect of dying should be anticipated daily – like the Stoics' *premeditatio* – so that when it inevitably occurred, it could be faced calmly and with due dignity.

The idea of altered states of consciousness where death is willingly sought is hard for the youth-obsessed West to digest. Nevertheless they exist.

> *Of all that is written, I love only what a man has written with*
> *his blood. Write with blood, and you will find that blood is spirit.*
> NIETZSCHE, *Thus Spake Zarathustra*

Last Day 🕐 *12.10 p.m.*

Gore Vidal claimed Japanese friends had described Mishima's seppuku as vulgar. An authentic seppuku, they said, was an aesthetic act of precise formalism carried out in private, not in front of so many witnesses. Indeed Mishima had investigated to see if there was any chance to televise it. Failing this he would have to make do with the men in General Mashita's office, and whoever might gain a glimpse from the adjacent rooms of the drama unfolding inside it.

If Mishima had looked up at those windows he would have seen a row of military and police faces gazing in disbelief through the glass part of the partition wall separating General Mashita's office from the outer office. More witnesses. Old Koga is leaning against the piled-up furniture which had been used to barricade the door. Tiny Koga is still positioned behind the General, although he no longer has a knife with which to threaten him – they are one knife down. Ogawa is still clutching his Tate no Kai issue metal truncheon. Morita, holding Mishima's sword, stands behind his kneeling commander.

'Please stop! This is madness! Do not kill yourself!' cries the General. He knows that his pleas will be ignored and that Mishima has decided to die. He has seen such determined looks before, but never in peacetime.

'*Tennō Heika Banzai!*' shouts the kneeling man.

Mishima slides the blade into his tightened gut. Nearly 4 inches of metal penetrate the man.[74] Too far, too deep a cut. Oral transmissions in ancient fencing schools counsel that no more than the equivalent of 2 inches of a knife should enter the belly when cutting your own stomach. Any more and the body will pitch forward. Mishima pitches forward, just as Morita brings the sword blade down, missing his neck and inflicting a terrible cut across Mishima's shoulders. Mishima sits back up, shaking his head to command the waves of pain. He stretches his neck, but again pitches forward as Morita strikes a second time, missing his target entirely and hitting the blood-soaked carpet. He looks on in horror. The audience looks on in horror. In the fullness of time, as the news goes welling out around the globe, the whole world will look on in horror.

In response to the pain Mishima has bitten his tongue and his mouth fills with blood. A third swing of Mishima's sword cuts into his neck, to collide with a sickening crunch against his jawbone, metal chipping bone. Some of the eyes staring down at the horrific scene look away. Morita turns imploringly to Old Koga, who at once takes the sword from his hand, balances his posture, aims and then with a single motion cuts off Mishima's head.

Morita retrieves the knife, pulls down his trousers, kneels and traces lightly across his abdomen with its sharp tip. A thin line of blood begins to flow. He nods, craning his neck a little to give a good target to Koga. A moment later he is dead.

The two severed heads are placed in front of the fallen bodies. The bodies are covered with their uniform jackets. All the surviving cadets begin to cry. Even General Mashita looks as if he might cry, but he does not, saying encouragingly: 'Go on and cry. It's right to cry. And try to say a prayer too.'

The General is untied and helped to stand. Everyone recites the *Nenbutsu* prayer for the dead – '*Namu Amida Butsu*', All Praise to Amida Buddha. The doorway is unbarricaded. Tiny Koga holds Mishima's sword, the edge turned towards himself, the sharp tip pointing towards the floor to show he is surrendering it, and together they troop outside to be arrested.

At 12.23 p.m. a police surgeon pronounces Mishima and Morita dead. Given that their heads are no longer attached to their bodies but rest on the floor of the office, this diagnosis is not difficult to make.

Two quotes from the *Hagakure* I should like to have asked Mishima about:

> It is useless to try to make the present age like the good old days a hundred years ago ... The error of people who are always nostalgic for the old ways lies in their failure to grasp this point.

> A person who is said to be proficient at the arts is like a fool ... The saying 'The arts aid the body' is for samurai of other regions. For samurai of the Nabeshima clan the arts bring ruin to the body. In all cases, the person who practises an art is an artist, not a samurai.

*It is not spontaneous, but comes about because someone has
planned, planted or incited it . . . It is planted primarily for the
immediate purpose of being reported or reproduced . . . Its
relation to the underlying reality of the situation is ambiguous.
Its interest arises largely from this ambiguity.*

DANIEL J. BOORSTIN, defining a 'pseudo-event'

Takao Tokuoka, having been alerted by Mishima that 'something was about to happen', was present during the balcony
address to the assembled SDF base personnel, and although not
a witness was near by whilst Mishima committed seppuku. He
learned at once that Mishima and Morita had been declared
dead by a police doctor and the details of how they died, that
their severed heads, resting next to their bodies, were still in
General Mashita's office. The bodies were not removed until
later that day, around 5 p.m.

Tokuoka called in his story, but no one would believe him.
He was told to go back and check the facts, and in the meantime
it was decided to run a cautious headline 'Injured Mishima
Rushed to Hospital' in the afternoon editions.

On the morning of 26 November the *Asahi*'s front page had
a huge close-up of Mishima's and Morita's severed heads. (The
same picture turned up in *Life* magazine – though not on the
cover – in its issue of 12 December 1970.) One Japanese academic reminisced to me that on arriving at her elementary
school, aged eight, she encountered the *Asahi* picture pinned to
the wall of her home room, with an admonition written by her
teacher – 'This is where right-wing politics leads.'

'You are right Mister Bond. That is just what I am, a maniac.
All the greatest men are maniacs. They are possessed by a mania
which drives them forwards to their goal. The greatest scientists,
the philosophers, the religious leaders – all maniacs.'

IAN FLEMING, *Dr No*

Alongside the usual hacks on the Diet beat was a new crowd of
journalists and photographers assigned to get instant responses
to the drama of the day. As Eisaku Satō, the Prime Minister,
emerged with his secretaries and four burly bodyguards from
the Special Protection Squad, a chorus of voices yelled: 'What
about Mishima's death, his suicide?'

In the circumstances Satō might have been forgiven for saying
nothing at all. He was a friend of Mishima. The Mishimas,
husband and wife, used to dine with the Satōs, and Mrs Satō,
who was more intelligent than her husband, was able to entertain
him. Yet Satō was a politician and his aides were weighing
damage-limitation. The Satō government had given permission
for Mishima to train with the SDF. They had wooed him as a
spokesman – at one point had even proposed that he run for
Governor of Tokyo. And now he had attempted a coup.

Satō turned as he was getting into his car. *Kichigai*, he said.
Mishima is *kichigai* . . . mad.

Kichigai is written using two *kanji*. The first is *ki*, spirit or
mind. The second is *chigai*, which comes from the verb *chigau*,
meaning to be different. *Kichigai* is the ordinary term in Japanese
for mad, but more literally it denotes 'a different mind', 'a
contrary spirit'. Perhaps the Prime Minister was right after all.

When my crow phone cawed I didn't recognise the voice at the end of the line. 'You don't know me,' he said. 'My name is Yamato and I have been told you are looking for the sword used to cut off Yukio Mishima's head.'

'Yes,' I said.

'I have it. The sword. If you wish, you may see it. But you will have to promise me certain things. Will you do that?'

'Yes,' I said at once, not waiting to find out the details of any promises he might ask for. 'Yes, I will.'

The sword is the axis of the world and its power is absolute.
CHARLES DE GAULLE

Yamato-san said he would drive me back to the station. I had to agree, to play along with the 'security arrangements', keeping my word in allowing him to remain anonymous and making no attempt to locate his home, beyond knowing the general neighbourhood. I'd agreed not to try to look for landmarks, or for any means to retrace our journey and find my own way back. But wasn't it a huge act of trust on his part simply to ask me to look down, to stare at the floor, rather than take the more obvious, if melodramatic, precaution of a blindfold? He had already decided that I would honour such a condition – and he was right. I re-examined the rubber mat on which my feet rested in the passenger foot-well of the car as we wound our way through labyrinthine streets.

After I had thanked the former policeman, had bowed

goodbye at the departing white car without taking in the numberplate, he drove away and turned a corner. I walked towards the station ticket machines to find my way back to Shibuya and Ken's. The sounds were ubiquitous. Trains are everywhere in Tokyo, and the sounds of train stations are the sounds of the city, comforting familiar sounds.

Although I'd brought along a disposable camera, Yamato-san had not let me photograph the rusted blade he'd shown me, the object he'd said was Mishima's sword. He'd send me a picture he said, it was better that way. He never did, or hasn't so far, and I have no way of knowing whether the rusted sword blade he showed me in his simply furnished living room is what I had been looking for, or was just a prop for a prank perpetrated to no obvious purpose. He had explained how he came by it. That he had been told to destroy it when no Mishima family member wanted it, but could not bring himself to do so; and had just taken it home one day. He was, he told me, now retired from the police. I wanted to ask him how he got my number, but something stopped me. The situation ruled it out.

On the way home my mind raced with the possibilities of what had just taken place. That I had handled Mishima's sword. A short, chipped and slightly bent ruined weapon. Or that I had been set up, perhaps in the hope that I would stop looking and leave Japan. The sword had matched what I knew of its size, shape and condition, but I had no way to be sure, and the idea of the sword finding me was improbable and disquieting.

Later that day I felt deflated. Nothing like triumphant. Mishima's sword was, I realised, more real to me as an idea, an archetype for some quixotic grasp at a fantasy past, and didn't seem to need to exist as two feet or so of decaying edged steel. It had, in my failure to find it, remained intangible, yet faintly still vital. Something that could never be completely lost or fully destroyed. Or ever, really, possessed.

*... a passion for extremism, in art and politics, is a veiled
longing for death.*

MILAN KUNDERA

Standing in the street just outside 109, a department store in
Shibuya. Not moving, just standing. Holding my mobile to my
ear, to explain my immobility. Looking down the hill, watching.

Walking towards me are hundreds, perhaps thousands, of
people. Girls and boys, in and out of uniform. Office workers
wearing dark blue suits. Teens in jeans, shopping. Middle-
aged ladies-who-lunch scurrying their individual ways to lunch
appointments. A woman walking a dog with a curly tail, cocked
like a musical base clef. A hurrying man in a hard hat holding
an *onigiri* rice ball. I am staring into their faces, but no one
notices this.

They are the faces of individuals. Frowning or smiling, lively
or tired. Mostly they look well; a few reveal tell-tale signs of
illness. Some mouths are drawn or clamped shut, others are in
motion, making brisk conversation with companions, as they
move up the hill towards me. A couple walk past holding hands,
as if merged. There is laughter. Fragments of speech, isolated
words quite divorced of context, waft past my ears – Yes; That's
quite right; You liar; She *is* cute, has her mother's eyes;
Tomorrow, OK, sure . . . Yes, yes, yes.

The faces and voices, as I look and listen, tell me they are
alive. Each of the individuals, who together almost meld into a
surging single mass of living matter, is alive. Vibrant, vital,
engaged, purposeful, they surge past me like breakers in a human
sea. I am a rock washed over by a living ocean.

This insight seems to provide validity for the idea that life
matters, matter matters, is imbued with meaning, even if that
meaning is beyond easy articulation. Life will continue in its
inevitable cycle of birth, death and rebirth, irrespective of your
fate or mine. One death, however significant to an individual

and those who might know him or her, is as nothing when set next to this gigantic ongoing truth. And it is quite enough to cancel out the bleak black bleating naysaying of nihilism. I am not and never will be a nihilist. Absorbed in my vision of that present moment in the Japanese sunlight, I had lost myself. Minutes pass before, grinning, I begin to move again, walking on down the hill towards home. I am no longer thinking of death.

> *Death is not an event in life: we do not live to experience death.*
> *If we take eternity to mean not infinite temporal duration but*
> *timelessness, then eternal life belongs to those who live in the*
> *present.*
>
> WITTGENSTEIN, *Tractatus Logico-Philosophicus*

NOTES

1 The term *iaidō* derives from a phrase, *Tsune ni ite, kyū ni awasu* – whatever we may be doing, wherever we may be, we must always be prepared for any eventuality. It differs from kenjutsu and kendō by commencing with a sword draw and ending with the resheathing of the sword. The major schools are Muso Jikiden Eishin Ryū and Muso Shinden Ryū, which trace their origins to the sword skills of the samurai Hayashizake Jinsuke Shigenobu (1542–1621).

2 There are two kinds of oil used to protect a Japanese sword blade. Camellia oil, *kurobara*, is regarded as the best, but clove oil is fine for an *iaitō*, where its anti-bacterial properties will inhibit the growth of moulds inside the *saya*, sheath.

3 The technique for assisting at a seppuku is called *kaishaku* in Muso Jikiden Eishin Ryū and *juntō* in Muso Shinden Ryū.

4 *Seiza* means 'upright sitting', and may once have fostered good posture among Japanese. Due to the widespread displacement of sitting on the floor by the introduction of Western chairs, this is becoming a lost skill, and sitting in *seiza* is now regarded as a near-torture.

5 In *iaidō kata* this move, called *chiburi*, takes one of several forms, the most common of which are a circular whipping of the blade to flick blood from the sword, or an angling of the sword to let the blood drip off. Neither method would work with real blood, which is viscous and inclined to congeal. A samurai would always wipe the blade of his sword before resheathing it.

6 Mishima insisted on the date 25 November for his premeditated suicide, refusing to change it when his original appointment at the Ichigaya base was cancelled. I spent a great deal of time researching a plausible reason for this date. There are various theories. Wakasa Sensei told me it was the date in 1948 when the death sentences against General Tōjō and his co-accused were formally announced. One biographer claims it is the date (adjusted for a change in calendar) of the execution of Yoshida Shōin in 1859. It was the date in 1948 when Mishima formally commenced his career as a full-time writer. None of these theories is very convincing. In his 1950 novel *Ao no Jidai* (The Blue Age) Mishima has a character called Yamazaki commit suicide on 25 November. From this I believe that the date had a

private meaning for Mishima, and it is unlikely that we shall ever know what this might be.

7 *Hagakure kikigaki* (What was heard in the shadow of leaves) is an eighteenth-century text by Yamamoto Tsunetomo, expounding a romantic idealistic kind of bushidō, the code of how a samurai should conduct his life.

8 . . . then I myself am the World.

9 Mino-den is one of the five regional sword-making traditions or *gokaden*, established in what is now Gifu Prefecture. The others were Yamashiro, Sagami or Sōshū-den, Bizen and Yamato.

   Sword classification divides swords into several categories according to when they were made. The oldest katana, or *kotō*, were made between the twelfth and the end of the sixteenth century. Swords made between the sixteenth and the end of the eighteenth century are called *shintō* (new swords). Those made between the end of the eighteenth century and late nineteenth century are *shinshintō* (new new swords). Twentieth-century and contemporary swords are *gendaitō* or *shinsakutō*.

   Seki no Magoroku is a term for two smiths working in Seki, a town in Mino Province (now Gifu Prefecture). They both signed their works Kanemoto and are known as Kanemoto I, who worked in the Kamakura Period (1185–1332), and Kanemoto II, who worked in the late Muromachi Period (1392–1572). Subsequent generations of smiths used the Kanemoto name, and are sometimes called Seki no Magoroku, but experts say this designation should be limited to the first two Kanemoto smiths.

10 The *habaki* is the collar moulded around the blade above the handle to secure it in the *saya*, the scabbard.

11 Respectively Shinmen Musashi Fujiwara no Genshin, commonly known as Miyamoto Musashi (1584–1645), and the fencing instructor to the Tokugawa Shōgunate and headmaster of the Yagyu-Shinkage Ryū school of swordsmanship.

12 See *The Unfettered Mind* by Takuan Sōhō (Kodansha, Tokyo).

13 I doubt if Mishima had in mind the Hōchō Masamune Tantō, or Kitchen Knife Masamune, so termed because it is shorter and wider than other Masamune *tantō* knives.

14 Sei-i-tai-Shōgun, Barbarian-Subduing Commander-in-Chief – the title of the military de facto ruler of Japan from the Kamakura Period until the Meiji Restoration.

15 All *meitō* are known swords whose manufacturing history and subsequent provenance is documented. There is no such thing as a newly discovered *meitō*. Some *meitō* have been destroyed and are classified in the third volume of the *Kyōhō Meibutsu Chō* as lost *meitō*.

16 These two were not contemporaries. Muramasa worked in the early Muromachi Period.

17 Tokugawa Ieyasu's grandfather Kiyoyasu was killed by a retainer using a Muramasa sword, an identical fate to that of Ieyasu's father Hirotada. Ieyasu was betrayed by his eldest son Nobuyasu, who was ordered to commit seppuku. The *kaishaku* used a Muramasa sword. During the battle of Sekigahara, Ieyasu was wounded by a Muramasa sword.

18 Supreme Commander for the Allied Powers, the occupation authority headed by General Douglas MacArthur.

19 Ian Buruma, author and cultural commentator, has written extensively on Japan – see for example *A Japanese Mirror: Heroes and Villains of Japanese Culture*.

20 *Mishima: A Biography* (Tuttle, 1974).

21 There is no official shortlist for the Nobel Prize for Literature, but the names of those in the running are leaked to the Swedish press and are usually thereafter described as being on a shortlist.

22 *Shichi Fukujin*. They are: Benzai, goddess of arts, entertainment and scholarship; Bishamon, god of success in war; Daikokuji, god of wealth; Ebisu, god of commerce and fishing; Fukurokuju, god of long life; Hotei, god of generosity; and Jurōjin, god of good health and longevity.

23 *Yōmeigaku* or *Oyōmei* is the Japanese term for the ideas of Wang Yang-ming (1472–1529), known in Japan as Oyōmei, the founder of the so-called Idealist School of neo-Confucianism.

24 Henry Scott Stokes, *The Life and Death of Yukio Mishima* (1975).

25 An edged, traditionally forged Japanese sword. There are *iaitō* made outside Japan, mostly in China, which have a cutting edge. Most *shinken* used in practising *iaidō* are rejected art swords or swords made by a swordsmith's *deshi*, apprentice, as a practice effort. *Gendaitō* are, in general, too valuable to risk damaging as a training weapon. And this is doubly so for older swords.

26 One of the oldest *koryū* martial arts and centred on the Kashima Shrine in Ibaraki Prefecture.

27 *Hōjō no Umi* (translated as *Sea of Fertility*) comprises four novels: *Spring Snow*; *Runaway Horses*; *Temple of Dawn* and *Decay of the Angel*. The device of the reincarnation of a central character who dies in the first volume to be reborn in each of the following novels in the series is taken from a classical model, the *Hamamatsu Chūnagon Monogatari*, The Tale of the Hamamatsu Middle Counsellor, an eleventh-century Heian romance attributed to Sugawara no Takasue no Musume.

28 *Taoyameburi*. The corresponding masculine-soul tradition is known as *masuraoburi*. Quoted from an interview with Philip Shabecoff published in the *New York Times Magazine*, 2 August 1970.

29 Peter Ackroyd acerbically opened his 1975 *Spectator* review of this volume: 'If the publishers are right and this is the "climax" of Mishima's work, I am very grateful to have missed all the

other novels, and if he is indeed "the most dynamic and outspoken writer of post-War Japan" then that crowded and polluted people should learn to concentrate on making pen batteries.'

30 According to the national studies scholar Motōri Norinaga, *mono no aware* is a direct form of perception, a sensitivity to things without the intervention of language.

31 *Kinjiki* (1951). The novel *Forbidden Colours* – a single volume in the English translation by Alfred H. Marks – was published as two connected novels in Japanese. The second volume, *Higyo*, translated as *Secret Medicine*, came out in 1953.

32 Literally 'standing reading' – the practice of reading whole books whilst browsing in Japanese bookshops.

33 Make-up was used by samurai. The *Hagakure* advocates using rouge to avoid a pale complexion which might be mistaken for cowardice.

34 C. L. Yates, *Saigō Takamori: The Man Behind the Myth*, p. 23.

35 The minor works, not as yet translated, are: *Bushidō Kosha sho* by Ogasawara Shōzō; *Shidō kokoroe sho* by Hōjō Chikuho; *Shidō yogi* by Matsumoto Kodō; *Bushidō yokansho* by Ishida Ittei; *Kokon bushidō ezukushi* by Hishikawa Moronobu; and *Shidō yoron* by Saitō Masakata.

36 *Shu shi*, a Confucian system that stresses obedience to government, was employed by the Shōgunate to justify detailed rules of feudal distinction. It covered every aspect of life from food and clothing to rights of travel and marriage.

37 Decisive battle in 1600 when Tokugawa Ieyasu defeated the Toyotomi and their allies and 40,000 heads were taken!

38 Examining some handwritten manuscripts by Mishima later, I found they had revisions – so perhaps he did this occasionally and not all the time.

39 *Angry White Pyjamas* by Robert Twigger, winner of a Somerset Maugham award and William Hill Sports Book of the Year.

40 This rebellion was in the tradition of *genkokujō*, a form of insubordination first noted in the fifteenth century. Traditionally, criminal acts were sanctioned to redress injustice or attack corruption.

41 General Sadao Araki was the leader of the Imperial Way faction in the army. Taku Mikami shot and killed Prime Minister Inukai in 1932 and was imprisoned for three years in 1961 for inciting a coup. Tameo Sagoya shot Prime Minister Hamaguchi in 1930; Hamaguchi died in 1931. Tadashi Konuma assassinated financier Junnosuke Inoue in 1932.

42 In 1969 Mishima got into a public argument with novelist Arima Yorichika. Arima commented on the 26 February rebels: 'Far from being misguided but pure revolutionaries [they were] out-and-out murderers.'

43 In English the title *Yūkoku* is usually rendered *Patriotism*, but strictly patriotism in Japanese is *aikoku*, literally 'love of country'. *Yūkoku* is subtly different, suggesting a sense of sadness on

witnessing the decline of the nation. A love of country, yes, but a disappointed love. In calling it his favourite story Mishima admitted that it contained the best and worst of his writing.

44 Tama Reien, plot number 10–1–13–32. Mishima's Buddhist death name, or *Kaimyō*, was *Shobuin Bunkan Koi Koji* (Buddhist Lay Spirit of Literature and Martial Arts, Mirror of Culture) *Kimitake*, an indication of wealth, in that each *kanji* must be purchased from the officiating Buddhist priest. The current cost is more than ¥ 100,000 a character.

45 The *kiku*, chrysanthemum, is also used in homosexual shunga pornographic woodblock prints to symbolize the anus, which it is thought to resemble.

46 The sword fighting in *Seven Samurai* is authentic, as Sugino Sensei of the Tenshin Shoden Katori Shinto Ryū, Japan's oldest surviving *Koryū*, was a technical adviser.

47 A feature of Yagyū Shinkage Ryū swordsmanship is to take the initiative, the literal meaning of *sen o toru*. However, Yagyū Jūbei further developed this principle so that he would wait for an opponent to reveal a weakness and then attack the weakness, or gap in spirit, *suki*.

48 Eighth dan, Dōjōchō of the Aikidō Yōshinkan Honbu Dōjō, Ochiai, Tokyo.

49 Language lacks sufficient precision to tell the truth. As Iris Murdoch famously pointed out, beyond requests such as 'pass the gravy' everything is an expression of falsehood, either wilfully or because language is not up to the job.

50 Though I was very surprised to learn that in 1995 6 per cent of all murders committed in Japan were by sword. Yakuza traditionalists?

51 John Yumoto in *The Samurai Sword* says the colour is that of the moon in June or July.

52 Takeo Okuno, literary critic and Mishima biographer.

53 *Forbidden Colours*, chapter 3, 'The Marriage of a Dutiful Son'.

54 A Japanese proverb states: 'A man who loves his wife is spoiling his mother's servant.'

55 According to Henry Scott Stokes, who was in the audience, Mishima repeated the remark that Yōko was entirely without imagination when addressing the FCCJ with Yōko sitting passively next to him.

56 A line of three cedar trees with one taller than the others, the signature *hamon* of Seki no Magoroku.

57 After a distinguished military career, General Nogi became headmaster of the Peers School, which Mishima was later to attend.

58 Women do not commit *seppuku*, but instead use a *tantō* to sever a neck artery or stab themselves in the heart. This is called *jigai*. Before doing so it is considered correct to tie up one's ankles to avoid being found in a vulgar posture after death.

59 Literally 'ten thousand years', and a contraction of *Tennō heika banzai*, May the Emperor reign for ten thousand years – i.e. for ever.

60 Living National Treasure is a common translation of *Ningen*

Kokuhō, more formally termed
'Important Intangible Cultural
Asset'.

61 Swords were traditionally
considered to fuse beauty of
form and function, an idea
known as *kinoubi* in Japanese
aesthetics.

62 'Among my incurable
convictions is the belief that the
old are eternally ugly, the young
eternally beautiful. The wisdom
of the old eternally murky, the
actions of the young eternally
transparent. The longer people
live, the worse they become.
Human life, in other words, is
an upside-down process of
decline and fall.' *Nīnīroku jiten to
watakushi*, Yukio Mishima.

63 *Mishima: A Life in Four Chapters*,
directed by Paul Schrader.

64 Mishima commented as follows
on his reasons for writing
Confessions of a Mask: 'This book
is my farewell message to the
realm of death in which I have
been living. Writing this book
has been for me a suicide in
reverse. If the film of a man
committing suicide by throwing
himself from a cliff is run in
reverse, the man will appear to
spring up with tremendous vigor
from the valley bottom to the
cliff and return to life. My
attempt in writing this book was
to learn the art of recovering life
in this fashion.'

65 Meredith Weatherby's 1958
translation of *Kamen no
Kokuhaku* gives Ko-chan rather
than Kimi-chan in the one place
in the text where the narrator is
named. I believe he is mistaken
and that Kimi, a diminutive of
Kimitake, Mishima's real given
name, is the correct reading of

this *kanji*. Chan is an affix used
to express friendly familiarity
towards younger intimates.

66 Abbreviation for Tokkōtai,
which is a contraction of
Tokubetsu Tokkōtai, or Special
Attack Forces, known in the
West as Kamikaze. Alternatively
called Tokubetsu Kōgekitai.

67 Presumably *Die Homosexualität
des Mannes und des Weibes*,
published in 1914.

68 Water trade – the demi-monde
of bars, clubs and entertainment
businesses over which the
yakuza prevail by various means,
such as protection rackets.

69 In the 30 November 1937
edition of the *Nichinichi Shinbun*,
the forerunner of the *Mainichi*
newspaper, an article appeared
about the Japanese army in
China. It was headlined: 'A
Contest to Cut Down 100
people! Two Lieutenants
Already Fell 80.' The article was
in the form of a dispatch from a
frontline reporter called Asami
who claimed to have happened
upon a competition between
two second lieutenants –
Toshiaki Mukai and Tsuyoshi
Noda – to see who would be the
first to kill 100 Chinese enemy
soldiers using only their
Japanese swords. Mukai's sword
was a famous meitō by Seki no
Magoroku and Noda's sword,
although unsigned, was said to
be an heirloom passed down
from his ancestors. The account
details a number of
engagements and provides a
running body-count. In a
solitary night-battle Mukai is
declared to have killed 55 men
with his Seki no Magoroku
sword.

A second dispatch from Asami followed up on the story, updating the total kills to 105 for one officer and 106 for the other. As neither man was sure who had passed 100 first, the contest was declared a draw. They were quoted as saying they might go on to try for a new total target of 150 kills. Mukai pointed out that his sword had only one small chip in the blade and was photographed holding the weapon in action. The picture caption suggested he was heroically unconcerned about incoming enemy bullets.

On returning to Japan after the war, Mukai learned of this newspaper account and was said to be 'astonished and ashamed'. He assumed no one in their right mind would believe such an obvious propaganda fabrication and voluntarily returned to China to stand trial. Both Mukai and Noda were tried in Nanjing, found guilty, and executed in due course. Asami, the journalist who had written about the sword-killing contest, seemingly untroubled by his conscience, refused to retract the story or help the condemned men by testifying in court.

70 A boy's fifth birthday is celebrated by dressing him as a samurai. In the past this was the age when a samurai boy would receive his first sword, called a *genpuku-tō*. Today this tradition is continued, usually substituting a toy weapon.

71 Yasukuni Jinja was built in 1869 as a *shōkonsha* – a place where the divine spirits who have made the supreme sacrifice are invited, i.e. a memorial to those who died defending the imperial cause, including, controversially, executed war criminals such as General Tōjō.

72 Article 9 of the post-Second World War Japanese constitution for ever renounces war as a means to settle disputes and renders illegal the maintenance of military forces. Despite the euphemistic term – Self Defence Forces – the Japanese military is regarded by experts in constitutional law as illegal.

73 Mishima and his Tate no Kai cadets rehearsed the event eight times in Room 519 of the Palace Hotel in Marunouchi.

74 The autopsy performed on Mishima at the Keio Daigaku Fuzoku Byōin stated the following: the cut he had made across his stomach was 13 cm across and between 7 cm and 9 cm deep; 60 cm of intestine had been exposed; he had bitten through his tongue, nearly severing it; there was a piece of the sword blade embedded in his teeth; cause of death – decapitation.

SELECT BIBLIOGRAPHY

Andō, Takeshi *Mishima Yukio no Shōgai*. Tokyo: Natsuke Shobo, 1998.

Buruma, Ian *A Japanese Mirror: Heroes and Villains of Japanese Culture*. London: Jonathan Cape, 1984.

Funasaka, Hiroshi *Eirei no Zekkyō*. Tokyo: Bungei Shunjyu sha, 1966.

Funasaka, Hiroshi *Seki no Magoroku*. Tokyo: Kōbunsha, 1973.

Hashimoto, Osamu *Mishima Yukio towa nanimono dattanoka*. Tokyo: Shinchōsha, 2002.

Inose, Naoki *Persona – Mishima Yukio Den*. Tokyo: Bungei Shunjyu sha, 1995.

Kapp, Leon, Kapp, Hiroko, and Yoshihara, Yoshindo *The Craft of the Japanese Sword*. New York: Kōdansha America, 1987.

Matsumoto, Tōru *Mishima Yukio Jiten*. Tokyo: Bensei Shuppan, 2000.

Mishima, Yukio *Confessions of a Mask* (*Kamen no kokuhaku*, 1949). Trans. Meredith Weatherby. New York: New Directions, 1958. London: Secker & Warburg, 1960.

The Blue Age (*Ao no Jidai*, 1950).

Forbidden Colors (*Kinjiki*, 1952). Trans. Alfred H. Marks. New York: Alfred A. Knopf, 1968. London: Secker & Warburg, 1968.

The Sound of Waves (*Shiosai*, 1954). Trans. Meredith Weatherby. New York: Alfred A. Knopf, 1956. London: Secker & Warburg, 1957.

The Temple of the Golden Pavilion (*Kinkakuji*, 1956). Trans. Ivan Morris. New York: Alfred A. Knopf, 1959. London: Secker & Warburg, 1959.

Patriotism (*Yūkoku*, 1960). Trans. Geoffrey W. Sargent. New York: New Directions, 1995.

The Sailor Who Fell from Grace with the Sea (*Gogo no eikō*, 1963). Trans. John Nathan. New York: Alfred A. Knopf, 1965. London: Secker & Warburg, 1966.

My Wandering Years (*Watakushi no Henriki Jidai*. Tokyo: Kōdansha, 1964).

Voices of the Heroic Dead (*Eirei no koe*, 1966).

The Way of the Samurai: Yukio Mishima on Hagakure in Modern Life (*Hagakure nyūmon*, 1967). Trans. Kathryn Sparling. New York: Basic Books, 1977.

In Defence of Culture (*Bunka Bōei Ron*. Tokyo: Shinchōsha, 1969).

Sun and Steel (*Taiyō to tetsu*, 1968). Trans. John Bester. Tokyo: Kōdansha International, 1970. New York: Grove Press, 1970. London: Secker & Warburg, 1971.

Spring Snow (*Haru no yuki*, 1969). Trans. Michael Gallagher. New York: Alfred A. Knopf, 1971. London: Secker & Warburg, 1973.

Runaway Horses (*Honba*, 1969). Trans. Michael Gallagher. New York: Alfred A. Knopf, 1973. London: Secker & Warburg, 1973.

The Temple of Dawn (*Akatsuki no tera*, 1970). Trans. E. Dale Saunders and Cecilia S. Seigle. New York: Alfred A. Knopf, 1973. London: Secker & Warburg, 1974.

The Decay of the Angel (*Tennin gosui*, 1971). Trans. Edward G. Seidensticker. New York: Alfred A. Knopf, 1974. London: Secker & Warburg, 1975.

Collected Works (*Mishima Yukio Zenshū*) in 41 volumes. Tokyo: Shinchōsha, 2000–.

Morris, Ivan *The Nobility of Failure*. London: Secker & Warburg, 1974.

Muramatsu, Takeshi *Mishima Yukio no Sekai*. Tokyo: Shinchōsha, 1990.

Nagayama, Kokan *The Connoisseur's Book of the Sword*. Trans. Kenji Mishina. Tokyo: Kōdansha International, 1998.

Nathan, John *Mishima: A Biography*. New York: Little Brown, 1974.

Okuno, Takeo *Mishima Yukio Densetsu*. Tokyo: Shinchōsha, 1993.

Scott Stokes, Henry *The Life and Death of Yukio Mishima*. New York: Farrar, Straus & Giroux, 1974. London: Peter Owen, 1975.

Shinoyama, Kishin *Mishima Yukio no Ie*. Tokyo: Bijutsu Shuppan, 1995.

Sōhō, Takuan *The Unfettered Mind*. Trans. William Scott Wilson. London: Kōdansha Europe, 1988.

Starrs, Roy *Deadly Dialectics*. Honolulu: University of Hawaii Press, 1994.

Tokuoka, Takao *Gosui no hito – Mishima Yukio Shiki*. Tokyo: Bungei Shunjyu sha, 1996.

Twigger, Robert *Angry White Pyjamas*. London: Orion, 1997. New York: Perennial, 2001.

Watatani, Kiyoshi, and Yamada, Tadashi *Bugei Ryuha Daijiten*. Tokyo, 1978.

Yamamoto, Kiyokatsu *Jieitai Kagenobutai*. Tokyo: Kōdansha, 2001.

Yates, Charles L. *Saigō Takamori: The Man Behind the Myth*. London: Kegan Paul, 1995.

Yoshida, Kazuaki *Yukio Mishima for Beginners*. Tokyo: Gendai Shokan, 1985.

Yourcenar, Marguerite *Mishima: A Vision of the Void* (*Mishima, ou, La vision du vide*, 1980). Trans. Alberto Manguel. London: Aidan Ellis Publishing, 1986. Chicago: University of Chicago Press, 2001.

Yumoto, John M. *The Samurai Sword: A Handbook*. Tokyo: Charles Tuttle, 1958.

GLOSSARY

bakufu Lit. camp, or tent. Government, the Shogunate, the military regime established in Kamakura by the Minamoto clan in the twelfth century.

battō-dō Japanese martial art. Sword-drawing and cutting. A term used in some schools in preference to *iaidō*. Nowadays the cutting of targets using a *shinken*.

bokken A wooden sword. Also *bokutō*.

bōshi The temper line in the *kissaki*, or point, of a Japanese sword.

budō Japanese martial arts.

bundan The literary establishment – writers, critics and academics.

bushi Warrior. The knightly class. Also samurai.

bushidō A code of conduct practised by *bushi*.

chi gung Chinese martial art skill, internal power.

chōji Cloves. Used to scent an oil applied to sword blades.

daimyō Lit. big name. Ruler of a feudal domain.

dao Chinese broadsword.

deshi Disciple, apprentice. Also *uchi deshi*, resident disciple.

dōgi Practice clothes worn to perform modern Japanese martial arts. Also *keikogi*.

enka A form of romantic song, a modern ballad.

fundoshi A Japanese loincloth.

funshi A form of seppuku performed to protest against injustice.

gaijin Lit. outside person. Non-Japanese. Also *gaikokujin*.

gendaitō Modern-era sword, late nineteenth century to the present.

genkan The entrance to a traditional Japanese house, where shoes are removed.

geta Wooden platform clogs.

gokaden The five schools of swordsmiths in the Kotō period (prior to 1596).

guntō   Lit. military sword. Usually refers to mass-produced swords made during the Second World War and mounted in a leather scabbard.

gwei lo   Lit. round eye. Chinese pejorative term for a Caucasian.

hachimaki   Headband worn to show resolve when engaged on an onerous task.

hakama   Large pleated and folded trousers. Worn formerly by samurai and still worn in Japanese traditional formal dress and in modern martial arts such as *kyudō* (archery) and *aikidō*.

hamon   Distinctive pattern of the temper line on a Japanese sword.

han   Feudal domain.

haori   A short-sleeved jacket worn as part of Japanese formal costume, usually showing a family crest or *mon*.

hara-kiri   Lit. belly cut. A means of formal suicide developed by the samurai. Also seppuku.

heijōshin   Lit. constant stable spirit. A quality sought by practitioners of *budō* and only attained after the slaughter of the ego.

hō   A form of magnolia wood used to make scabbards and sword handles.

hōjō jutsu   A rope-tying martial art. Still practised in some older systems, such as Shindō Musō Ryū.

iaidō   A sword-based martial art where all techniques originate with the draw of a sheathed sword and conclude with the return of the blade to the sheath.

iaitō   A dull, non-edged sword used for practising *iaidō*.

ikebana   Japanese flower-arranging systems. There are several distinct traditions.

irori   A sunken charcoal hearth or fireplace.

jigai   Lit. self-harm. Suicide. Women do not commit seppuku but instead cut their throats with a knife, an act termed *jigai*.

jihada   Surface pattern on the grain of the steel of a Japanese sword.

jōdō   A martial art using a stick of approximately 128 cm (or 4 *shaku*, 2 *sun*, 1 *bu*) length.

jūken dō   A modern martial art employing a rifle with an attached bayonet.

jūmonji   An extreme form of seppuku involving both horizontal and vertical cuts, in the shape of the Japanese character for the number ten.

junshi A form of seppuku on the death of a daimyō performed by close retainers. Banned since the early seventeenth century.

juntō Term in Shinden Musō Ryu for the form for assisting at a seppuku.

kaishaku Assisting at a seppuku where you cut off the head of the principal. Term in Musō Jikiden Eishin Ryū for the form to do this.

kaizen Continuous improvement of a service or product by requesting suggestions and feedback from staff and customers.

kakun A code of conduct of a feudal domain. Also *kun*.

kami Divine qualities. Animist spirits. Gods of Shinto.

kamikaze Lit. divine wind, referring to a wind that sunk an invading Mongol fleet in the fourteenth century. Also refers to the Tokkō special attack planes (and manned torpedoes) used on suicide missions towards the end of the Second World War.

kamiza In Shinto, a shelf where various objects of ritual significance are displayed to attract the presence of *kami* and towards which prayers are directed.

kanji Chinese characters used to write Japanese.

kanshi A form of seppuku which acts to remonstrate with a feudal superior.

kata A form or sequence of fixed or prearranged actions, a method.

katana A Japanese sword. A long sword. Also *uchigatana* or *daitō*.

kenshi A swordsman. A practitioner of kendo, kenjutsu or *iaidō*.

keppan An oath sworn by shedding blood. A blood-sealed promise.

kiai Lit. spirit blending. A loud shout uttered when striking or blocking in various forms of *budō*.

kichigai Lit. different spirit. Pejorative term for crazy, mad.

kissaki The tip or point of a Japanese sword.

kōban A small police station or police box.

kobuse Low-carbon steel that forms the core of a Japanese sword.

koryū Ancient forms of Japanese martial art.

koshirae Sword furniture: the handle, scabbard, mountings and fittings.

kun See *kakun*.

makoto Sincerity. Also *shisei*.

meishi A name card, a visiting card.

meitō A named sword. A sword made by a famous smith.

mekugi A small, usually bamboo, pin used to secure the blade to the handle in a Japanese sword.

mon A unique crest indicating a particular samurai family.

mugi-cha Barley tea.

mukansa Lit. not submitted (to the judging panel). Beyond judgement. The highest level in sword appraisal competition.

mumei Nameless. An unsigned sword.

nagako The tang or hilt end of a sword which fits into the handle.

nasake Compassion, a samurai virtue. Also *bushi no nasake*.

ne waza Ground-fighting techniques in judo and jujutsu.

niniroku Lit. 226. The 26th of February, referring to a military rebellion that broke out on 26 February 1936. Also *niniroku jiken*.

nishinoya A stone lantern found in Japanese cemeteries.

nuguikami Special paper used to wipe the blade of a Japanese sword.

o-furo A Japanese bath.

omura Sandstone in powdered form used in forging a Japanese sword.

o-nigiri A rice ball wrapped in seaweed.

oroshigane Moving *tamahagane* around in a forge to alter its carbon levels.

rāmen Chinese-style noodles in soup.

sam jeet kwun Chinese weapon, a three-sectional staff.

satetsu Iron sand. Ferrous oxide, a raw material for making steel.

saya A scabbard or sheath for a Japanese sword.

sayashi A craftsman who makes *saya*.

seitō A person committing seppuku, the principal.

seiza Upright sitting. Formal kneeling posture.

sempai Senior in social hierarchy.

senryū A form of comic poem, similar to a haiku.

sentō A Japanese public bath.

seppuku Belly cutting. Formal method of suicide developed by samurai. Also hara-kiri.

shiai A duel or contest.

shibakama Death costume. The clothes worn by someone committing seppuku.

shichishō Seven lives. Abbreviation of the phrase, to die seven times and each time to be reborn to serve the nation.

shidō   Way of the Samurai. Code of conduct of the bushi. Also bushidō.

shindoku   Self-scrutiny. A Confucian meditation exercise.

shinjō   A true heart. A quality aspired to in Confucian practices.

shinken   An edged Japanese sword. A live blade.

shirasaya   A plain wooden scabbard used for sword storage.

shisei   Sincerity. Also *makoto*.

sogai   Being aloof from mainstream culture. Haughtiness.

sonnō jōi   Lit. Restore the Emperor, expel the barbarians. The slogan of a nineteenth-century political movement.

sori   The curvature of a sword blade.

suburi   Practice cuts in *iaidō*, kendō or kenjutsu.

suki   A gap in defence.

tabi   A kind of sock where the big toe is separated from the other toes.

tamahagane   A form of raw steel used in making Japanese swords.

tameshigiri   Sword testing by cutting various targets.

tantō   A short knife or dagger with a blade less than 12 inches long.

tatara   A special smelter for making *tamahagane*.

Tate no Kai   Shield Society. Militia with fewer than one hundred members formed by Yukio Mishima in 1968.

Tennō heika banzai   Lit. (May) His Majesty the Emperor (reign) ten thousand years, i.e. for ever. Also *Banzai*.

toki   Japanese crested ibis.

tokonoma   The alcove in a Japanese room reserved for flower or other displays to indicate a season or formal event.

tsuba   Sword guard.

tsuka   Sword handle.

tsukamaki   Handle wrapping and the methods used to do this.

utsuri   Reflection of the temper line on the surface of the sword between the *shinogi* ridge line and the *hamon*.

uwagi   A jacket worn in modern forms of budō.

wa   Harmony. Avoidance of conflict.

wakizashi   A short sword worn as a companion sword to the long sword, two swords being the badge of a samurai. Also *shōtō*.

washi   Hand-made Japanese paper.

yakuza   A Japanese gangster.

yoroidōshi   A heavy knife designed to penetrate armour for battlefield hand-to-hand combat.

yūkoku   Patriotism. A feeling of sadness at the decline of the spiritual condition of the nation.

zanshin   Mind remaining. A quality of attention emphasised in budō.

zōri   Straw sandals.